Acclaim for MICHAEL WILDING

The Prisoner of Mount Warning: With a detective called Plant and a journey from Sydney to the dope fields of Byron Bay, the private eye novel has come a long way from Raymond Chandler … the detective novel's move into an era of magic mushrooms and free love. – *Sydney Morning Herald*

The Magic of It: The truth in this fiction is at least as entertaining as what has been invented. This a clever, offbeat rendering of a crime story with a smattering of illustrations by the great Australian artist Garry Shead and a protagonist who surely will be back. – Emma Young, *Sydney Morning Herald*

Superfluous Men: You have a way of being gloomily funny that speaks for all the early-retired and those who cannot avoid weary contempt for the bureaucrats both in and out of the universities. – Frank Kermode. A brave new world of political correctness gone mad. – Ross Fitzgerald, *Weekend Australian*

Academia Nuts: Wilding at his absolute satirical best. – David Williamson. A witty campus novel? In 2004? It seemed as likely as a holiday romance set amid the tropical delights of Guantanamo Bay … But it is very funny. So funny that I had to stop reading it in bed in case my roars of laughter were disturbing the neighbours: so funny that it deserves to be the final great campus novel. It is unlikely to be challenged. For what Wilding's aged unreconstructed dons are playing with such absurd brio is unmistakably the last waltz. – Laurie Taylor, *Times Higher Educational Supplement*

Aspects of the Dying Process: One of the best writers of short stories in Australia today. – *Australian Book Review.* The short story writer as sociologist, the short story writer as photo-realist … Wilding can accurately pace a story and make a woman ironical and elusive in just a few sentences. – *Times Literary Supplement*

Scenic Drive: Takes you on a trip that shouldn't be missed … I laughed until I cried. It's rare that I enjoy a book as much as I enjoyed *Scenic Drive* – it's a memorable book, sexy and funny. Once you read it, you'll want to turn all of your friends on to it. – Dianna Pizza, *L.A. Star.* Wilding is fast becoming a well-known figure to the U.S. underground … It's first-rate fiction. – Dick Higgins, *Newsart*

This is for You: 21st century writing for 21st-century people. – J.P. Donleavy. Erotic, fiercely intelligent and mordantly funny. – Janette Turner Hospital. His stories subvert and transcend not only sexual and social conventions … but story-telling itself. – Jim Crace

Living Together: Is it really about a ménage a trois? – Princess Margaret. A very funny book and a perfect picture of the people, the time, the place. – David Marr, *Bulletin*. He is so exhilaratingly adept with narrative you cannot put the book down … Wilding's pen is sharp as a rapier. – Jan Meek, *Vogue Australia*

National Treasure: Michael Wilding has form … Witty and genuinely funny … But don't be conned. This is fiction with more truth than lies. – Christopher Bantick, *Weekend Australian*. Thoroughly enjoyable, sometimes hilarious … But it is not lightweight: it is tough, well-calculated, smoothly witty. – Brian Matthews, *Australian Book Review*

Pacific Highway: Readers can recognise that much the narrator recounts issues from his consumption of hallucinogenics … But just how much? Where in his account of events does the actual end and his paranoid perception of it begin? And could his suspicions that global conspiracies are behind unwelcome developments in this otherwise near Arcady or Eden be justified? … humorous … menacing … – Brian Kiernan, *Running Wild*

The Phallic Forest: Elegantly written and evocative … an undercurrent of sensitivity and searching for truths. – Jean Bedford, *National Times*

Raising Spirits, Making Gold and Swapping Wives: the True Adventures of Dr John Dee and Sir Edward Kelly: The story of Queen Elizabeth I's necromancer, John Dee, as transcribed from original documents interspersed with Michael Wilding's own words. A piece of esoterica designed to startle and delight the modern reader. – Peter Porter, *The Economist* Books of the Year

The Short Story Embassy: A Novel: Considerable entertainment. – *Times Literary Supplement*. Excruciatingly funny. – Frank Devine, *National Times*. The best of the talent emerging from down under. – *San Francisco Review of Books*

Somewhere New: New & Selected Stories: What strikes one first, apart from the impressive merits of individual stories, is Wilding's keen sense of literary integrity … Wilding's voice in these stories is always one to attend to: an ironic, witty, highly educated, and in its indirect way, passionate authorial persona who has believed in literature as a life of principle, has seen many of the bases of that belief assaulted by abstruse theory, trendy anti-realism, and sinecure-seeking cynicism, and yet still in the face of everything, is able to make the affirming act through the agency of fiction … No one in English writes better fiction about the process of writing than Wilding. – Don Graham, *Studies in Short Fiction*

Wild Amazement: Anyone interested in how contemporary Australian writing came to be the way it is, with its strengths and follies, its cliques and patrons, and the challenges it faces, will benefit from reading Wilding's sensitive, sometimes bitchy, often funny and always intelligent tracing of his life's trajectory. – Peter Corris, *Quadrant*

Wildest Dreams: Deserves to be thought of as a contemporary classic. – Adrian Caesar. An *Australian* Book of the Year

Michael Wilding's fiction includes *Living Together*, *The Short Story Embassy*, *The Men of Slow Feeling*, *The Paraguayan Experiment*, *Wild Amazement*, *Academia Nuts* and *Superfluous Men*. His private-eye Plant previously debuted in the pilot *National Treasure* (2007) and *The Prisoner of Mount Warning* (2010).

Michael Wilding, novelist and critic, was born in Worcester, UK and read English at Oxford. He has taught English and Australian Literature and creative writing at the University of Sydney, where he is now emeritus professor, and various universities internationally. He has also been a milkman, postman, apple-picker, newspaper columnist, *Cosmopolitan* Bachelor of the Month, Fellow of the Australian Academy of the Humanities, and Chair of the New South Wales Writers' Centre.

Also by Michael Wilding

Australians Abroad (ed. with Charles Higham)
Aspects of the Dying Process
Living Together
The Short Story Embassy
The West Midland Underground
Scenic Drive
Marcus Clarke
The Radical Reader (ed. with Stephen Knight)
The Tabloid Story Pocket Book (ed.)
The Phallic Forest
Political Fictions
Pacific Highway
Reading the Signs
The Paraguayan Experiment
The Man of Slow Feeling
Dragons Teeth
Under Saturn
Great Climate
Her Most Bizarre Sexual Experience
Social Visions
The Oxford Book of Australian Short Stories (ed.)
This is for You
Book of the Reading
Somewhere New: New and Selected Stories
Wildest Dreams
Raising Spirits, Making Gold and Swapping Wives: The True Adventures of Dr John Dee and Sir Edward Kelly
Academia Nuts
Best Stories Under the Sun 1–3 (ed. with David Myers)
Wild Amazement
National Treasure
Cyril Hopkins' Marcus Clarke (ed. with Laurie Hergenhan and Ken Stewart)
Superfluous Men
Heart Matters (ed. with Peter Corris)
The Prisoner of Mount Warning
The Magic of It
Wild & Woolley: A Publishing Memoir
Wild Bleak Bohemia: Marcus Clarke, Adam Lindsay Gordon and Henry Kendall

ASIAN DAWN

Michael Wilding

ARCADIA

This Project has been assisted by the Australian Government through the Australia Council, its arts funding and advisory board.

The Press On series of novels was founded by Michael Wilding and Phillip Edmonds. Edmonds was the managing director of Wet Ink, the magazine of new writing, and Wilding is Press On's commissioning editor.

Press On – 16

First published 2013 by Arcadia
the general books' imprint of
Australian Scholarly Publishing Pty Ltd
7 Little Lothian Street Nth, North Melbourne Vic. 3051
TEL: 03 9329 6963 FAX: 03 9329 5452
EMAIL: aspic@ozemail.com.au WEB: scholarly.info

ISBN: 978-1-921875-39-7

A Ctaloguing-in-Publication entry is available
from the National Library of Australia.

Cover art Tanya Crothers
Design and typesetting Art Rowlands
Printing and binding Tenderprint Pty Ltd

Set in Fairfield LH 45 Light 11pt

To Pira Sudham

1

'Mr Plant?' said the voice on the phone.

'Uh-huh.'

'You do research and investigations?'

'Uh-huh.'

That was what his card said, more or less. Research Assistance. Investigative Reporting.

'Is that a yes or a no?'

It was a strong, peremptory, female person voice. He was never good with them. Liable to turn to jelly.

'Well,' he said, as if to begin, while avoiding doing so.

'I have an investigation and I require assistance.'

'I see,' said Plant.

'I don't see how you can,' she said. 'I haven't told you anything yet.'

'Go ahead, then,' said Plant.

'It's not something I can explain on the phone.'

It rarely was.

'You don't list an office address,' she said.

'No,' he admitted.

'But you're on the coast.'

'Pretty much,' he conceded.

She said nothing. His trick, and he fell for it.

'A bit inland,' he said.

'Well, I'm on the coast,' she said.

The Gold Coast. She gave him an address. One of those high-rise apartments overlooking the ocean at Broadbeach.

'Did you write that down?'

'No,' he admitted.

'Would you, please. Do you have pen and paper?'

As if she were about to provide them, download them from the phone line.

'Sure,' he said.

She repeated the address.

He wrote it down.

She gave him her phone number.

He wrote that down.

'It's a complex matter,' she said. 'It may involve travel.'

'Travel,' he said.

Outside the window the wallaby was chewing the unmown grass. A laid-back kind of chewing. Who would want to travel when you could just be where you were?

'Asia,' she said. 'Would that be a problem?'

'I'd have to think about that.'

'Sleep on it and meet me tomorrow. Eleven o'clock.'

'A.M.?' Plant checked.

'Yes,' she said frostily, 'A.M.'

Asia. It covered a lot of territory.

Plant was vegetating. Rusticating. He had got himself his hideaway and was hiding away in it and thinking his green thoughts and enjoying it. He looked at the wallaby chewing grass and the wallaby looked back at Plant smoking grass and a fine contentment reigned. They could go on like this for twenty minutes at a time, Plant and the wallaby. The wallaby's ears would rotate at distant sounds, lock onto them, and it would freeze there listening, apprehensive. Plant shared the apprehension. But no one came, nothing happened, and they both relaxed back into contentment. An alert contentment, perhaps. Certainly on the wallaby's part. Plant carried on smoking and became less alert. That was why he was in his hideaway, not to have to be endlessly alert.

At first Plant had thought the isolation would be difficult. Soon he found he was relishing it. He had thought that never seeing anyone, he would be bored. But he found, looking back on it, that seeing people had been the boring thing. In general. The meetings for a drink, a meal, and the same stories, the same situations, he wondered how he had ever put up with it. With it all no longer there he felt a great relief. At first he had thought he would need to contact people. He had written down phone numbers of people at Byron Bay, people on the Gold Coast, people near Nimbin. People within a range of a hundred kilometres. But he called none of them. Once or twice he had considered it. But before he had picked up the phone, the impetus had gone, the utter predictability of what would be said had borne down on him like the dead weight of the past. It was the dead weight of the past. He called no one. Except the wallaby, who chose not to respond. And the frogs at night, who called back. Croak, croak, croak, they called. Croak, croak, croak, he called back, working on capturing the exact pitch, the exact timing. Croak, croak, the frog called. Croak, croak, Plant responded. Soon he was initiating dialogue. When the sun had set he would be out there talking to them. Croak, Plant would call. Croak, the frog responded. He wished he knew what it meant. Maybe not a lot. Maybe no more than all the urban dialogues that lay behind him.

He tended his seedlings. He looked at the stars. He read a bit, tried catching up on what he had failed to read in the past. He watched a bit of television, but less and less as the days passed. He wrote down reflections in a notebook, but they didn't fill many pages. Most things seemed less and less necessary, things that had once seemed so important.

So when the phone rang, he had answered it without much eagerness.

If it hadn't been for the bulldozers Plant might never have taken on the job. If he lived economically and grew his own he might never need to work very much again. Maybe. It was a delirious world of happiness free from everything and everyone. And then the bulldozers shattered it. Their motors roaring, their metal tracks jingling and jangling, their remorseless destruction of the bush shattering his peace as they cleared some block along the valley. First thing in the morning. And then when they were finished the building would start. Hammer, hammer, hammer, clang, clang, clang.

Visions of Asia, gentle temple bells, silently meditating monks, opium dreams, Thai sticks, to soothe the shattered morning.

He got in the car and drove to meet her.

2

'Mr Plant?' she said.

'Yes,' he said.

'Alice Ackerman,' she said.

Plant shook her hand. Soft. Moist. He hated shaking hands. Ever since an expert on dog flu told him viruses were transmitted by body contact. Holding paws. He'd thought of wearing gloves, like the Queen. A Malaysian businessman sitting beside him on an airplane once explained to him that that was why the Queen always wore gloves. So nothing untoward could be transmitted. And why she had an official birth date. So the black magicians couldn't work magic spells based on her real birth date. The things people told him, uninvited.

Alice Ackerman looked him steadily in the eyes as she held his hand. Oh spare me those piercing looks. What could she read in the bloodshot whites? Was she some sort of iridologist?

She invited him in and told him to sit.

'Do come in. Do sit down.'

He did.

'My husband has gone away and not come back.'

She had that tall, elegant, well-groomed look of wives who hired private investigators to search for missing husbands. Expensive hair. Expensive linen dress. Expensive Italian shoes. A fair bit of gold distributed around the extremities. Earrings. Necklace. Bracelet. Watch.

'I don't really do divorce cases.'

'It isn't a divorce case. It's a disappearance.'

'Missing persons,' said Plant, to find a category, define it into officialese.

'Do you do missing persons?'

'Well …'

'Or isn't that classy enough either?'

'Well …' he tried again.

'Professor Oates recommended you.'

'Ah, yes.'

'He said you were a good lad for someone who wasn't a footballer.'

'Nice of him.'

'I'm not looking for a footballer.'

'Well isn't that fortunate,' said Plant.

'He said you do academic investigations.'

'Research assistance, investigative reporting,' Plant quoted. 'Archives, data searches, academic and general,' he expanded. It was meant to distinguish him from all the spouse, teenage activities, missing persons, de-bugging and surveillance stuff listed in the yellow pages. A specialist niche. Broaden the client base. Or thin it out. Classy, as she put it.

'My husband was an academic.'

'Was?' said Plant. 'You think he's dead?'

'What makes you say that?'

'The way you put it,' said Plant. 'When people say someone was, it can suggest they think, or know, someone is dead.'

'That old trick,' she said.

'That old trick,' he agreed.

He could have said, 'You said it,' but didn't. Remember the bulldozers, he told himself. Think of the temple bells.

'He took early retirement,' she said. 'That is why I said was.'

'When?' Plant asked.

'When what?'

'When did he take early retirement?'

'Oh, a year or so ago, eighteen months back.'

'Why?'

'Why? Because he was tired of it. The university had changed and he hated it.'

'Hated?'

'Does that sound too strong?'

'Not at all,' said Plant. 'Not necessarily.'

'So why did you query it?'

'People who hate often inspire hate. It could be a motive to explain his disappearance. That's all.'

She said nothing.

'Where does Professor Oates fit in?' Plant asked. 'Did your husband work with him?'

Tricky old Oates, Emeritus Professor of Evasion, who seemed to imply he might have had connections in intelligence, but there again might not.

'No, he's just a friend down here on the coast. An acquaintance really. I bumped into him and happened to tell him Alec was missing and I didn't know what to do, and he said he knew someone who did this sort of work.'

Maybe.

'It's always better if someone recommends someone.'

Maybe.

'So what did you husband do?'

'He was a sort of historian.'

'Sort of?' Plant asked. Why was nothing straightforward?

'That was his department. But he specialised in Asia.'

'An Asian historian.'

'Political and economic.'

'Ah,' said Plant.

Murky waters. Especially with tricky old Oates in the background. Nothing ever quite as it announced itself. An academic who was no longer an academic. An historian who was only sort of an historian. Not a lot of money in it, history. Not a medical or a legal or a business studies academic. Not a full pension if he took early retirement. Not the sort of income to fund much of an Asian investigation. Not to cover the time for the bulldozers to bulldoze and the building to finish.

'And how long has your husband been missing?'

'A couple of months or so.'

'Or so,' said Plant.

'Two and a half, maybe.'

'So quite a while,' he said, looking at her.

'Quite a while,' she agreed.

'And have you made any inquiries?'

'I didn't know what to do. I kept thinking he'd turn up. I tried calling people, but ...'

'But?'

'I didn't get anywhere.'

'Can I ask what you do? If anything?' Plant asked.

'Is that pertinent?'

It was for the economic base.

He smiled. His least impertinent smile. 'Just background.'

'I run an art gallery.'

'Run it?'

'Own it.'

That sounded better.

'What sort of art?'

'Asian primarily.'

'You were a student of your husband's?'

The Asian connection. And her age. Late thirties, he estimated. Early forties.

'Why do you say that?'

To be impertinent. To piss her off, basically. To try to retain the upper hand.

'It's often the case in academic marriages.'

'It wasn't an academic marriage.'

'Uh-huh.'

'It was a real marriage.'

'Was?'

'Is,' she said.

'And this gallery,' he said. 'It makes money? Or is it more like ...?'

She cut him off.

'It is not a hobby, if that is what you are thinking. It makes more than my husband ever earned. If anything, he was the hobby. I can afford to pay you, Mr Plant, if that is your worry.'

Not your typical academic wife.

'Good,' he said.

'Is it?'

'Is it what?'

'Your worry.'

'Yes,' he said simply. One of them, anyway.

'I like a man who is honest,' she said.

I think you'd like one who was dishonest too, Plant said to himself. I think you probably like men in general. And in particular.

She was attractive. There was no denying that. And she knew it. No denying that, either. And she used it. Probably all the time, probably that was her normal manner of hustling through the world, round the art galleries of the world, through the art dealers of the world, nothing personal in it at all.

'So now we've established I can afford you, Mr Plant, what else do you need to know?'

'Pretty well everything,' said Plant. 'So far I don't know much at all.'

'Would you like a drink?'

'A coffee would be fine,' he said.

She seemed to be the sort of person who would make a decent coffee.

3

The coffee was good. At least he had been right about that.

She leaned towards him as she poured it, the neck of her dress dropping down. How to win friends and get them to look for your missing husband. The sooner he got to Asia the better. Assuming he was going to take the case. Which it seemed like he was going to.

'He woke up one morning and decided he'd had enough. They were running down History. They wanted to destroy History so they could control the future. That was how he put it. They were shedding jobs and anyone over fifty-five was being targeted. Taken in for counselling and told to go. He worked out he would be no worse off financially if he went. I'm still working. We're not rich but we're not impoverished. So he went.'

'Went?'

'Left the university. Well, he stayed on as an honorary associate. They let him keep a room. A shared one. But there was no more teaching. No more staff meetings. He was much happier. Despite everything.'

'Despite what?'

'He was unhappy at what had happened to the university. To his subject. He felt a whole tradition of learning had been destroyed. He didn't mind not teaching. But the research, the accumulated body of knowledge ...'

She gestured. She was good at gestures. Had she been to drama school before taking up fine art? Finishing school? Or was that what they used to teach them at private girls' schools in her day?

'And then there was all the trouble with the series.'

'Series of what?' Plant asked.

'He edited a series of monographs.'

'Monographs?' said Plant. 'You mean like books?'

'I mean like monographs,' she said. 'It was a series of books on Asian studies.'

'Who was the publisher?' Plant asked.

'He was the publisher. He and Ghosh.'

'Ghosh?'

'He was one of Alec's colleagues. They set up the series years ago. And then Ghosh got sick and retired and Alec retired and they found they couldn't keep running it. Or didn't want to. It was getting too hard. They couldn't get the funding any more. The university used to give them assistance in the past, a bit of a subsidy and postage and all that sort of thing. But that had all come to an end. And with neither of them working there any more they couldn't get any secretarial help. Administrative assistance. They don't call them secretaries any more. So Alec handed it over to this American publisher and Ghosh got all hysterical about it.'

'Why?'

'He said he didn't trust them. He thought they were ...'

She searched for the appropriate word. Another gesture. These were not things normally a part of her own elegant, rarefied world.

'Crooks,' suggested Plant.

'Untrustworthy,' she said.

'In what way?'

'He didn't say in what way. He felt most publishers were' – she searched for the word, as if it were unfamiliar – 'crooks, as you put it. In general. In general Ghosh seemed to feel that way about most things. But he didn't have any better idea. Alec had been working on ways of keeping it going and Ghosh just had one of his emotional fits and went off and left it to him. And then complained at what Alec had done.'

'Was there money involved?'

'Of course. You can't publish without money. That was the problem. Neither of them was any good with money and they couldn't afford auditors and the new tax laws required all this reporting and they were worried the whole thing was going to blow up in their faces.'

'In what way?'

'Nothing criminal, if that's what you're thinking.'

'I'm not thinking anything. I'm just asking.'

'Just in terms of book-keeping. And the society.'

'The society?'

'Technically the series was published by a society with members and all that. At least it was originally. But the society had effectively collapsed, like everything else at the university. There were no meetings. No one was paying any subscriptions. In effect the society no longer existed. Alec was afraid that if they didn't have proper meetings and elections they would be technically in breach of things. Tax and things. But Ghosh could never get it together. Nor could Alec.'

'What were they afraid of happening?'

'Academics are jealous people. Not a very nice breed at all.'

Breeding, reflected Plant.

'Envious little men. And women. It just needed someone they'd offended, someone whose work they had rejected, to make a complaint to the university. Ask for audited accounts.'

'So it was a matter of embezzlement?'

'There was no embezzlement. There was nothing to embezzle. Any money the series made on sales went back into printing the next volume. It was all hand to mouth. That's why Alec was trying to find somebody to take it over so it could keep going.'

'And he did.'

'Yes.'

'But Ghosh didn't approve.'

'No.'

'And that upset your husband.'

'He was used to Ghosh. It's no big deal.'

'But it was one of the things that depressed him.'

'One of the many. You just asked me to fill in the picture.'

'It all helps.'

'Does it?'
'We'll see.'
'I hope so,' she said.
'Anything else?' Plant asked.
'Then Bowles called.'
'Bowles?'
'He was a student of Alec's. A former student. He had got himself some sort of a job in Thailand and he called Alec up to see if he would fly over and give a lecture.'
'Just one lecture?'
'Yes.'
'A long way to go for just one lecture.'
'Alec was a distinguished scholar in his field.'
'OK.'
'They were paying. It was some public lecture or something. I don't know. He was a devious little weasel.'
'Bowles?'
'Yes.'
'Is that what you husband felt about him?'
'Yes.'
'Why?'
'Because he was.'
'In what way?'
'In every way. He was doing a Master's degree, or not doing it, more to the point, and they were about to throw him out. Then Alec took pity on him and got him through, which was a big mistake.'
'Why?'
'Because then he stayed on and enrolled for a doctorate and asked for Alec as supervisor.'
'And did your husband supervise him?'
'Yes.'
'Even though he disliked him.'
'Mistrusted him.'
'Mistrusted him. For any reason?'
'Does there have to be a reason?'
'There must have been one.'
'He thought he was devious. Apart from the fact that his stepfather or his grandfather used to run the secret service.'
'Which secret service?'

'I don't know. Does it matter? How many are there?'

'And this worried your husband?'

'I didn't say it worried him. Why should it?'

'You tell me.'

'It just added to the general air of deviousness and manipulativeness that Bowles exuded.'

'And was Bowles himself in the secret service?'

'I shouldn't have thought so. I can't imagine anyone employing someone like him.'

'But you don't know.'

'How would I know?'

'What did your husband think?'

'I've no idea. I never discussed it with him.'

'Bowles completed his doctorate?'

'After much time-consuming hassle, yes.'

'And got a job in Thailand.'

'Apparently.'

'And invited your husband to give a lecture there.'

'That's what I told you.'

'Could there be a secret service angle to your husband's disappearance?'

'I can't imagine why.'

'He didn't have those connections?'

'No.'

'You're sure of that?'

'Well if he did, he didn't tell me,' she said. 'But then he wouldn't have, would he?'

'Possibly not.'

She offered no response.

Nor did Plant. With Oates in the background, he wasn't sure that he could believe her. Or anything else.

'And your husband accepted this invitation from Dr Bowles?'

'Yes.'

'And?'

'And nothing. That was the last I saw of him.'

'What was?'

'When he set off for the airport.'

'He never came back?'

'No.'

'Did he get there?'

'I don't know.'

'Didn't you call Dr Bowles?'

'Of course.'

'And?'

'He wasn't there.'

'Who wasn't there?'

'Bowles, of course. He'd gone on leave or something. I don't know. I couldn't get any sense out of anyone. No one seemed to speak English. Not enough to get any sense out of them. It's hopeless trying to do anything by phone with a university. You just sit waiting while someone puts you through to someone else. The lines go dead. You never get anywhere.'

'You didn't go over there?'

'That's what I want you to do.'

She gave him her suffering look. The imploring look. The dewy-eyed look.

'If you would.'

The catch in the voice.

It worked. It always did. The catch in the voice. Together with the bulldozers. He wouldn't have put it past her to have hired the bulldozers. One of her ways of making sure the earth moved.

'So, to sum up, you haven't heard from your husband.'

'No.'

'You don't know whether he's alive or dead.'

'No.'

'What about money? Is his bank account still being accessed?'

'I don't know. We have separate accounts.'

'You haven't asked the bank?'

'How could I?'

Easily. But he left it unsaid.

'I don't think banks like you asking about other people's accounts. I don't know how to go about it. That's why I'm hiring you.'

'Fair enough,' said Plant. 'What about Foreign Affairs?'

'What about them?' she snapped.

'Did you contact them?'

'Them? Oh, I see what you mean. No.'

'What did you think I meant?'

'Nothing,' she said.

'That your husband was having one?'

'Having what?'

'A foreign affair.'

'Not at all.'

'What else did you think I meant?'

'I had no idea what you meant.'

'So why didn't you contact Foreign Affairs?'

'Why? Should I have done?'

'If your husband disappeared overseas.'

'If he's disappeared what would they do? If he'd been found dead they would have contacted me. Otherwise I can't imagine they would take any interest. He could be anywhere.'

'Anywhere?'

'He knew people all over Asia.'

'So he might have left Thailand?'

'Yes.'

'You think he has?'

'I don't know.'

'But you raise the possibility.'

'Of course. He was always travelling. He might have stopped off on the way back.'

'Are there any stop-offs?'

'Or taken a side trip.'

'That's what you think?'

'I don't know.'

'Foreign Affairs might.'

'How?'

'Passport control. Immigration.'

'For other countries?'

'They could ask.'

'I don't want to make a big issue out of it,' she said. 'It might be nothing. I don't know how to go about asking Foreign Affairs. If you think that's the way to go about it, then do it. That's why I'm hiring you.'

Plant nodded. Was that why? He didn't know either. Here were two of them, neither knowing anything.

'If you'll take the job, that is,' she said.

The imploring mode.

'I'll take it,' said Plant.

She leaned over and poured another coffee.

4

It was not just a matter of hopping on a flight to Asia. Oh that it had been. The bulldozers rent the early morning. Plant considered pouring sugar into their gas tanks, joining the Greens, buying a Stinger missile in an Asian street market. In the immediate, he resolved to make some quick enquiries. Check out Ackerman's university. He could have phoned. He thought of it. Apart from his personal aversion to the telephone, he thought of Mrs Ackerman's assertion of the hopelessness of trying to do anything by phone with a university. Maybe. Sometimes phoning was better than a personal appearance. It was difficult these days to know what personal appearance he should cultivate. The club tie and blue blazer no longer necessarily worked. Baggy T-shirt, body piercing, and an overweight androgynous look seemed favoured by the current breed of academics. A fast food, hormone-laced meat diet was the way to go.

He stood in front of his bathroom mirror until the roar of the bulldozers forced him into arbitrary and accelerated decision. Personal appearance it would be. The clumsy shave, the un-ironed shirt, the crumpled slacks. No point in ironing or pressing, he would be crumpled again by the end of the two-hour drive, he always was.

He talked his way in through the gates and parked in sight of the brutalist great court. Not quite up to Mussolini's aesthetic vision, but adequate for Macarthur's headquarters in World War II. A good base from which to occupy and subdue Australia and forge an economic alliance with Japan. He wondered what sort of Asian history Alec Ackerman taught.

The directory outside the History department still listed Professors Ackerman and Ghosh. The administrative officer was a classic Queensland blonde, hard, athletic, tough. She just needed to put her hair up and she could be a policewoman or an Olympic athlete. It was a type that always gave Plant a frisson of something or other. Attraction. Or horror. Or fear. Or all three. It worried him, his response.

'I think he might be on leave,' she said.

'On leave?' said Plant. 'I thought he had retired.'

'He did,' she said. 'But he came back.'

'Came back?'

'As a visiting professor,' she said. 'They generally do.'

'As visiting professors?'

'Or an adjunct professor. Or an honorary associate. Or a research fellow. Or an emeritus.'

'I see,' said Plant. 'Retired, come back and then gone away again on leave.'

She said nothing.

'Why would he be on leave if he's retired?' Plant persisted.

'Travel insurance,' she said. 'If he is overseas on university business he's covered by university travel insurance.'

'What sort of university business?'

'Study leave,' she said.

'Not official business?'

'No,' she said. 'Conferences. Visiting lectures. Research.'

'The privileges of office,' said Plant.

She gave no response. A loyal servant of the system.

'And how long is he on leave for?' Plant asked.

She consulted the data base on her computer. It took a while. Plant studied her reflectively.

'A year,' she said.

'And Professor Ghosh?'

She clicked a few more keys.

'A year.'

'Any idea where?'

'Professor Ghosh is in Kolkata.'

'Kolkata.'

'You probably know it as Calcutta. It's called by its Bengali name now.'

'And Professor Ackerman?'

'He's listed Bangkok, Singapore, Manila, Kolkata, London.'

'Do you have an address?'

'No, just his email address,' she said.

'Nothing else?'

'Most staff keep in contact by email now.'

'And Professor Ackerman? Has he kept in contact?'

'I don't know,' she said. 'I haven't seen anything.'

'So you've no idea where he is?'

'Not really,' she said.

'And you haven't heard from him, you said.'

'We wouldn't expect to,' she said. 'He was never one for using email. If he wanted anything he'd just look in at the office.'

'And he hasn't looked in?'

'No,' she smiled, sweetly.

'The monograph series he and Professor Ghosh edit,' said Plant. 'Do you sell copies here?'

'Not any more,' she said. 'We used to.'

'But not now?'

'No.'

Another sweet smile. The negative seemed to bring out the best in her. He wondered if she ever said yes.

'Where could I get hold of them?'

'You could try the bookshop.'

'Would they have them?'

'Probably not.' A sad smile, a sweet, sad smile.

'So how could I get them?'

'You could try emailing the editors.'

'But Professor Ackerman doesn't use email, you said.'

'No,' she agreed. 'You could try Professor Ghosh.'

'Does he use email?'

'He uses everything,' she said. And everyone, her tone seemed to imply.

He dragged himself away regretfully, giving his sweetest smile.

Walking through the campus, picking his way between entangled students on the lawns and scavenging birds pecking around them for lunch scraps he ran back over the dialogue in his head. She had been amazingly helpful for a university person. Forthcoming. He had never found the breed forthcoming in the past. Or helpful. Having to deal with recalcitrant students day after day made them generally uncooperative. Usually they gave nothing out and took everything in. As with hotel keepers and bar staff, he worked on the assumption university administrative officers had to be informers. Police. Special Branch. Security. Keeping a check on the intelligentsia. He could picture her in a uniform. He could picture her in a uniform more easily than out of it. The blue skirt, blue blouse. Matching her eyes. The whistle. The riot stick. The holster at the hip. The police service revolver. It was not good, imagining these things; not that it was good suppressing them, either. It raised the likelihood that her cooperativeness could only have been to encourage him to ask more questions. Perhaps someone was keeping a tab on Ackerman and on whoever might be asking about him.

She was right about the bookshop. No monograph series. Nothing in the history section by Ackerman or Ghosh. Nothing much at all. The end of history.

The bank was a bit trickier. It took a while and some ID confirming and a call to Mrs Ackerman and other carrying on. But in the end he got something, even if it was only nothing. Ackerman's pension was paid in every fortnight. But nothing had been withdrawn from the account since he had flown out of Australia. No credit card transactions. Nothing. So much for the money trail.

He checked with the airline. More bureaucracy. But he talked his way through. He had his methods. Yes, Professor Ackerman had departed for Bangkok. A return ticket. Valid for one year. Return booked for twelve months from departure. Return date unchanged. Still unused. Still valid.

Plant called to arrange another meeting.

'Is it absolutely necessary?' she said.

The bulldozers groaned and roared and smashed down trees, the power-saws whined and howled.

'It would be best to get everything straight while I'm here,' he said. 'I don't want to find myself in Asia without some crucial information I could have got before I left.'

'I can't imagine what it might be,' she said. 'I've told you all I know.'

'I'd like to run through it one more time.'

'Play it again, Sam,' she said.

He let that pass.

'Is there anything in particular that you want?' she asked.

'It would help to know what your husband looks like.'

She groaned.

'Do you have a photograph?'

'I'll see if I can find one,' she said.

'And I'd like to have a look at something your husband might have written. Something in the monograph series he published. The bookshop didn't have anything.'

'Did you try the library?'

'I don't have borrowing rights,' he said.

'Of course you don't. Well, in that case you'd better come here. We can nose along the bookshelves together.'

It sounded delightful.

5

She handed him a photograph. A passport style mug shot. The books were on the table waiting for him. A couple of books. So much for nosing along the shelves in tandem, the accidental, fleeting contact, the glasses removed, the hair let down. He had read it somewhere. Many times. But it never seemed to happen like that.

'Try not to lose them,' she said. 'The books are out of print. They're impossible to replace. And all the monograph back-list is away in some warehouse in Woop Woop or Karachi or wherever they got sent.'

'I don't lose books,' Plant said.

'You imply you lose other things.'

'No.'

She smiled at him.

'Not even your temper.'

He smiled back.

'I'm sorry, Mr Plant,' she said. 'Forgive me if I sound tetchy. It has all been rather a strain. I'm trying to keep up a brave face. But it makes me very edgy. And bitchy. It's nothing personal.'

'That's all right,' said Plant.

'It isn't,' she said. 'And I know it isn't. I'll try and behave better. How about a drink?'

It was too early. It was too hot and he had to drive. It wasn't at all what he wanted. But she was making a gesture and he had to accept it. One of those gestures of goodwill, of lowering the tension, that let her still retain the upper hand. Imposing her will even as she implied surrendering it. It all went through his head as she poured him a Margaret River Verdelho. She diluted hers with mineral water. He would have done the same if she had left room in his glass. But she hadn't.

Or was he imagining it all? Projecting games that were not there, to defend himself against someone who seemed too attractive and who had no interest in him at all, to defend himself against himself by making her the enemy. Plant, you have vegetated too long, you must move more in the company of women, you must experience how they really behave rather than fantasizing fearful projections in your hermit's retreat. You have to stop imagining that every attractive woman is coming on to you and resenting them in case they aren't and you're making a fool of yourself.

She wasn't fazed by his researches.

'It doesn't mean anything. Taking study leave doesn't mean you have to be away. Quite often people don't go anywhere. You take the insurance cover for if and when you travel. If you come back early you cancel it. It's easier to apply for the whole year in one go than keep on changing plans. And you list anywhere you might possibly go. Just in case. It doesn't necessarily mean he was going to go to any of the places he named.'

'So you don't think it means he was planning to stay away.'

'No. He was just flying over to give a lecture and coming back.'

'And the ticket? Return in a year?'

'That doesn't mean anything either. You have to have a return date for the computer. You can't just have it open-ended. Bowles would have had it issued like that. Then Alec would have changed it to the return date he wanted when he knew what it was. He would have stayed on after the lecture. He wouldn't have got straight on a plane and flown back. And he wouldn't have wanted to pin down a date until he was there. He'd have wanted to see how long he could put up with Bowles, see if anything turned up. It's not as if he had to get back for classes any more.'

'And the bank account? No withdrawals.'

'That's why I'm worried. How is he living without any money?'

She left the unspoken, that he wasn't living. That he might have planned to disappear, she absolutely denied.

'Why would he just vanish?' she asked, her fixed gaze holding Plant's eyes. Would you? she seemed to be saying. Would you not return to me? But it was unvocalised so he did not have to reply.

'So,' she said, 'end of question time. Or have you more to ask?'

'Just odd things,' said Plant.

'Go on then.'

'Does your husband have a life insurance policy?'

'I've no idea.'

'No idea?'

'Why would he? He had his superannuation. He'd been in the fund a long time. The old fund. It was a good one. Why do you ask?'

'Just covering every angle,' said Plant. 'If he had one the insurance company would need proof of death before paying out. Or reasonable likelihood. Proper investigation.'

She looked at him in disgust.

'I am not hiring you so that I can cash in on my husband's life insurance.'

'Which you say he didn't have anyway.'

'Which I have no reason to believe he had. I certainly didn't insure him, or hire an Asian hit-man to kill him so I could claim on it.'

'I didn't mean that,' said Plant.

'What did you mean?'

'I don't know what I meant,' said Plant. 'I was just thinking aloud.'

'And why were you having those thoughts? I've hired you to find him. Alive.'

'You believe he's alive.'

'What does it matter what I believe?'

'Often what people believe is true,' said Plant.

'I hope so. I sincerely hope so,' she said.

'You want him back?'

'I want to know what's happened.'

'You don't want him back?'

'I need to know … Of course I want him back. But I'm not stupid. It's been so long. I can't let myself … entertain false hopes.'

'So you think he might be dead.'

'I don't think anything. I can't let myself think anything. That's why I need to know. So I can stop thinking. Stop these thoughts.'

She stood at the window looking out over the sea. The iridescent blue. The wide horizon. If you dropped your gaze you could see the surf and the surfers. But if you stayed sitting where Plant was sitting you just saw the long, level line of the ocean, the clear salt emptiness, and the tall slim woman in the expensive linen dress, glass in hand, hair immaculately brushed down to her shoulders.

'Did your husband commute from here to the university?' Plant asked.

'No. We have a house in Brisbane.'

'So this is like an investment property?' Plant asked.

'No, this is not an investment property. This is a vulgar, old-fashioned weekender.'

'Very nice,' said Plant.

'It has appreciated in value since we bought it, but that was not why we bought it. It was just somewhere to get away to.'

'You felt the need to get away.'

'No, not that either,' she said. 'But we both like the beach. We like to swim. The Gold Coast was here. Why not enjoy it?'

'Why not?' said Plant. 'And do you?'

'Do I what?'

'Do either of you enjoy it?'

'Yes,' she said. 'We both do. Doesn't it seem enjoyable to you?'

'Oh yes,' said Plant. 'And do a lot of academics do the same?'

'If you mean enjoy things, I rather doubt it. If you mean do they have property on the coast, yes, I would think so. Some go for the hills behind, some prefer the bright lights.'

'You prefer the bright lights.'

She smiled sadly at his crudity.

'And your husband?'

'Is this some sort of grilling?'

'Just routine,' said Plant. 'I need to get some sort of profile of him to know where to look for him. Asia's a big area. I'd like to narrow it down. Bright lights or jungle. Urban centres or coastal resorts.'

'Why don't you just say what you want, Mr Plant, instead of …'

'Instead of?'

'Instead of whatever you're doing. Insinuating. Being devious.'

He topped up his wine with mineral water, now he had cleared some space.

'Or is that your technique?'

'I guess it's my technique.'

'You don't like asking straight questions?'

'They don't always elicit straight replies.'

'And you want straight replies.'

'Not necessarily,' he said. 'I'm just trying to build up a picture.'

She gestured at the art work covering the walls.

'Take your pick,' she said.

'Your husband liked art, too?'

'Not especially,' she said.

'What did he go for?'

'He was more like you, Mr Plant. He went for the economic base.'

'A Marxist?'

'Is that what you are, Mr Plant?'

'For the moment I ask the questions,' he said.

'To understand modern Asian politics you need to know your Marx.'

'Is that so?'

'That was what Alec said.'

'And did he?'

'Did he what?'

'Know his Marx?'

'He was a political historian, Mr Plant. He had necessarily read his Marx and his Mao. And his Confucius and his Sun Tzu.'

'A well-read man.'

'He is.'

'Back to the present tense,' said Plant.

That was when she began to cry. She didn't rush out of the room, so he got up and put an arm round her and said he was sorry. She fitted snugly into his arm. For a while it was all very cosy. Then she broke away.

She turned her mascara-streaked gaze towards him.

'I have to fix my make-up,' she said.

He drained his glass while she fixed it.

'Why don't we get some lunch?' she said when she came back into the room.

'You'll have had quite enough Asian food before you're finished,' she said, taking him past the Chinese and Indian and Japanese and Korean and Thai restaurants and leading him into an Italian trattoria. Her regular, clearly. The padrone came over and embraced her. He was wearing a gold-braided yachting cap with Venezia embroidered on the front, so Plant assumed he was the padrone. A kiss on each cheek, a long sustained bear-hug. The waiter polished glasses behind the bar and winked at Plant. The padrone shook his hand solemnly.

'Mr Plant is looking for my husband,' she said.

'Excellent,' said the padrone. 'And when you find him and kill him, you tell me and I marry the lady and give you a reward.'

'I wasn't planning to kill him,' said Plant.

'No problem,' said the padrone, 'that can be arranged. Just find him and make him get a divorce. That's all right. Just so I can have her. You still get a reward. Maybe not such a big one.'

He pulled out a chair for her to sit down.

'Pinot grigio, aqua minerale,' he said, only the slightest note of a question. The waiter was already bringing them over, attaching the ice bucket to the table's edge. Her table.

'You need a menu?' the waiter asked.

'Just tell us the specials,' she said.

'You know the specials,' he said.

'I like to hear you tell them,' she said.

He rolled his eyes and recited them.

It was all very cosy. The starched tablecloth, the chilled white wine, the naked lady on the mineral water label. Santa Vittoria, pray for us now.

'I come here often, yes, if that's what you're asking.'

'I thought you might,' said Plant.

'I like the familiar.'

'Fair enough.'

'When Alec didn't come back it was a terrible shock.'

'When was that?' Plant asked.

'What do you mean, when was that?'

'Did you expect him on a particular day, and he didn't show?'

'No, he hadn't given me a specific date. But when he wasn't back after a couple of weeks, I started to get anxious. And then, as the weeks went on ...'

'More a sort of developing, cumulative shock rather than a sudden one.'

'What are you getting at?'

'I don't know,' said Plant. 'I'm just trying to get the picture clear.'

'He expected to be away about a week or so.'

'He expected to or you expected him to?'

'I don't know, what's the difference?'

'Did he say he would be away a week?'

'I don't know, now you ask. It was what I assumed. There was no reason he'd be gone any longer. He was only giving the one lecture.'

'He didn't have anything else he was doing?'

'No.'

'No private business.'

'No.'

'He wasn't seeing anyone else?'

'No. Not that he said.'

'But he didn't give a definite return date.'

'Not definite. But it wasn't going to be for long.'

'You weren't picking him up at the airport?'

'We never pick each other up at the airport.'

Plant looked across the table at her.

'We never did. Airlines are so unreliable. The planes are always delayed. Alec was always travelling, it was no big deal. It was much easier just to pick up a cab.'

'I see.'

'I don't think you do.'

'It makes sense,' said Plant.

'But you think it's odd.'

He shrugged.

'Look, there was nothing wrong with my marriage. We were very happy. We had separate careers but our marriage was very close. Don't take any notice of Frankie, he goes on like that with everyone.'

'Frankie?'

'Francesco. The restaurateur. It's part of his act. Like his hat. It's all theatre. All restaurateurs and waiters are actors.'

'I thought they were all hit-men.'

She held on to his wrist.

'Please don't get me wrong,' she said.

The firm grip. The deep, steady gaze. The low-cut, expensive dress. The repaired make-up. Frankie at the door greeting some new arrivals.

'Bellissimo.'

Plant held her gaze and she relaxed from imploring his trust to offering a gentle smile, one of those smiles actresses worked on for years. She loosened her grip and her fingers slid down over his. He found it hard not to get her wrong.

She recommended the duck and the suckling pig and the snapper and the barramundi and risotto pescatore, and chose swordfish herself. Plant stuck to his vegetarian principles and ordered funghi al gorgonzola and stuffed zucchini flowers.

'You close your eyes to the anchovies in the stuffing,' she said.

Plant conceded that he did.

She ordered an arugula salad and ate most of it herself, Plant not feeling obliged to eat salad just because he didn't eat meat.

'How was it?' asked Frankie.

'Beautiful,' she said.

'Excellent,' Plant agreed.

Frankie smiled at them in appreciation.

'You enjoy it then.'

'Absolutely,' she said.

'That is good. That warms my heart.'

He stood behind her and squeezed her shoulders with both hands in some sort of massaging action.

'How about that?'

'Heavenly.'

He grinned at Plant. His teeth were chipped.

'Some woman,' he said.

'I like a man who likes his work,' she said. 'Do you like your work, Mr Plant?'

Plant said that he did.

6

Plant sat himself down in the foyer bar of the hotel and ordered a draught Singha beer. It was happy hour. Order one beer, get one free. He was never one to refuse a bargain. Not even on expenses. A girl sang sad songs to an electronic keyboard accompaniment in what seemed to Plant's unpracticed ear a particularly mournful way. She looked too thick-set to be Thai. Chinese-Russian-Jewish from Harbin, perhaps. Or Mexican-American-Filipino from Los Angeles. Her accompanist looked like a Taiwanese Buddy Holly. Or his glasses made him look that way.

Plant crunched his complimentary peanuts and sipped his beer. There seemed no point in brandishing Ackerman's photograph to the busloads of Japanese and Korean tourists trooping in and out. He would ask the manager in the morning. It seemed somehow uncivilised to check in and start quizzing the staff immediately. Have you seen this man? He didn't imagine it would lead to anything. But even when you have a thousand kilometre walk ahead of you, you start with the first step.

The hotel was one where Ackerman usually stayed in Bangkok, Mrs Ackerman had told him. No, she didn't know if he stayed there last time. No, she didn't know if Bowles had arranged accommodation. Plant chose to stay there since he had nowhere else in mind. He might as well stay where Ackerman had stayed, or might have stayed. Soak in the ambience. Sniff out the trail. Put himself in his quarry's shoes. Would Ackerman have sat down in the foyer for happy hour, the frequent flyer, the experienced Asia hand? He had no idea.

He drank his second beer and ordered a third, which would make four in the end. Assuming happy hour had not passed. He chewed his peanuts and tried to think of what to do. He had no idea what to do. Whatever it was would have to wait until the morning, when it might become clear. He watched the singer. She watched him back impassively. The songs seemed especially lugubrious. Lost love and missing persons. The fourth beer arrived. It must still have been happy hour. When she launched into 'Strange Fruit' he figured it was over.

He woke feeling dreadful, jet-lagged, hung-over, disoriented, not a shred of happiness to show for all the happy hours he had put in. But a shower and a breakfast of noodles and fresh fruit restored him. He gave thanks for noodles and fresh fruit. Even the most distant scent of fried egg, black pudding, slaughtered pig, fried bread would have been too much. He was in the east, rejecting his heritage.

The girl at reception cupped her hands together slightly underneath her chin and bent her head in the namaskara gesture. Plant gave a smile and a stumbling nod and asked for the manager.

'No problem, I hope,' said the manager. Chinese. Impassive.

'No problem at all.'

'Everything satisfactory.'

A statement rather than a question.

'Excellent,' said Plant. 'Breakfast was beautiful.'

The manager waited. Of course it was beautiful. He registered no satisfaction at the obvious.

'Do you know this man?' Plant asked, producing his photograph of Ackerman.

The manager considered.

'He is a guest?'

'Often,' said Plant.

'Often,' said the manager.

'Regularly,' Plant expanded.

The manager let that pass. Not a word for the oriental tongue.

'Western faces,' said the manager. 'Very difficult.'

'I understand,' said Plant. 'All look the same.'

'You understand,' said the manager.

'Yes,' said Plant.

'He in trouble?' asked the manager.

'No,' said Plant.

'Police look for him?'

'No. He is missing.'

'You police?'

'No,' said Plant. 'Private investigation. He came here a couple of months ago. And then vanished. Never came home. His wife is very worried.'

'Ah, wife,' said the manager.

Plant produced a photograph of Mrs Ackerman. She had given him a hard time before she let him have it. 'Why do you want my photograph? It's Alec you're looking for.' 'It might come in useful,' he'd said. 'You want to keep it in your wallet next to your heart?' she'd asked. 'Put it under your pillow in strange bedrooms?' 'Something like that,' Plant had conceded.

'Attractive woman,' said the manager.

'Yes,' said Plant.

'Why he run away from her?'

The manager waited but Plant could offer no suggestions.

'I wondered if you could check your records,' said Plant. 'He was booked to stay here. I wondered if he ever arrived.'

'Maybe not check in,' said the manager.

'Exactly.'

'You see police?'

'No,' said Plant.

'You police?'

'No.'

'Your name please.'

It sounded like police again.

'Plant.'

'You stay here?'

'Yes.'

He keyed it into the computer.

'How long?'

'Until I find him.'

The manager looked at him. 'Maybe long time.'

'I hope not,' said Plant. 'But it's a nice hotel to stay in.'

'Huh,' said the manager, focused on the monitor.

'OK, his name.'

'Ackerman.'

The manager keyed it in.

'Ah, Professor Ackerman. Yes, he stay here.'

Plant's spirits rose, such as they were.

'When?'

'Oh, many times. Ah, Professor Ackerman.' He looked at the photograph. 'Now I see him. Good man. Very good man. He had special rate.'

'Special rate?'

'Australian government rate.'

'Really?' said Plant.

'Yes.'

'Did the Australian government arrange that?'

'No, he pay.'

'So why a government rate?'

'Special rate. Cheaper. Here often.'

'I see,' said Plant. He didn't. But one thing at a time.

'When was he here?'

'Like you say. Two months ago.'

'For how long?'

'I think three days.'

He read out the dates.

'Then he checked out?'

'Yes.'

'And you've no idea where he went?'

The manager smiled in weary disbelief. How could he?

'How did he pay?'

The manager looked at the screen again.

'Cash.'

'Did he always pay cash?'

The manager opened his hands.

'Could be. Could be not. I only have this record.'

'And the other times he stayed?'

'Not on file any more.'

Plant left it at that. If he needed past records he could try again. He couldn't see that he would. He started to write down the details. The manager raised a forbidding hand.

'I print it for you.'

'You're very kind,' said Plant.

The manager smiled.

7

Plant took a cab from the hotel to the university. He could have phoned. No doubt. But, apart from Mrs Ackerman's alleged difficulties, he had no reason to expect he would achieve successful communication. He wasn't sure whether he believed Mrs Ackerman or not. But with no knowledge of Thai the thought of trying to deal with a university switchboard, and a departmental secretary let alone an administrative officer, and a university, where no one could ever be found, that was the nature of the beast, deterred him from any attempt. And then there was the element of surprise. Rather than alert Bowles to his inquiries, he would just front up. Already he was thinking of Bowles as someone who had to be trapped by surprise. Already he was seeing him as suspect. Suspected of what? Abduction? Manslaughter? Kidnapping? Assassination? Was this the best way to go about his inquiries?

The cab wound through a network of narrow alleys, threatening to run down moped riders, tip over handcarts, crush dogs and small children, until it connected with the highway. Then it became stationary, waiting to enter. And having nosed its way into the traffic stream, continued to remain stationary along with the rest of the clogged traffic. Plant practiced patience, rehearsed his questions. Slowly the miasma of fear dissolved, the alien threat broke down into its component parts. He began to register the pattern of street stalls, juice, fruit, grilling meat, fish, shirts, ties, wallets, watches. Shops of Indian tailors and Chinese gold merchants. The fumes were choking, the traffic was appalling but no one ran into anyone. There were blasts of horns and imprecations and gestures. But there was no collision, no impact.

The cab driver found the university, the guard at the gates directed him to the department, the secretary pointed him to Bowles' room, the door was open, and Bowles was there, feet on desk. Plant knew it was Bowles from the R.M. Williams boots. Australians abroad.

'Dr Bowles,' said Plant.

The feet crashed to the ground and Bowles stood on them, not quite to attention, nor especially at ease. He was tall and young and callow, red haired, with the pallid skin that often goes with red hair. The pallid, puffy look of a goldfish. Short-sleeved tan shirt, open at the neck. Light fawn cotton slacks, not quite military. But close enough.

'Plant,' said Plant.

There was no reason why it should mean anything, and it seemed not to.

'Do you have a moment?'

'Well,' said Bowles. The airmail *Guardian Weekly* lay on his desk, open at the crossword. About a third of the clues completed. About as far as Plant had ever got. Know the mental capacity of your adversary or at least his crossword-solving skills.

'I don't want to take up too much of your time,' said Plant. 'I'd just like to ask you a few questions.'

His best police-procedure procedure. It rarely failed to unnerve. Not that Bowles didn't seem congenitally unnerved, his mouth open in alarm, his jaw wiggling from side to side. If he had been a smoker he would have reached for a cigarette, but a politically correct sign pinned to the wall announced No Smoking. After all the efforts the USA had made to open Thailand to American tobacco products. Successfully. And now Bowles was trying to thwart them.

'It concerns Professor Ackerman,' said Plant. And left it at that.

'What about Professor Ackerman?'

'He's disappeared,' said Plant.

'Disappeared?'

'Disappeared.'

'What do you mean disappeared?' Bowles asked.

'Disappeared. Vamoosed. Vanished,' said Plant. 'And you were the last person to see him. It appears.'

'Me?' said Bowles.

'You,' said Plant.

Outside the window temple bells rang, or maybe classroom bells, and young girls in pure white blouses and respectable navy blue skirts went by giggling and chattering. Bowles sat at his desk, jaw sagging vacantly. Plant's shock tactics had achieved their effect of shock but not much else. He followed up what was supposed to be his advantage.

'When did you last see Professor Ackerman?'

'He gave a lecture here,' said Bowles. 'A couple of months ago.'

'You arranged it?'

'Yes.'

'And then what happened?'

'What happened?' said Bowles. 'I don't know.'

'He gave the lecture?'

'Yes,' said Bowles.

'And then where did he go?'

'I don't know,' said Bowles. 'Back to Australia I suppose.'

'He never returned.'

'To Australia?'

'Or anywhere else.'

'Heavens,' said Bowles.

He looked round his room as if there might be some trace of Ackerman hanging there.

'Well, I really don't know. And I was the last person to see him?'

'Yes.'

'Are you sure of that? I mean, how do you know no one else saw him somewhere.'

'They may have,' said Plant. 'But so far you're his last known contact.'

'Crikey,' said Bowles.

He scratched at his pimples between his mouth and his chin. Then he rubbed his nostrils.

'I say, do you have time for a coffee? Or a juice? The coffee isn't very good.'

'I've all the time in the world,' said Plant.

They sat among the students on wooden benches beneath a shingled roof. Bowles recommended mangosteen, star fruit and watermelon juice. Plant complied.

'You mean he's really disappeared? No one knows where he is?'

'That's right.'

'How extraordinary. I mean, how terrible. How is Mrs Ackerman taking it?'

'She's hired me to find him.'

'Have you had any luck?'

'Would I be out here asking you questions if I had?'

'No, I suppose not.'

'Tell me everything you know about him,' said Plant.

'Everything?' said Bowles. 'That's quite …'

He tailed off.

'Quite a lot?'

'I don't know whether it's that much, actually. I just don't know where to begin.'

'Begin at the beginning,' said Plant.

'And go on till you come to the end,' said Bowles. He grinned happily.

'Alice,' he said.

'Actually, it was the king.'

'Well, yes,' said Bowles. 'Are you a fan of Lewis Carroll?'

'Not especially.'

'Oh,' said Bowles.

Plant waited until he found a beginning and began.

'He was very good to me. They were going to throw me out of the M.A. course. But he stepped in and took me over and straightened me out and arranged the examiners and everything. And I got my degree. Then I enrolled for a doctorate under him.'

'He must have been pleased.'

'I don't know. I don't think he really liked supervising. Or maybe he didn't really like me.'

'But you liked him.'

'He was inspirational. In his way. I'd just been doing the M.A. for something to do really. But when I got it, that inspired me. That's why I enrolled for the doctorate.'

'For something else to do?'

'No. No. Because I'd got caught up in it. He'd made it seem meaningful.'

'You got on well with him?'

'I suppose so. It was hard to tell. He was sort of distant and moody sometimes.'

'But he thought you were a good student.'

'I don't know. I don't know that I was. I think he was glad I passed because that scored off the director of graduate studies. She'd wanted to throw me out.'

'So it was all politics.'

'Academic politics. Yes, in part.'

'And you kept in touch with him after you'd finished.'

'Not really. Well, sort of. For references and things.' He laughed. 'There were quite a lot of those. Till I eventually got this job.'

'And why did you take this job? Why here?'

'I love it here.'

'Is that why you came?'

'Not initially. Initially it was a matter of getting a job anywhere. But I got to love it.'

'Why's that? The sex? The drugs?'

'I'm married,' said Bowles. 'I don't do drugs.'

'So what is it you love? The weather?'

The sun beating down on the shingled roof. The sweat dripping off them in the humidity.

'The people.'

'The masses?'

'The individuals,' said Bowles.

'And what do you teach?'

'Mainly it's English language teaching. Conversation. Civilisation. But that's really a way of getting them proficient in the language. We read through *Kim* together.'

'Asian civilisation?'

'No. European. Western.'

'But your degree was in Asian studies.'

'My doctorate was on colonialism in the novel.'

'I thought Professor Ackerman was a historian.'

'Yes. But he didn't believe in arbitrary disciplinary boundaries. He saw literature as historical data. The novel offered documentation of colonialism.'

'But Thailand was never colonised, was it?'

'Not formally. Not politically. But economically ...'

He tailed off.

'Economically?'

'All Asia is economically colonised.'

'Was that Ackerman's line?'

'It's no particular person's line,' said Bowles. 'It's just the way it is.'

8

'Tell me about the intelligence services,' said Plant.

'The intelligence services?'

'I understand your stepfather was head of one of them.'

'My father, actually,' said Bowles. 'But my parents divorced. I only found out when I tracked him down.'

'Tracked him down?'

'There was this terrible Christmas. A family row. There were always rows. My mother was a very strong woman. One Christmas there was a sort of scene. I was having an argument with my father. Well, the man I'd always thought was my father. And she said, "You can stop calling him father, he isn't your father." Then it came out she'd been married before. I never knew. So when I was in England doing research for my doctorate, I decided to track my real father down. Used my research skills. He was quite impressed. It turned out he was head of this secret agency.'

'Which one?'

'I don't think I'm allowed to tell you.'

'So was he impressed enough to give you a job?'

'It would be hard to do something like that after working under Ackerman.'

'Because they wouldn't have you?'

Bowles laughed. 'Yes, well, there could be that. They're not too keen on chaps like him. No, what I meant was the values he instilled.'

'What values?'

'I suppose you'd call them progressive.'

'That's the coded word for Marxist.'

'No, not at all. Well, it might be, I don't know. It's not what I meant.'

'You don't know the term?'

'No.'

'How extraordinary,' said Plant. 'Not even after being taught by Ackerman.'

Bowles said nothing. For all his seemingly callow appearance, he knew enough to know when to say nothing. Intuition? Plant doubted it. Training? He wondered.

'How about your mother? Is she in intelligence too?'

'My mother?' He laughed. 'I never thought of it. She's more the special services type. Direct action.'

'Is that a yes or a no?'

'I've no idea,' said Bowles.

'Why did you invite Professor Ackerman to give a lecture?'

'It was the least I could do,' said Bowles. 'He'd been good to me. Spent so much time on me. And we had the funds. For a public lecture by a distinguished specialist. And he is distinguished in his way.'

'Wasn't it expensive to fly him out just for one lecture?'

'It would have been more expensive to have him give more,' said Bowles. 'Anyway, he probably wouldn't have wanted to. We had the funds to pay for one public lecture. We didn't have funds to put him up for more than two or three days, though.'

'You put him up at the university?'

'No, we gave him a per diem. That's what he asked for. He arranged his own accommodation.'

'So did he just come for three days? Or was he going to stay on?'

'I don't know,' said Bowles. 'He might have stayed on. I just arranged the flight and the honorarium. It was up to him what else he did.'

'He didn't have any plans?'

'None I could detect.'

'You were into detection.'

Bowles gave a boyish grin.

'He just seemed to have come for the ride.'

'What did he talk about?'

'Nothing much. Gossip about the department. He didn't seem happy with the way it was going.'

'I mean his official talk. The lecture.'

'Oh, that,' said Bowles. 'Let me see.'

He tapped his teeth with a pencil.

Oh that. Bowles had flown his old professor some thousands of kilometers for a lecture and couldn't remember what it was about. Was that credible? Plant wondered. Probably. Probably it was. The academic gravy train. Who ever took any notice of the ostensible purpose or the official subject?

'The usual things, I guess,' said Bowles. 'Tiger economies. Social justice. Regional security. The war on terror. Free markets. Pros and cons, you know. Nothing controversial.'

'He wasn't controversial?'

'Not in a public lecture.'

'In private?'

'He could be.'

'Was he this time?'

'I didn't get to talk to him much.'

'Did he stay on after?'

'I don't know. I think I already told you that.'

'Did you expect him to stay on?'

'I didn't really think about it.'

'Really?'

'The paperwork arranging just that was quite enough in itself. I didn't really have time to think of anything else.'

'You said it was a public lecture. Did the public come?'

'Yes. Parents. Alumni. Embassy people. You know the sort of thing.'

'I don't.'

'Oh well, the faculty and graduate students, a few people from other campuses, overseas research students, that sort of thing. It was a decent enough crowd.'

'And then?'

'We had a dinner.'

'On campus?'

'At a hotel in town.'

'And he seemed all right?'

'Yes.'

'He didn't collapse with food poisoning?'

'No.'

'Didn't get drunk and have to be carried off?'

'No.'

'Didn't disappear with a local beauty.'

'No. Well, not that I noticed.'

'And you never saw him again?'

'No. I saw him that evening at the dinner. And I'd had lunch with him the day before. And that was it. He knew his way around Bangkok. He didn't have to be nursemaided or anything. I was caught up with family at the weekend.'

'Your father visited? Your mother?'

'My wife's family. She's Thai.'

'So you never saw him again.'

'No.'

'And how did he seem when you did see him?'

'He seemed like he always seemed.'

'Not depressed? Excited? Distracted?'

'No, none of those.'

'You didn't get the impression he had something on his mind? Preoccupied with something.'

'No,' said Bowles.

'Take your time.'

'He seemed like he'd always seemed.'

Plant handed him a card from the hotel.

'Give me a call if you think of anything else.'

'How long are you staying?'

'As long as it takes,' said Plant.

Merely to sound menacing. He didn't mean it. At this rate it could take for ever.

That and the drive back was enough for one day. He took a cab back to the hotel and had lunch there. More noodles. He considered spending the afternoon in more inquiries but he couldn't think where to inquire. He considered doing the tourist thing, visit the royal palace or the temple but he didn't feel like another bout of traffic.

He went up to his room and dug out the books from Ackerman's series that Mrs Ackerman had reluctantly lent him. Now he finally looked at them they seemed not actually to be written by Ackerman. They had his name on the cover. But both books seemed to be conference proceedings. Selected papers on South East Asian Culture and Society. Edited by Ackerman and Ghosh, but not actually written by them. Neither of them contributed a paper to the proceedings. Unless they used pseudonyms, which seemed unlikely. Each volume had an introduction signed jointly by Ackerman and Ghosh. But neither introduction was more than a couple of pages. Barely made the top of the second page in both cases. And in both cases the introduction simply summarised what the ensuing papers were about. So much for finding out the map of Ackerman's mind from his writings. Maybe there weren't any writings. Maybe there wasn't any mind. Or maybe it was a mind carefully concealed behind other peoples' writings. Or maybe he was one of those generous impresario-like academics, committed to showcasing the work of their colleagues and modestly keeping out of the limelight themselves. Were there such? Plant could not recall ever having met any.

He took a beer from the mini-bar, despite his resolution never to use hotel mini-bars. But he needed something to accompany his researches. He tried reading some of the contributions to the books. They were hard to read and as far as Plant could make out not saying very much. Perhaps that was the art of the academy. Perhaps Ackerman was a master of the art, not even writing empty nothings but saying nothing by simply editing other people's sweet nothings. Or perhaps he was just lazy.

The first beer went down more easily than the conference proceedings. He walked over to the mini-bar and took out a second one. Exhaustion or tedium or alcohol soon overwhelmed him. The answer was to surrender to a recuperative afternoon's sleep. He surrendered. He had read quite enough. Later he would explore.

9

The evening traffic on Sukhumvit was clogged to a standstill, three lanes each way, none moving. He joined the throng of pedestrians on the sidewalk and strode past it. He blundered along in the flow, another pink Caucasian sweating in the crowd, aimlessly gawking around. Terror overwhelmed him, terror of crowds, terror of the alien. But no one picked his pocket, no one mugged him, no one harassed him. People walked purposively about their business. Thai people. People like Plant, farang, swung their necks from side to side, looking for directions, looking for street stall bargains, looking for sex, looking for reasons for being where they were.

'Is traffic like this in your country?'

'Sorry?' said Plant, turning.

A smiling Thai man in a short-sleeved brown shirt and tan trousers was walking along beside him.

'You have traffic like this where you come from?'

'Not like this,' said Plant.

'Where you come from? Europe?'

'Australia,' said Plant.

'Sydney?'

'Gold Coast.'

'Ah, Gold Coast. Nice name. People there must be very rich.'

'Not me,' said Plant.

'You have all the gold in Australia, you buy Mercedes, you take cab, still quicker to walk.'

'Much quicker,' Plant agreed.

Was this going to be a 'you like my sister?' routine, 'you need a guide, you want sex, boys, girls?'

'Always the same. Every day. Every night. Always the same.'

'Really,' said Plant.

'They build railway.' He gestured upwards at the rail track above them on its concrete pillars. 'No difference. Every Thai must have his car. Status symbol.'

'Same everywhere,' said Plant.

'Same everywhere maybe, but traffic jams worse here.'

'Yes,' Plant agreed.

'You here on business? Holiday? Stop over?'

'Bit of both,' said Plant.

The man laughed. 'Which both?'

'All three,' said Plant.

'Combine business with pleasure and stop over, good idea.'

'Yes,' said Plant.

He decided to switch himself into question mode. Despite the heat, the humidity, the traffic fumes. When being questioned, ask questions back.

'And you? You work here?'

'Oh yes. Off to work now.'

'What do you do?'

'I am a police captain,' the man smiled.

'Here, in Bangkok?'

'Yes, here. This is my precinct.'

'Ah,' said Plant.

'You need directions? Hotels? Shopping?'

'Ah,' said Plant. Again. Anything. Yes. 'Maybe shopping,' he said.

And the sooner the better.

'Hotel shopping mall, very good.'

He pointed.

'Excellent,' said Plant, turning towards it. 'I'll take a look.'

The police captain smiled.

'Enjoy your visit,' he said. 'Business with pleasure with stop over.'

He laughed.

Plant laughed with him.

Then he ducked into the hotel, shudders running down his spine. The chill of the air-conditioning, maybe. He walked round the shops with their array of international names. Gucci, Hermes, Versace, Dunhill, elegant windows of things he would never want and no doubt could never afford, a cold sweat congealing beneath his shirt. He did a circuit of three floors and then went out into the heat and crowds and headed back to his hotel. Everybody always said how friendly the Thai people were. So why wouldn't police captains be friendly? Chatting to passing strangers. Catching up with strangers to chat to them. Did they talk to every passing stranger? At random? Or was there a specific purpose? Just checking. Just warning. Just letting you know. A cloud of traveller's paranoia enveloped him. Was that why airport bookstalls specialised in thrillers and espionage, to complement and reinforce the adrenalin buzz of it all?

He sat in the foyer and listened to the sad, sultry singer sing her sad, haunted songs of strangers and loneliness and separation. He drank down a beer in no time at all and ordered another one. He didn't check whether happy hour was over. He suspected it might be.

On the way back to his room he stopped by reception to see if there were any messages. The girl made the namaskara gesture and gave him a slip of paper. Bowles had called. She indicated a courtesy phone.

'I just remembered,' said Bowles. 'I wasn't the last person to see Professor Ackerman alive.'

'We don't know that he's dead yet,' said Plant.

'No, of course, no, let's hope he isn't. But my point is I think you should give this fellow Prem a call. I just remembered he was at the lecture. I'm pretty sure Prem gave Bowles a lift after the dinner.'

'Are you now?' said Plant. He sounded like a provincial policeman in an English crime drama. He wondered if he sounded like that to Bowles. 'Do you have an address?' he asked, suppressing an impulse to add 'sir' to the question.

'I have his phone number. Do you have pen and paper?'

'Hold on,' said Plant, trying to keep up with Bowles' eagerness. He searched through his pockets.

'He should be able to help you,' said Bowles.

'You think so?'

'Oh yes.'

'Who is he? What does he do?'

'He's some sort of journalist,' said Bowles. 'Look, I'm about to go out, I can't talk now.'

'Thank you for phoning, anyway,' Plant said.

'My pleasure,' said Bowles, and hung up.

I bet it was, thought Plant. Dob in someone and get yourself off the hook. The convict tradition. The tradition that never worked for the convicts, simply impaled them more firmly on the hook, swinging there ever vulnerable to further employment.

10

Plant stood at his twentieth floor hotel window and looked down at the fishponds in the gardens below. He could see the golden carp swimming there. He could see something, anyway. The ponds gave an air of tranquility in gardens shut away from the clogged streets. High-rise hotels and office blocks stood up amongst them as far as the eye could see, many uncompleted, under construction or the developers bankrupt. Down on the roads close to the hotel thatched shacks and roadside stalls lined the pavements. A storm blew over the city. He watched the rain approach like a grey curtain. On the pavement pedestrians put up bright umbrellas. He decided against wandering the streets again. He wasn't a tourist. He did not have to do tourist things. He had nothing to do. He had no idea what to do. He went down to breakfast.

After he had eaten he phoned Prem, who said his office was close by so why didn't he come round to the hotel midday.

'I'll be in the foyer,' said Plant. 'I'm wearing a pink shirt.'

'Not too shocking, I hope,' said Prem.

'And I'll be reading the *Guardian Weekly*.'

'Ah, parlour pink,' said Prem.

Plant settled down in his room with Ackerman and Ghosh's edited volumes and then switched to the *Guardian* crossword. Jet lag lulled him to sleep before he had solved more than a couple of clues. He was woken by the phone summoning him to the foyer.

A slim, composed, figure greeted him, pressed white shirt and light grey trousers. He made Plant feel crumpled and shapeless. But then, Plant often felt that way. Sometimes it served to discompose people. But Prem seemed perfectly composed.

He accepted a beer but declined the peanuts.

'Economy class fodder,' he said. 'I have a friend in nuts. He tells me they develop a fungus which is very bad for you. So they treat the fungus with a chemical which is carcinogenic and even worse for you. Every year the fungus gets worse and more chemicals are used.'

Plant choked on the mouthful he was chewing.

'I am sorry,' said Prem. 'I did not mean to alarm you.'

I wonder, Plant wondered.

'But Professor Ackerman. Missing. Now that is alarming.'

'You think so?'

'Of course? You must be alarmed to be inquiring.'

'I didn't know him.'

'But you are inquiring after him.'

'His wife hired me.'

'Ah, the accomplished Mrs Ackerwoman. And how is she taking it? Well?'

'I don't know her well enough to say.'

'I don't think anyone ever would. She has amazing control, that lady.'

'Yes?'

'Like the late Queen Mother,' said Prem.

'I hadn't thought of that.'

Prem chuckled, almost giggled.

'She probably would prefer a younger comparison. But I admired the late Queen Mother.

'And Mrs Ackerman? Do you admire her?'

'From a distance, oh absolutely. I would never dare not to.'

'So tell me,' said Plant, 'about Professor Ackerman. Dr Bowles suggested you were the last person to see him alive.'

'Ah, Dr Bowels. What an energetic young man. So young. So innocent.'

'I don't know about that,' said Plant.

'Well, until he is proved guilty we must presume he is,' said Prem.

'His father is a secret service chief.'

'My father is a poor peasant farmer who cannot read or write. We do not all follow our father's path.'

'True enough,' said Plant.

'Only enough?'

'Dr Bowles said you were at Professor Ackerman's lecture. And drove him home.'

'I had no idea he was so observant. I thought he had eyes only for young girls. I would never have thought he noticed us old men.'

'He likes young girls?'

'Perhaps we can talk about that later. For the moment let us talk about Professor Ackerman.'

'Did you drive him back from the dinner?'

'Yes.'

'To his hotel?'

'First to my home. We drank a bottle of wine together. A bottle of Grange. I had been saving it for his visit.'

'You were good friends?'

'We have known each other a long time.'

'How did you come to know him?'

'Nothing improper,' said Prem. 'My father was a poor peasant farmer.

Very poor. And I was the runt of the family. Weak. Delicate. No use in the fields. So they gave me away to the monks. What else can a poor family do? I became a temple boy.'

'An acolyte.'

'A servant. You can call it an acolyte. I had to wait on the monks. Clean up their rooms. Just an unpaid servant. They provided lodging. But I was always hungry.'

Plant looked at the peanuts.

'Even now I can feel that hunger. This hotel has an excellent chef. Have you had lunch?'

'No,' said Plant.

'Why don't we eat?' Prem suggested. 'It is more civilised to talk over a good meal.'

They moved to the dining room.

'I don't eat meat,' said Plant.

'You are a Buddhist?'

'No. I just don't like killing animals.'

'That is good,' said Prem. 'When I was a monk I ate no meat. But now …'

He smiled.

'But not a lot. Not a lot. However, I will speak to the chef. I will ask what he can prepare for you.'

He called the waiter over who went and brought the chef out. The chef greeted Prem like an old acquaintance. He cupped his hands together and bowed to Plant. Prem spoke to him in Thai.

'It is all arranged,' he said.

'They know you here.'

'I usually book my visitors into this hotel.'

'Is that why Professor Ackerman stayed here?'

'I arranged the special rate for him.'

'The Australian government rate?'

'Is that what they call it?'

'Apparently,' said Plant.

'Then that must be what it is.'

'Did Professor Ackerman work for the government?"

'Possibly,' said Prem. 'Who knows? In some countries either you work for the government or you do not work at all. Perhaps Australia is not like that.'

'Perhaps not,' said Plant.

'The lucky country,' Prem giggled.

'How did you get to know him?'

'I was telling you,' said Prem. 'My parents sold me to be a temple boy. They hoped that way to achieve merit. And perhaps to help me be what they could never be. The monks educated me. I was good at my studies. But I saw that there was no future for me. I did not want to become a poor monk. I had no connections. No patrons. No family who could help. In those days there were the Colombo Plan scholarships. The generals' sons and daughters and the rich businessmen's sons and daughters and the politicians' sons and daughters all went to study in Harvard and Yale and Oxford and Cambridge. I could see I would never get one of those scholarships. But there were also scholarships to New Zealand and Australia. They were not countries any general's son would want to study in. You understand. The universities did not have the social prestige. I hope I am not offending you. This is the way it was here. The way I saw it. I thought, perhaps if I applied for New Zealand or Australia I might win a scholarship. I could then learn English fluently. To be a success in business I would need English. What else could I do? I could not go back to my village, there was no work there for me, my parents barely grew enough to keep themselves alive. And so. That is how it was. I became an overseas student. A perpetual student. Like in those Russian novels. The scholarship would support me until I completed my degree. Naturally I never finished my degree. How else could I live? Living and learning fluent English were more important to me than collecting a few letters after my name. Not everyone understood. But Professor Ackerman, he had a generous spirit. He collected lame ducks. He is not one of those professors whose students hold chairs in Harvard and Princeton and Oxford and London. But he helped a lot of people. He helped me. He never insisted that I complete my course. He understood. That is how we met. That is how we became friends. That is why I shared a good bottle of wine with him when he visited.'

'And then what?' Plant asked.

'Then we strolled down to the red-light district. Not to participate, you understand, just to observe. Then he returned to his hotel and I went home. The next day I took him up to my village for a few days and then I brought him back to Bangkok and said goodbye.'

'Another bottle of Grange.'

'I am not that wealthy.'

'Where did he go?'

'I thought back to Brisbane. But perhaps he went to London. He might have gone anywhere. Bangkok is a hub. Wherever you want to fly.'

'Or he might have stayed.'

'He might. I cannot imagine why.'

'You stay.'

'I have my business.'

'Exactly what is your business?'

'Exactly public relations. I handle a couple of big corporations. A few other smaller contracts.'

'Dr Bowles said you were some sort of journalist.'

'Some sort.' He laughed. 'Did Dr Bowels say what sort?'

'He said some sort.'

'What a charming young man is Dr Bowels. So generous with his definitions. I will present you with a sample of my work so you can see for yourself. I am sure I have copies in the car. Unfortunately after lunch I must go and earn my living. No doubt you must too. But this evening, if you are free, perhaps I should show you some of Bangkok.'

'That would be nice,' said Plant.

'Perhaps,' said Prem. 'Perhaps not. But it might be informative.'

'I need all the information I can get,' said Plant.

'I think you do,' Prem agreed.

Prem suggested they should stroll down to the red-light district. Not to participate, just to observe. Follow the tracks Professor Ackerman took. Reconstruct his last known days. Wasn't that what they did in crime shows on television? Not that they need suspect any crime.

All human life was on sale. Boys, girls, transvestites, standing along the streets, standing outside the bars, calling them in. Crumpled, sweaty Australian and English and German men walking hand in hand with beautiful young Thai prostitutes, topless girls gyrating to disco music inside the bars, tourists stumbling around in groups gawking, pimps accosting them, all the cacophonous competing music, all the flashing neon and strobing lights from dance floors and bars

'Welcome to Thailand,' said Prem. 'The nicest people that money can buy.'

'You come here often?' Plant asked.

'Only with visitors from overseas,' said Prem. 'I bring them down and make sure they get out safely. It is good for them to see it if they wish to understand Thailand. But I do not recommend that they participate. If you wish to participate you should consult Dr Bowels.'

'He told me he was married.'

'Ah yes. One of his pretty young students. I had forgotten he had reformed.'

'Reformed?'

'Let us hope so. For his pretty young wife's sake.'

Prem looked at his watch.

'It is too early to check,' he said. 'Maybe later, two o'clock, three o'clock. By then the girls are getting desperate. They are waiting around and they have no customers. They need money. That is when Dr Bowels comes to strike a bargain. Sale price. A third off. Maybe half price, if they are desperate enough. And usually one of them is. They have to live. They know nothing else. They are recruited from their villages. Their parents sell them. The parents do not have enough land to support themselves and their children. I was fortunate. I was given to the monks. I was not pretty enough for this life. I do not think Dr Bowels would have bought me even at seventy-five per cent off.'

He laughed.

'The girls work in the bars,' he explained. 'If you want to buy one, you have to pay the bar owner a price to take her away. So Dr Bowels comes down at two o'clock or three o'clock, just before the bars close. He waits outside, sits on the step outside so he does not have to buy a drink or pay the bar owner. When the bar shuts and the girls come out, those who have not gone off with a customer, then he bargains. It saves him a lot of bahts. It means he can come down every night. He should be teaching economics, your Dr Bowels. The free market. The laws of supply and demand.'

'Isn't Professor Ackerman an economic historian?' Plant asked.

'Of the theoretical kind,' said Prem.

'He wasn't down here buying and selling?'

'No,' said Prem. 'He is a nice man. I do not imagine he ever needed to buy sexual favours. But even if he did, we should not think ill of him. Not for coming down here. The men who come down here, look at them, the factory slaves of Western Europe, the victims of economic miracles. Their lives are hard, their pleasures are few, their horizons are circumscribed. This seems like paradise to them. Beautiful young bodies. Some fall in love with them. Take them back to Germany with them. Dr Bowels bought a girl for a week and took her back to Australia.

To meet his mother.

'No, they are not bad people. The customers are victims as much as the boys and girls. Victims of the same forces; the same businesses; the same investors, probably. It is all about money. All about greed. If sex brings a little relief, who can complain? A little relief, a little distraction, and more money for the generals and the bankers who own it all.'

'They own it all?'

'Of course. They own everything. They own the airlines that bring in the sex tourists. The hotels where they stay. The restaurants where they eat. The food wholesalers that buy the food from the peasants. The real estate that the bar owners rent. The breweries that supply the beer. The importers that distribute the wine and spirits. The drug cartels that control the drug traffic. The latex corporations that produce the condoms. The banks that provide the loan capital to the airlines and the hotels and the breweries and the drug dealers. All owned by the same people.'

It was a vision of hell and it haunted him. Not that Plant believed himself a puritan. Not that puritan. He had fought the work ethic, said yes to drugs, espoused free love and contraception. He lay sleepless in his bed, the remorseless Afro-American beat of a discotheque somewhere resonating through the hotel. Was it the free market that he recoiled from? The fleshly materializations of Mrs Thatcher, soliciting from her corner shop. The amnesiac, slick-haired hipster Ronald Reagan peddling his Hollywood arse outside the pool hall. No doubt Mrs Thatcher and President Reagan had no less prostituted themselves than the poor village boys and girls. As for Blair and Clinton and Bush and Brown and Howard and Obama and Rudd and Cameron and Clegg and Gillard, could they have been no less available for the right price? A higher price perhaps, along with the rise in executive salaries and bonuses. But all for sale.

He gave up on sleep and began to read Prem's book. It was not journalism, but fiction. But it was fiction that seemed all too factual. It was all there, the same streets, the bar girls, the pimps, the transvestites, the impoverished peasants, the grasping landlords, the usurious moneylenders, the grinding poverty, the obscene wealth, the murderous businessmen, the gunmen they hired, the idealists they killed, the massacred protestors, the assassinated schoolteachers, the tortured peasant organisers, the crushed resistance, the corrupt politicians. He sat up most of the night reading it. And when he stopped reading as the cockerels crowed in the breaking dawn, it all revolved again in hideous dreams, and he was down amongst the dead men with Dr Bowels and Mrs Ackerwoman and the go-go dancers and the endless bars with their strobing lights. And it was not as if it did not allure him. That was the horror of it, too.

11

He was awoken by the telephone ringing. A brisk and cheerful Prem.

'You had a good sleep?'

'Not especially.'

'Oh, what happened? You didn't go back down to the bars.'

'No.'

'That's good. I was afraid I might have led you astray. Led you into temptation and delivered you into evil.'

'No, I couldn't sleep so I sat up and read your book all night.'

'Oh dear. Even worse.'

'Not at all,' said Plant. 'I enjoyed it. Well, maybe not enjoyed. But I thought it was excellent.'

'Good enough for a sort of journalist.'

'No, truly, it was amazing. Powerful.'

'You make me blush.'

'It was most insightful. It helped me understand things.'

'Instruction with delight,' said Prem. 'Isn't that the purpose of all writing?'

'Not that I've noticed lately,' said Plant.

'Perhaps I am old fashioned then.'

'I think so.'

'Oh dear,' said Prem.

'It was meant as a compliment.'

'Then I shall take it as such.'

'You should,' said Plant.

'The reason I telephoned,' said Prem, 'is that I have to leave town and go to my village. Today. Just for a quick visit. I thought if you were not busy you might like to come with me. In a way it will be following your trail. Who knows, something might come back to me. Some remembered conversation. Some clue.'

Plant considered. What else would he do? Struggle with the *Guardian* crossword until happy hour. Drown the sorrows of the singer in endless draughts of draught beer. Stroll down to the bars and the pool halls and the prostitutes.

'Why not?' he said.

'Excellent. I will pick you up in one hour,' said Prem. 'Does that give you time?'

Time for what, Plant wondered.

'An hour and a half perhaps,' said Prem, when he hadn't answered.

'An hour and a half,' Plant agreed.

It gave him time to shower and eat his noodles and fruit and check out and be waiting in the foyer when Prem arrived, dapper and trim, to take him to the waiting Mercedes.

The poor peasant returns to his village.

They had just pulled out onto Sukhumvit and were crawling along in the barely moving traffic when a man ran out into the road ahead of them, stood in the middle lane, and took a photograph. The flash made Plant duck. And then the man was back on the pavement and lost in the crowds. A tall man. Caucasian.

'What was that?' Plant asked.

'He must have liked my new Mercedes,' said Prem. 'I am flattered.'

'You think?'

'A Mercedes stuck in traffic amongst the Toyotas and the tuk-tuks. It amuses the tourists.'

'I think he was photographing us,' said Plant.

'Two good-looking young men, why not?' said Prem. He brushed his hand over the hair at the back of his head.

'You don't think it was odd?'

'Odd?' said Prem.

He gestured at the traffic, the clutter of stalls lining the street, the towering hotel blocks, the poverty, the wealth.

'What isn't odd?'

'It doesn't worry you?'

'It does no good to be worried,' said Prem. 'To be careful, yes. To be worried, no.'

'What about your books?'

He had established from the 'by the same author' page that there were several.

'Oh yes. I worry about them. I worry they might not be good enough.'

'They are. Or at least the one that I read is.'

'Thank you.'

'You're not worried they might get you into trouble?'

'As long as I write in English I am not spreading subversion,' said Prem. 'I try to be careful. They are fiction. Not a sort of journalism.' He laughed. 'I do not name the generals and businessmen. Besides, everyone knows who they are. That tall building there, that is drug money. That development, further along, that is owned by army officers. That hotel is part of a chain owned by a drug baron. He is quite famous. He is on the Americans' wanted list. Perhaps they want to share his profits. Everyone knows these things.'

As they drove through the city Prem pointed out the landmarks. Landmarks of corruption. Landmarks of the drug trade. Landmarks of development.

'It is just money. How you make your money is all the same. Drugs. Sex. Factories. Shopping malls. It is all interlocked. That way you stay rich. And the poor die on the streets.'

He pointed out groups of people standing at street corners.

'They are waiting to be hired. Some get hired. The rest starve. They come in from the country looking for work. They are hired for building sites. Factories. There are so many of them. It keeps the wages down.'

In the country he pointed out the eucalyptus forest projects that had sucked up the water from the soil and made the neighbouring peasants' land barren. And the salt pans for Japanese glass manufacturers that had leached into the neighbouring peasants' land and killed the crops.

'Then the land is worthless. They sell out to the companies for a pittance. No one else will buy the land. Then they go to the city and look for work. The boys wait on street corners. The girls become prostitutes. The old people die. But I have already told you all this.'

They stopped for lunch in a huge multi-storeyed hotel at the side of the road. It stood alone, no village, no settlement in sight. It seemed deserted. Drug money, air force generals, Prem explained. 'I do not usually like supporting such places. But the food is good.'

They sat in the empty dining room and ate lunch. The food was good. Bean curd shaped like pieces of chicken in a coconut sauce. Stir-fried vegetables. And not another soul there.

'Why did they build it?'

'Perhaps someone owned a construction company and needed a contract. Perhaps some money needed to be laundered. Perhaps one day they expect tourists. Perhaps they diverted a development grant from somewhere.'

It was extraordinary, a concrete folly.

'While I am here,' said Prem, 'I will try to sell them my books.'

He picked up his briefcase from beside his chair.

He patted the back of his head, brushing down his hair, and headed for an empty shop in the empty lobby. Silk shirts, wooden carvings, souvenirs, postcards were displayed in the window and on the counters. There were one or two books: Jim Thompson and the silk trade, *Secrets of Thai Cooking*. Plant leafed through them while Prem talked to the woman sitting there. He showed his samples. She ordered two of each title and Prem collected them from the boot of the Mercedes.

'You always carry copies of your books?'

'Always,' said Prem. 'Thais are not good business people. They do not have the drive. But when I came back from my years away, I worked for a Chinese businessman. I watched him and I learned. In England, you go for lunch and the restaurant is open but they say, "Lunch is off." With the Chinese, the restaurant has closed, they see you coming down the street, they open up especially for you. Never miss a chance of a sale. Everybody has something to teach us, even our enemies. Especially our enemies.'

They made one other stop at the site of an ancient temple. A smaller, unpublicised Angkor Wat. They walked round the ancient stillness, crumbled stone, fractured weathered carvings.

'It is important that you see some traditional sites,' said Prem, 'even if much has been looted and stolen. Otherwise you will think it is all drugs and prostitution and big business and greed.'

On the way out they stopped at the souvenir stall and Plant bought a cast of the seven-headed serpent, the Mahanaga, while Prem checked his books. He was happy. There was only one copy left. The tourists had been buying them. He went to the boot of the Mercedes and replenished the stock.

12

It was dark when they arrived in the village. Prem's house was in a long, flat street of houses, in its own block, a large block, a small house. He drove into the driveway and a girl came out and shut the gates behind him. She bowed, her hands together, and came to the car. She limped.

'We'll carry our own bags,' Prem said.

They sat in a dark, cool room, the ceiling fans revolving above them.

'I will get you a drink,' said Prem.

He selected a heavy Australian red, a Shiraz, and opened it.

'This one Professor Ackerman brought me,' said Prem. 'He brought me a case. He knows my foibles.'

'He was travelling light?'

'Perhaps he paid excess baggage,' said Prem. 'Or perhaps he bought it at duty free and smuggled it into the cabin. It worries you?'

'I was looking for indications of his plans,' said Plant. 'Whether he was intending to go straight back, or did he have a longer stay in mind. The amount of luggage he brought might have given a clue.'

'Ah, a clue,' said Prem. 'Ever the investigator. You remind me of Dame Agatha Christie. I used to read her books to understand Anglo-Saxon ways.'

'You found she helped?'

'Nothing ever helped,' said Prem. 'Fortunately I enjoy mysteries.'

'What about the mystery of Ackerman's disappearance?' Plant asked.

'That is not so enjoyable.'

'Did he say anything to you about his plans?'

Prem shook his head.

'Did he seem worried about anything?'

'He always seemed worried,' said Prem. 'About the state of the world, the state of the university, the state of his health.'

'The state of his marriage?'

'That was something he never talked about.'

'But he talked about the rest?'

'Endlessly,' said Prem. 'You might even say remorselessly.'

'What in particular?'

'The way the university had become like everything else, only concerned with money. They wouldn't support his publishing programme any more. So he had handed it over to these international publishers.'

'I heard his co-editor wasn't too happy about that.'

'For good reason, I would think.'

'Why's that?'

'The same people approached me. A couple of years ago. They wanted to buy me out. I was not interested.'

'Buy you personally?'

'I am not so pretty. No, my publishing company.'

'You have a publishing company?'

'Only for myself. And a couple of art books that keep on selling. When I wrote my first book I went to a publisher here. He offered me terms. They were terrible but I accepted them. I wanted so much for my book to be around. I wanted people to buy it. But he was a crook. He hardly sold any copies. Or if he did, he lied about it and paid me nothing. In the end he went bankrupt. I bought the company from the administrator. It was worth nothing, but I got my rights back. Along with the two art books. After that I vowed never again. I would do my own publishing. That was why I wasn't interested when these people approached me. Besides, they showed me their standard contract. They insisted on taking all world rights in all languages. With no time limit. That is unacceptable. Most publishers ask for world rights or English language rights for a year, but if they don't sell them within that period the unsold rights revert to the author. Not Legal and Visual International. They wanted total rights for all markets in perpetuity. So I said no. I negotiate my own translations. I was not about to surrender my rights again, not once I had got them back.'

'Who were they? What do you know about them?'

'Americans, naturally. They said they were expanding. Globalizing. They were looking for a company to buy. In the end they found one and took it over.'

'Why not just set up a new one?'

'You tell me.'

'They wanted to buy you up so they could suppress your books?'

'You think so?'

'It has been done before.'

'Possibly,' said Prem. 'But I don't think so. I am not so subversive.'

Plant said nothing. Who knew what counted as subversive?

'There was no doubt some reason involving foreign capital or transferring funds. They had companies everywhere. Companies and foundations. They seemed to have a string of foundations. New York, Amsterdam, Geneva, Liechtenstein, Kolkata, Hong Kong. They wanted an affiliate in South-East Asia.'

'Why?'

'Playing the currency exchange. Laundering drug money. Who knows?'

'You don't?'

'No, I don't know; but those are the usual reasons. Something fishy.'

'You think?'

'What else? Foundations mask a multitude of sins.'

'Did you say that to Professor Ackerman?'

'Yes.'

'What did he say?'

'He said, "Very likely." He had already thought of it, naturally.'

'Did he know for sure?'

'It is very hard to know these things for sure. Everyone knows these things in principle. But hard evidence is something else.'

'Did he try to find out?'

Prem stood up and poured another drink.

'You think he went asking questions about them and they eliminated him?'

'It could be.'

'It could be indeed,' said Prem. 'It is not expensive to kill someone here. A few thousand baht.'

'What do you think?'

'He asked me what I knew about them. But I knew nothing. I was not interested in selling so I had no reason to find out about them. I couldn't help him.'

'And he didn't ask you to try and find out?'

'No,' said Prem. 'But if he wanted to, he could find out as well as I could. Perhaps more easily. He knew his way around. He was a trained researcher, after all. That was his profession.'

'I suppose it was,' said Plant, reflectively. He hadn't thought of Ackerman in that way.

'Oh yes,' said Prem. 'He was always more interested in research than in teaching or writing. He was a kind man. He was kind to his students. But they were not his first love.'

'Not like Dr Bowles.'

'Ah, Dr Bowels, I think Dr Bowels' first and last love is himself. Not that love would ever be a significant motivation for Dr Bowels.'

They breakfasted on papaya and watermelon on the verandah. The gates were open and a line of villagers sat and squatted along the driveway.

'They know I am back,' said Prem.

The girl with the limp brought them a pot of tea.

'I am sorry that I cannot offer the morning paper,' said Prem. 'Let alone the *Guardian Weekly*.'

'I am relieved,' said Plant.

'I will show you round later,' said Prem. 'Do you think you can entertain yourself for a while? I shall have to see some of these people. They get themselves into trouble and think I can help.'

'What sort of trouble?'

'Of course, trouble is your business,' said Prem, 'you have a professional interest. What happens is that they get into debt. The Chinese middle-men cheat them on their harvests. The Indian middle-men cheat them on the silk cloth they weave. They have more children and cannot support them. They gamble. Chinese gamblers travel through the district and cheat them of all their savings. Then they lose their land. They come to me and beg me to buy it back for them. What can I do? If I give them the money they will lose it again. So I buy their land to get them out of debt, and then I let them work it and they keep half of what they grow for themselves. Soon I shall be the biggest landowner in the village.' He laughed. 'What can I do with more land?'

'Have all these lost their land?' Plant asked.

'Oh no. Some have sick children. Born with harelips. Or a hole in the heart. I try to help. You saw the girl with the limp. She had a withered leg. I used to see her, dragging it after her, following the other children down the street. It was heart-rending. So I arranged for her to fly to Australia for an operation. Such a simple operation, when there is money for it. I approached some friends, rich tourists, who had read my books and written to me. Germans, Australians, Swiss. We set up a foundation. They make donations. It saves them taxes. It means comparatively little to them and so much to these children. Now she can walk properly. Just a slight limp.'

Plant looked at the gate. Old men. Young mothers. Children playing in the dust.

'So,' said Prem, 'if you will excuse me I will go and minister to my charges. Cross your fingers I do not come back with more fields I do not want.'

He brushed the back of his hair with his hand, pulled himself upright, stiff, and went down the driveway. Later he took Plant on the tour. The schoolhouse he had built in his grounds, where he taught the children in the school holidays.

'They learn English. They learn to type. Keyboard skills. Soon we will have computers. This way they learn some skills. Otherwise ...'

He left it unsaid. He had already shown Plant the alternatives.

They walked round the village. Flat streets, houses on stilts, some with satellite dishes where the men had gone away to Saudi Arabia as guest workers and sent back money. They walked round the fishpond that had been constructed collectively to conserve the monsoon rains and, stocked with fish, provided some protein. A couple of villagers came up and showed them the other source. They were carrying a bucket and in the bottom were half a dozen black beetles. They pointed to them and smiled.

'Protein,' said Prem. 'They collect them from water buffalo dung. Otherwise, this time of year, there is nothing but rice and a few grasses. That is all.'

He took Plant back through the village. Beneath the pole houses women were weaving silk cloth. They called out to Prem, showing him samples. He suggested Plant might like a shirt. 'Every tourist needs a Thai silk shirt,' he laughed.

'Where would I get it made?'

'I will show you,' said Prem. 'Perhaps you should buy one ready-made. There probably isn't time to get one bespoke.'

They declined the lengths of silk and walked round to the tailors' shop.

Plant bought two shirts. It was the least he could do.

13

Back at the hotel in Bangkok he collected a message that had come while he was away. It was from Bowles who proposed they meet for a drink. Plant phoned him and Bowles suggested later that evening.

Plant waited in the foyer. Bowles arrived and accepted a beer and looked round appraisingly at the people at the other tables while he chewed the complimentary peanuts. The sad singer turned to them with beady, blank eyes and launched into 'Love for Sale.'

Bowles leapt up.

'Let's go out to a bar,' he said. 'Somewhere more authentic. These hotels are too expensive.'

They went down to the red-light district and chose some dubious dive, somewhere Plant would have been wary of entering on his own. Girls lined the walls.

'You've been out of town then,' said Bowles.

'Yes.'

'Go far? Up to the border?'

'Not that far.'

'What took you there?'

'Prem took me there.'

'Oh, the journalist bloke.'

'The writer. Yes.'

'Visiting the flesh-pots? Pattaya?'

'No. No flesh-pots.'

He waited a bit but Bowles said nothing. They listened to the disco music.

'Prem's village, actually,' said Plant. There was no point in not telling him. He no doubt knew if he had intelligence connections. And if he didn't, what did it matter?

'Did you find Professor Ackerman?'

'No, I didn't actually. Is that where he is?'

'Can't help you, sport. Not a clue.'

'I thought by putting me onto Prem you might have had something in mind.'

'Something in mind, cobber? Can't say I do. Just seen them together a few times. They seemed pretty thick. Thick as thieves, that is, not thick as, you know, thick. In a manner of speaking.'

'Whose manner would that be?'

Bowles laughed.

'Idiom,' he said. 'Been teaching idiom all afternoon. Idioms for idiots. Such is life. Bad show. Stick to you like burrs. Hard to shake them off.'

Plant nodded sympathetically, searching for the right word in the right place.

'Must be tricky,' he said.

'Tricky,' said Bowles reflectively. 'You know Professor Ackerman went up to Chiang Mai?'

'No.'

'He was up there not so long ago.'

'Is that so?'

'That's so. You know what that means. Or what it could mean. No proof, of course.'

'Tell me.'

'You know Chiang Mai.'

'A town in the north of Thailand.'

'Next to the Golden Triangle.'

'Yes,' Plant agreed. 'On the Lao border.'

'That only means one thing,' said Bowles.

'What's that?'

'There's only one reason to go to Chiang Mai.'

'To go to Laos?'

'Drugs. Can't believe you don't know.'

'Ah,' said Plant.

'Hard drugs.' He leaned on the hard.

'Really?'

'So what would Ackerman have been doing up there?'

'I'm sure I can't imagine,' said Plant.

'Doesn't it strike you as fishy?'

'Funnily enough that's what Prem said about the foundation that took over Ackerman's monograph series.'

'Said what?'

'It was fishy.'

'Utter nonsense,' said Bowles.

'Different kettle of fish altogether?'

'Absolutely.'

'More fish to fry,' said Plant.

'What's that?'

'Fish seem to be omnipresent. Must be the effect of that Thai fish paste they cook everything in.'

'Fish paste?' said Bowles. 'What on earth are you talking about?'

'Ackerman's publishing operation. I gather his co-editor wasn't too happy about its being taken over.'

'What was he unhappy about? They bailed it out, didn't they? The series was moribund. Bloody bankrupt.'

'Bankrupt?'

'A manner of speaking,' said Bowles. 'Broke. They couldn't keep it running. The new chap came to the rescue.'

'Like a White Knight,' said Plant.

'Absolutely. Jolly decent of him. Now there might be a chance to make something of it.'

'Turn a profit for altruism,' said Plant.

'Altruism, who said anything about altruism?' The word was clearly not part of current idiom. 'It's a business operation. They bailed out Ackerman and Ghosh, but only because they could see how the series could be developed. Bring in a new editorial team. Bring it into the twenty-first century. Ackerman was a decent enough fellow, in his way, but he was stuck in the past. Starr's a professional.'

'Starr?'

'He runs the show.'

A hostess came over, offering her services. Bowles brushed her away without looking at her.

'Later, maybe,' she said. 'You want I come back later? You want I bring girl for your friend?'

Bowles refused to acknowledge her.

'Bad mood tonight?' she said, sweetly. 'You want something make you happy? Thai sticks? You want to shoot up?'

'I said no, go away,' said Bowles.

She giggled and went back to join the other wallflowers.

'You didn't, actually,' said Plant.

'Didn't what?'

'Say no. You didn't say anything.'

Bowles scowled. Plant looked across at the wallflowers, careful not to smile invitingly. Oh yes, he could see the appeal. All too well. And then AIDS and an early death. Or a later lingering one. But Thai sticks, on the other hand, that sounded good. Not with Bowles there, though. Still, now he knew where to come.

'So you've no idea where Ackerman is?'

'Sorry, cobber, not a clue. Why don't you try Kolkata?'

'Kolkata?'

'Calcutta that was. Sounds like the old hippy dope trail, doesn't it?'

'Why Kolkata?'

'You hear things.'

'Where did you hear that?'

'Can't say.'

'Can't, or won't?'

'Hard to tell,' said Bowles.

'Why would he be in Kolkata?'

'Up to something with that dreadful old villain Ghosh, maybe. Who knows?'

'Somebody presumably does,' said Plant.

'Possible,' agreed Bowles. 'Can only pass on what a bloke hears. Take it or leave it.'

Down among the bar girls he exuded a different manner from the diffident academic. Something harsher and nastier. Something with a distasteful aura, something brutal, something with the force of authority behind it, the authority of force.

They sat there, conversation running out, the girls patiently waiting. It had been a long evening. It reminded Plant of those awful years when you were trying to crack onto a girl and some other male kept sitting there and wouldn't go away. Maybe Bowles felt the same. Almost certainly Bowles felt the same. They sat there, each trying to out-sit the other. The hostess cruised past a couple more times. There was no sign Bowles was going to leave. In the end Plant got up.

'I'll just stay on for a nightcap,' said Bowles, 'before I set off home.'

Plant nodded and walked out into the street. After he had gone what he judged far enough he dropped into another bar and bought another beer that he didn't really want.

'You want nice time?' the girl asked.

The thumping disco music, the strobing lights, the drunken Australians and Germans and British slumped at the bar eyeing off the go-go girls. It was better than beetles in a bucket, but still not his idea of a nice time.

'Not tonight,' said Plant. 'Maybe a couple of Thai sticks.'

'You wait,' she said.

Plant waited. This was when you never knew. Was she going to come back? Or would it be a couple of police? But she came back.

'Have a nice day,' she said. 'Enjoy.'

Just like McDonalds. About the same age as McDonalds' counter staff, too.

Plant sat in his hotel room, rolled up a smoke and turned on the television. Helicopter gunships swooped in on a jungle retreat. A missile scored a direct hit on the private jet parked on the landing strip. Kick-boxing narcotics agents were fighting with kick-boxing drug barons and their henchmen. He hadn't heard of any henchmen around Ackerman. No bodyguard chauffeur. And if Ackerman had been the mastermind of a drug ring, why did he need a special discount rate for his hotel accommodation, and a free ticket from Bowles to fly to Bangkok? Cover. It could all be cover. But who would fly economy class if he didn't have to? He hadn't even arranged an upgrade on the ticket.

If it hadn't been for Bowles he would never have thought of it. Was that gross negligence? Shouldn't he have wondered why Mrs Ackerman was hiring him to look for her husband, rather than going directly to Interpol or whoever? Because she couldn't deal with the authorities for fear of what they might unearth? It was a possibility. But if they were that loaded with Swiss bank accounts, wouldn't she have hired some bigger outfit? Plant was not afflicted with too much false modesty. He knew he wasn't amongst the top ten inquiry agencies. Not even the top hundred thousand.

He couldn't see it. It would make a nice story. It would do for the Sunday papers. But it didn't add up. Did it explain Ackerman's apartment on the Gold Coast and house in Brisbane? Two incomes explained that easily enough. Especially Mrs Ackerman's gallery. Another potential laundry, of course. But it hadn't seemed such an expensive lifestyle from his recollections of the apartment. Compared with Plant's own anchoritic cell it might seem rich. But Plant's lifestyle was no norm. No norm at all. He rolled another smoke. It could have been richer if he hadn't smoked it all away. But if he hadn't smoked it all away he would only have drunk it away. Or paid it out in alimony. Of course, Ackerman might have billions stashed away in some Swiss bank account. And of course he had not met Ackerman. Nor at the present rate of progress did it seem that he ever would.

You could manufacture any sort of theory once you got going on it. Especially with a little bit of help from the herb. It was all very exciting stuff to read about in an airport lounge. Yet another international bestseller. As for participating in it, Plant was less sure. No, he wasn't less sure, he was absolutely sure. He didn't like it. He didn't like it one bit. Especially Bowles. He had come back from Prem's village depressed about rural poverty, as Prem had intended, but uplifted by what the human spirit could do. Now he felt dragged back down into the mire. He felt tacky. He felt the ectoplasm of fear and conspiracy and crime and death reaching its tendrils all over him. He felt waves of paranoia engulfing him. It was something bad dope could do to you. It was something good dope could do too: offer you a correct perception. As they used to put it in the good old days, just because you're paranoid doesn't mean what you're thinking isn't true. He wasn't in fact at all sure what he was thinking. He didn't want to think whatever it was any deeper. Any more. There was something nasty going on and he wanted to get away from it. If Bowles was giving him a warning, he would take it. If it was a threat, he would take it too. He would go to Kolkata and see Professor Ghosh. It was only three hours away, after all, and Ghosh might fill him in on Ackerman and the publishing series, which might not be relevant but what else did he have to go on? Who knew, he might even see Ackerman. And it would get him out of this miasma of suspicion and give him a chance to get a perspective on things. Why not? He had never been to Kolkata. It might be a nice change. And they had good dope in India, too. So people said.

14

'The situation was quite clear,' said Professor Ghosh, 'we could not continue, there was no way I could continue, I am far too sick, I can hardly get around, I collapsed in the street, my legs simply gave way under me, how can I have the responsibility of the accounts when I am so sick? I called a meeting, I wrote to all the members of the society, personally, I emailed them all, I spoke to them in the faculty club. Do you know how many came? Nobody came, not even Ackerman came, he said he knew what I was going to say so why come. He said I had his proxy. How can I continue if nobody comes? And Ackerman refused to do anything, he said he was retired now and that was it, he absolutely refused to do any more.'

They sat in the cool, dark space. Ghosh had opened the door to him and launched into an immediate tirade, which carried them along dark corridors and up dark flights of stairs until at some seemingly arbitrary point they had stopped, Ghosh still talking, and sat down. It might have been a landing or a hallway or a sitting room or a waiting room, shrouded in darkness and gloom that excluded the heat and frenzy of the world outside, furnished, or part furnished, with an assortment of couches, chairs and carpets, all dark and faded and haphazardly positioned. Plant could not tell whether this was because the house was half-abandoned, furniture partially removed, no one living there, except Ghosh, temporarily squatting, or if this was how Ghosh always lived, in some characteristic style of old Calcutta. Outside were the street noises, traffic, horns, voices, cries, but in here nothing. Plant looked round at the faded furniture, the dark doorways leading into dark corridors. Outside was the glaring heat and the chaotic traffic and the beggars and the wandering sacred cows. Outside it was like hell on earth.

'I cannot get to you, you will have to come to me,' Ghosh had said when Plant phoned. Sitting there he was amazed that the phone had worked, amazed that there was a phone. Here was the faded splendour of the nineteenth century, the prosperous upper bourgeoisie of the vanished Raj, standing there three storeys high, solid, cool, dark, lost in time, and Ghosh there lost within it.

'I would call for a drink but there is no one to call, the servants are all gone. I remember when this house was filled with servants, my father would just have to raise a hand and a drink would be put in it, now it is all gone, and soon I shall be gone with it. And Ackerman comes worrying me about this silly bloody series of books, who was going to store the books, who was going to do the accounts, I told him, my father had fifty clerks to do his accounts, now you expect me to do them when I cannot even walk across the room without fearing I am going to collapse. I cannot risk the anxiety, I will not let the worry drive me to an early grave.

'"Not that early," he said, most offensively, typical of him. "You are not going to take over the accounts, are you?" I said. "No," he said. "So what should we do?" I said. "I have a good offer," he said, "I intend to take it." "And what is this offer?" I asked. "We enter into a partnership with Legal and Visual International," he said. "They are an international group of publishers with world wide affiliates. They are looking to expand. They will take all the books and they will distribute them internationally. They will continue to publish the series and we shall remain as advisors if we wish." "And who are these people?" I asked, "What do we know about them?" "They have branches everywhere," he said, "in New York, in Bangkok, even here in Kolkata." "In Kolkata?" I said. "Artworld Orient," he said. "Artworld Orient," I said, "they are pornographers, I went to university with the publisher, he was a filthy little beast then, now he publishes dirty picture books, or he did until he went bankrupt." "They took him over," he said. "And you want us to link up with pornographers?" I said. "Have you got a better idea?" he asked. "Give me time to think," I said. "There is no time," he said, "I want to get out of it now." "I think it's a bad idea," I told him. "Why?" he asked. "I don't trust them," I said. "Who do you ever trust?" he said, "you don't trust anybody, what don't you trust about them, what do you know about them?" "That is what I don't trust," I said, "I don't know anything about them." "So you know nothing. You know nothing bad about them," he said. "I know nothing good about them," I said. "When did you ever know anything good about any publisher?" he said. "What does it matter? Good, bad or indifferent, they have agreed to take on the series, they will pick up the backlist and they will fulfill the orders. We can close the account with the bank and we shall be in the clear."'

'How much was in the account?' Plant asked.

'Almost nothing.'

'And did you close it?'

'Yes,' said Ghosh.

'You didn't object?'

'Of course I objected.'

'So what happened?'

'So what could happen?' Ghosh asked, exasperatedly. 'He went ahead, what could I do, I could not take on the responsibility, we had no support from the university, the society was dead, the university is dead, all those years that I put in, I gave my life to it and then what, no recognition, no gratitude, you can apply to be a visiting fellow, they said, what an insult.'

'Did you?'

'It is necessary to have some sort of status. These things count in the eyes of the world. As soon as they gave it to me, I took special study leave and came back here, to this, my family home. Any day now they will knock it down, they will bring in their cranes and those great iron balls and bam, the walls will go down around me.'

He said it with great certainty and satisfaction.

'You intend to stay here while they knock it down?'

'Where else should I go, to our summer estate, you know what has happened there?'

'No,' said Plant, but Ghosh was not one to wait for a reply.

'I thought, I shall come back and retreat to the country, my father laid out the grounds with fruit trees and lawns and tennis courts, I would sit on the verandah at night, drink gin toddies, my manuscript beside me, listening to the birds calling. And now the bloody guerrillas have taken it over, bloody Maoist guerrillas. If you are not living there they take it over in the name of the peoples' revolution. What bloody people? What bloody revolution? I fought for the revolution all my life, I joined the party, I sheltered communists, I devoted my life to the revolution and now these bloody Maoists come and steal my land.'

'So you can't go there?'

'Oh, I can go there, if I want to be ambushed I can go there, I said to Ackerman, why don't you go there, talk to your precious revolutionaries at first hand, see how you like it, it would be a perfect place to write your bloody memoirs and you can get your pornographers to publish them.'

'Did he go?'

'If he did they would have taken him hostage.'

Ghosh laughed. It could have been hysteria or it could have been high satisfaction.

'They would soon learn their mistake, who would want to buy him back, the university, his precious lady wife? If they took him hostage they are stuck with him. Perhaps he will become their political philosopher, he would like that, the white man leading the revolution, Lawrence of bloody Arabia, then the Americans and the British can go in pursuit of him after they have mopped up the rest of the world and put him on trial as an unlawful combatant, no more prisoners of war, now they call them unlawful combatants, that would show him.'

'What was he doing here anyway?' Plant asked.

'Giving his lecture, what do you think he was doing?'

'Giving what lecture?'

'The lecture he gave in Bangkok, of course, mileage he called it, he was a great one for mileage, never give the same lecture once if you can give it a dozen times, that was his principle. He wrote to tell me he was giving a special lecture in Bangkok so I arranged his fare from there.'

'Was that his idea or yours?'

'I arranged his fare with the university here.'

'But was it his idea to come or did you invite him?'

'I invited him, of course; he said he would come so I invited him.'

'And that was all he came for, just to give the lecture again?'

'What else would he come to this bloody place for?'

'To see old friends?'

'What old friends?' Ghosh exploded. 'Who has friends any more, old or young?'

'Business, then,' Plant suggested.

'Business, what sort of business?'

'Dr Bowles suggested drug business.'

'Drug business?' said Ghosh, in amazement. Even amidst the emotionally charged pitch of his tirades, amazement stood out starkly. 'Bowles said that? That horrid little bounder, that treacherous little cad, after all that Ackerman did for him, what utter bloody nonsense.'

'You don't think it could be true?'

'How could it be true, the drug business is big business, how would Ackerman be involved in that?'

'Bowles said he had gone up to Chiang Mai.'

'To buy a kilo of opium and carry it back in his suitcase, I suppose?' said Ghosh. 'What bloody nonsense, you know what happens if you try to do that in Thailand, they execute you, who would be so idiotic, except idiots?'

'People still buy drugs,' said Plant.

'Of course they do,' said Ghosh, 'the entire economy is built on drugs, but you can't think someone like Ackerman would be involved in it.'

'So Bowles is just being mischievous.'

'Mischievous? Trouble-making, trying to discredit Ackerman for his own devious purposes, I never trusted him, I warned Ackerman, I said you're playing with fire supervising that little boy, he is trying to discredit you, he is trying to use your contacts, it's what they do all the time, and they succeed.' He thumped his walking-stick on the tiled floor. 'They discredited Ackerman, they discredited me, where are we now? Retired. Ruined.'

The thumps echoed round the house. The sound seemed to give Ghosh a bitter satisfaction. He thumped again and called out 'Ruined.'

The cry echoed along the gloomy dark corridors and down the stairwells.

'So there is no reason to think Ackerman is mixed up in the drug trade?' Plant persisted.

'Let me tell you about the drug trade,' said Ghosh.

'Go ahead,' said Plant, but Ghosh had already gone ahead.

'My grandfather was an opium trader, this house was built on the profits from opium.' He gestured round the haunted, hollow room. 'Not as big a trader as the Tagores, who were the suppliers to Queen Victoria, not as big as Jardines, but big, very profitable, it was licensed, you worked with the British government, the intention was to undermine China, to force opium on the Chinese so they would open up China to trade, make them sell their raw materials to buy opium, it was political from the beginning and it has never changed.'

‘I thought it was crime cartels now,’ said Plant. ‘The Mafia, the Triads.’

‘Puppets,’ said Ghosh, ‘they are merely the mechanics, they are hired to do the dirty work. Mussolini destroyed the Mafia and then the Americans invaded Sicily and restored them. The Triads’ big business is running dissidents and illegal migrants in and out of China, they are just the puppets for political action. The Corsicans were hired to break up the communist control of the Marseilles waterfront so that the Americans could get the Marshall Plan running which was their way of controlling Europe, and the Corsicans were paid off with the license for the Indo-China drug trade, everywhere it is the same pattern.’

‘So who controls it?’

‘It is run at the highest levels of government and military, everywhere, Morocco, Colombia, the Middle East, the Golden Triangle, Pakistan, how otherwise could it survive, it is controlled by governments and bankers and air forces and intelligence agencies and their private armies, there is no room for gentlemen amateurs, leaving aside the question of whether Ackerman was a gentleman, it is a global business, drugs for arms, Lebanon, Bosnia, Afghanistan, and the arms are sent according to foreign policy priorities, why do you think the drug producing countries have such savage laws for traffickers taking drugs out of the country, why should they care what happens somewhere else, why should they worry how many bloody foreigners become hooked and die on the streets?’

‘I agree it’s strange,’ said Plant.

‘They don’t care at all, what they care about is preventing independent operators from cutting into their trade and reducing their profits, it is big business like everything else, oil, automobiles, media, alcohol, pharmaceuticals, maybe a dozen big businesses world wide, soon it will be down to five or six, oligarchy capitalism. The military, the politicians, the developers all have their investment in the market, and the usurers, the insurance companies and the banks finance them. Anyone else who tries to buy in is removed, anyone else who tries to buy wholesale quantities is immediately informed upon, they are either arrested on the spot, or at the airport, or followed in their home country to see what contacts they have.’

‘And this is generally known?” said Plant.

‘Of course, by those who wish to know.’

‘And you wish to know?’

‘It is my subject,’ said Ghosh, ‘Asian history and politics, it is my business to know it, it is necessary for an understanding of the economic base, any serious scholar knows it. Not silly people who write on Orientalism and never even mention drugs, and even they may know and may simply be dissimulating.'

'Dissimulating?'

'There is much disinformation in politics, naturally.'

'So Ackerman would know all this.'

'Of course, it was one of his areas of expertise, as they call it.'

'Did he write about it?'

'It is unlikely. He never put a lot in writing.'

'What about Bowles? Would he know?'

'Of course,' said Ghosh, 'lazy and idle as he is, since he no doubt is working for the government.'

'You think?'

'I have no doubt,' said Ghosh. 'In the East these things are clear, we have no false illusions like the Western democracies, this is the country of the Great Game as you would remember if you had read your *Kim*.'

'Dr Bowles teaches it as a set text.'

'Of course,' said Ghosh.

'So what game is he playing? What is the purpose of bad-mouthing Professor Ackerman?'

'It could only be the highest purpose,' said Ghosh, 'the line from on high, the official line, an official warning, to tell you not to look for Professor Ackerman, perhaps.'

'You think?'

'I know.'

He leant his chin on his walking-stick handle.

'So I shouldn't look any further.'

'Not here,' Ghosh laughed. 'If Dr Bowles told you Ackerman had left Bangkok for Kolkata, I would go back to Bangkok and look there.'

'But he was here.'

'Yes, I told you, he gave his lecture.'

'And then?'

'And then he went back to Bangkok.'

Plant brooded on what Ghosh had told him.

'But if you don't buy wholesale quantities, it's all right to buy drugs here, isn't it?'

'Absolutely not,' said Ghosh, appalled. 'Not at all, the Americans have put pressure on the government, now they are cracking down on the local trade, it is no longer available.'

'Not even soft drugs?' said Plant.

'It would be highly dangerous,' said Ghosh, 'most ill-advised, and they are no longer available.'

15

Ghosh took him down to the street and hailed a taxi and gave instructions in Bengali to the driver.

'Sightseeing?' the driver asked, turning round to examine Plant, oblivious of the traffic ahead.

'No, just the hotel.'

'You don't want sightseeing?'

'Not today,' said Plant. He was averting his eyes from the sights he could see, the emaciated rickshaw wallahs, the maimed and sick begging along the crowded pavement, spilling over onto the crowded road.

'Nice Bengali girl, you like nice Bengali girl?'

'No, thank you.'

'Very young, very beautiful.'

'No thanks.'

'Very clean girls,' the driver assured him.

'No.'

'You like boy?'

'No,' said Plant.

'What you like?' the driver asked, turning round ingratiatingly.

He was going to have to think of something, wasn't he, Plant told himself, otherwise this would never end.

'I wouldn't mind some ganja,' said Plant.

'Ganja. You want ganja?'

'If it's possible.'

'How much you want, one tola, two tola?' The issue of possibility dispensed with, ignored.

Plant had no idea how much a tola was.

'Better make it two,' he said. He hoped that wasn't wholesale quantities.

The taxi swerved across to the side of the road and pulled up to a screeching stop beside some ramshackle huts. Children sat in the dirt. Dogs scavenged. Dust rose and settled.

Now I shall be mugged or taken hostage or arrested, Plant reflected. But he wasn't. He was the happy possessor of two tolas of ganja. They drove on.

'Where would I get papers?' Plant asked. The hotel, maybe, but he didn't want to buy cigarette papers where he was staying.

'Papers? You want papers? *Times of India?* English paper? *Guardian Weekly?*'

'No, no,' said Plant. 'Spare me. No, rolling papers.'

'Rolling papers?'

The driver looked round.

Plant gestured with his fingers, miming a rolling action.

'To smoke with. For the ganja.'

He mimed smoking.

The driver came to another squealing stop beside a stall.

'Papers? Tobacco too? Matches? I get them for you.'

Now he had everything.

He wondered if Professor Ghosh's information on the higher reaches of the drug trade was more accurate than his street level knowledge. As soon as he got back to the hotel he would roll a smoke and consider the question.

The ganja after all was a legitimate charge on expenses. It opened the doors of perception. It stimulated the speculative imagination. It was all part of the process of finding Ackerman. After all, Bowles had implied Ackerman was mixed up in drug business. How else was he going to find him, anyway? So far it had been an interesting enough tour, but what had he discovered, what had he established? He rolled himself another smoke, a great thick one, he'd probably overdone it buying two tolas, one would have been enough. He rolled himself a generous three-paper bumper joint and lit up again, and let thought pass over him. It passed over him and away. He really had no idea what to do. Except work at smoking through the huge stash of ganja, since it would be too dangerous to even think of taking it out of the country. He would have to smoke it all here.

The phone rang in his room. Plant looked at it in mild amazement. He could think of no one who would know to call him. Not first thing in the morning. Nor at any other time. Maybe another offer of a beautiful Bengali girl. He picked up the receiver.

'You would never believe it, it is an outrage, an outrage, unbelievable, are you there, can you hear me?'

'Who's speaking?' Plant asked.

'Professor Ghosh, I am in the lobby, I need to see you at once, you cannot believe it.'

'Believe what?'

'I will show you, what room are you, there is no time to waste.'

'It's all right,' said Plant, 'I'll come down, I'll see you in the lobby.'

The room reeked of ganja. He probably reeked of it himself. The windows were open but the fumes hung there. He rather liked them. Sweet, enticing, it was a shame to leave them. But he switched on the overhead fan and splashed water over his face from the wash-basin and cleaned his teeth and got into his clothes. He stuffed the ganja deep into his suitcase and locked it. Punctuating each activity with a few more puffs on the joint smoldering in the ashtray.

The phone rang again.

'Are you coming down or shall I come up to you?'

'I'm on my way,' Plant assured him. 'Just had a couple of things to do. I'll be right down.'

A couple of deep drags, and he stubbed out the joint, slipped the roach into a box of matches and the box into his trouser pocket. You never knew when it might come in handy.

Professor Ghosh was sitting in the lobby, clasping a silver headed walking-stick with one hand and a sheet of paper with the other, eyes fixed on the lifts, impaling Plant with his gaze as he emerged from the metal doors. Plant began an apology for the delay, but Ghosh cut across him, brandishing the paper in the air.

'Look at this, look at it, it is unbelievable, I cannot believe it, if you had told me this I would not have believed you.'

He flapped it around angrily.

Plant sat down. The paper passed to and fro before his eyes. Even with the accelerated, augmented vision of the herb there was no way he could read it.

'I can't quite see what it says,' he said.

Ghosh thrust it at him and then drew it back as if unwilling to let it go. He reached to take his glasses from his pocket and dropped his walking-stick. Plant picked it up for him while Ghosh fiddled with the spectacle case and put the gold-framed lenses astride his nose.

'"Media release",' he read, 'what pretentious nonsense, media, why cannot they just say press, "Media release, the South East Asian Library of Current Affairs announces the appointment of Doctor" – no, I cannot say it, I refuse to say it, I will not let his name pass my lips, you will have to read it yourself.'

He folded away his spectacles, still holding onto the paper.

'It is an outrage, an outrageous bloody outrage, my pills, where are my pills, they will kill me these people.'

'May I read it?' Plant asked.

Ghosh reluctantly handed it over and began searching through his pockets. His stick clattered to the floor again. He produced a pill bottle, retrieved his stick, and waved it in the air. A uniformed hotel employee came over.

'Water,' said Ghosh peremptorily, 'bring me water.'

He turned to Plant. 'Read it out,' he ordered.

'"Media release",' Plant began.

Ghosh swore.

'"The South East Asian Library of Current Affairs announces the appointment"—'

'No,' Ghosh shouted. 'Don't say it, I cannot bear it, it will kill me, where is that boy? Water, where is my water?'

Plant read on silently: '—the appointment of Dr Roger Bowles as editor in chief of its Studies in History and Society monograph series'.

'Ah, Bowles,' he said.

Ghosh grabbed the sheet of paper back.

'Enough, that is enough, that boy, I knew him when he was in short trousers, practically in nappies, I nursed him through his second year, and then he turned against me, and now, now, I cannot believe it. Water!' he roared again, with a quite impressive delivery.

'This is the series you and Professor Ackerman used to run.'

'My series, yes, for twenty years, for twenty years I built it up and now this, how could they do this?'

The water arrived. Ghosh took a swig and held it in his mouth, then tossed in a couple of pills. The Indian way of taking pills, as opposed to the western way of putting the pills in first and then adding water. Plant watched entranced. These significant cultural differences, they fascinated him, so much to watch. He stretched back in the cane chair. He felt a warm glow of contentment. Maybe he should suggest Professor Ghosh had a smoke to calm himself down. Then again, maybe not.

'Scoundrels,' said Ghosh. 'These people are scoundrels, arrant scoundrels, we must go and speak to these filthy pornographers now, this is unacceptable.'

Ghosh led the way, turning round at intervals to beat off the beggars that swarmed around Plant by brandishing his walking-stick at them, children, lepers, amputees, cripples, mothers with babes in arms.

'This never happens to me,' said Ghosh, 'you must attract them.'

He laughed, a particularly humorless laugh.

They went down crowded wide pavements, through crowded narrow lanes, food smells all around from pavement stalls, traffic fumes from the congested roads, a kaleidoscope of colours from the bright and garish to the dulled and dun, faded nineteenth-century buildings like Manchester or Melbourne draped with all the drapes and banners and accretions of the bazaar. The ganja helped, Plant was sure. Otherwise he would have been terrified. He was terrified, indeed, but in an interested, distanced sort of way. The sheer crowded fecundity of it all, that other sense, sometimes it seemed absence, of personal space, Professor Ghosh forging ahead in Austin Reed blazer and Oxford University tie and pressed grey trousers.

16

'Professor, how splendid to see you, you look so well, what an honour to have you visit us, you have come to see our books, perhaps to offer us one, don't say your magnum opus is completed already, you catch us unprepared.'

It was an office absolutely without feature. It looked as if it had only just been moved into. Or, alternatively, was about to be vacated. There was a desk that might have been a reception desk, but no chairs. They stood.

Ghosh brandished his sheet of paper. 'Have you seen this?' he demanded.

'Ah yes, indeed, I have one too.'

'What do you mean by it?' Ghosh demanded.

'What do I mean by it, dear fellow? I mean nothing at all. I am as ignorant as you. Much more ignorant, of course. You after all are a distinguished academic and I but a humble publisher.'

He looked anything but humble, tall and sleek in an elegant silver grey suit, fingers and cufflinks and teeth and spectacles flashing gold.

'Is this your doing?' Ghosh demanded again.

'Not at all,' said the humble publisher. 'This is from our Bangkok affiliate. We are of course all one big happy family. But we run our own lives, as it were. Cousins under the skin but independent as to what we do. Though our strength is in our unity, as we used to say in our militant days.'

He laughed, comfortably distant from those days.

'I have to sit, I am about to collapse,' Ghosh announced.

The humble publisher clapped his hands and called out something in Bengali. A chair was brought in and Ghosh sat on it, plunged into gloom and silence. Plant took the opportunity to be an investigator.

'Legal and Visual International,' said the humble publisher proudly. 'They are our parent company, specialising in business law, tax law, and international law. We are the icing on the cake. The superstructural adornment. The visual arts. Once, when we were independent, it was all art. Erotic sculptures, the Kama Sutra in colour, I am sure you know the sort of thing. But fashions change. Fashions change but the economic base remains the same. Cash flow. It is all about cash flow. And when the cash ceased to flow what could we do? Our tears might flow but they cut no ice in the frozen hearts of our bankers.'

Plant smiled sympathetically. He felt a warm sympathy for all humanity, safely insulated from the streets.

'So what happened?' he asked.

'We surrendered our independence. I do not regret it. How else would we have survived? We needed a patron with deep pockets, someone who would let us proceed in our traditional way, whom we could oblige in some other.'

'What other?'

'A partnership. The regulations governing foreign ownership have been strict. It is all a matter of equity. We had a company that needed capital. They had capital but needed a company that was Indian owned. We entered into a partnership. Technically we retain the majority shareholding. Now our books are distributed internationally and we publish our affiliates' books throughout India. It is satisfying to everybody. As I told Professor Ghosh, this is the way to go, you have your splendid series, but how will you keep it going now you are retired? You should explore a partnership. I was happy to facilitate the connection.'

'Happy?' Ghosh called out. 'How can you even say the word? Have you seen this?'

The media release was waved through the air yet again.

'Indeed yes, I have told you, I have a copy here. Like you, I am merely the recipient of the information. I had no part in the decision. I am merely the publisher. I am not responsible for these editorial decisions. I assumed you had arranged it.'

'Never,' said Ghosh.

A girl in a sari brought in tea and some brightly coloured sweet cakes, vivid greens and pinks. Plant stood there, politely sipping and chewing, Ghosh sitting on the chair and banging his stick on the ground.

'We were at university together,' the publisher told Plant. 'Even then he was emotional. He is an impassioned man, Professor Ghosh, are you not, sir?'

It was as far as they got. They went over it several times, round and round and back and forth but there was nothing more to be learned about Bowles' appointment. Or if there was, it was not disclosed.

Ghosh continued to seethe. Bubbles of rage rose through his trembling frame and erupted in explosive utterance. He brandished his walking-stick at the world as he pushed through the streets. He steered them into one of the big hotels, sailed on into the restaurant. Plant had hoped for some exotic dive but that did not seem to be the pattern. As Ghosh explained, the rich had servants who cooked for them, so why go to restaurants when you had servants? Restaurants were not that much part of the life of the rich. So there were not traditionally many of them, just street stalls. And Professor Ghosh was not about to eat at a street stall. Absolutely not. Plant bore with the spreading, empty room, the sterility of globalised, sanitised sameness. He ordered jackfruit curry, because it sounded interesting, and it was. Ghosh ordered goat.

'That horrid little boy, it is appalling they should appoint him editor, what does he know, he is an ignorant fool, I shall protest, Ackerman was right about him.'

'I thought he was Ackerman's protégé.'

'Protégé, what do you mean protégé?'

'Didn't Ackerman save his M.A. thesis?'

'Only to get rid of him, he was stuck with him, like all the rubbish they gave him to supervise. The head of department always kept the best students or gave them to her cronies, and we got the rubbish, utter rubbish. Ackerman helped him with his thesis to get the bloody thing finished so he wouldn't be stuck with it dragging on for the next ten years.'

'Then he enrolled for a doctorate.'

'A spook, a spook in the night, Ackerman always said he was a spook, the only students who spoke to us were spooks, all the rest were warned away, suddenly they would be avoiding us in the corridors, somebody had spoken to them and spooked them, only the spooks remained.'

'Why?' Plant asked. 'What were they trying to find out?'

'These are Asian studies, dear boy, three quarters of the people in Asian studies work for the intelligence services, the other quarter they put their spooks onto to find out what we are thinking, who our contacts are.'

'Who are this they?'

'They? The British, the Americans, the Indians, the Chinese, and their Australian counterparts.'

'And Bowles is a spook.'

'Of course he is, who do you think pays his salary?'

'I thought he had a university lectureship.'

'And who pays him?'

'I assumed the university did.'

'Nonsense,' said Ghosh, 'rubbish, it is a special project, it is funded by ASEAN and Australian Foreign Affairs and the U.S. State Department.'

'Really?'

'No one else would give that little boy a job, they arrested him in Iran.'

'What for?'

'Going where he shouldn't have gone, talking to dissidents, he is trouble, nothing but trouble, now he has control of the series, I was right. People laughed at him, but then five years later it would turn out I was right. That bloody Legal and Visual International, I said that they didn't add up, they had to be a front. I said, "Why would the forces of repression want to publish our series? It is against everything they represent. It can only be so that they can monitor the opposition, see what manuscripts come in." "You are insane," he said, "you know what rubbish comes in, who would want to monitor that, we can hardly get anything worth publishing, except what we edit ourselves." "Then they'll put something through," I said, "some phoney stuff to give somebody credibility, they'll kill some authentic radical and use his manuscript to give some boneheaded operative a publication." "Why would they publish something radical if it was so subversive that they had to kill the author?" he said. "They'll sanitise it," I said, "they'll cut out the guts and leave enough jargon to make it look like their dummy author is a radical sympathiser, or an Islamic fundamentalist." He said that seemed totally improbable. I said if they killed villagers in the Philippines and drilled holes in their throats to make it look like the vampires had got them so the peasants would think the guerrillas were vampires, why would this seem improbable? "You'll see," I said, "you've sold us to the enemy," I said, "not even sold us, given us away, we'll live to regret it," I said and I do, now I do, now they give my series to that little blood-sucking vampire in short trousers I see it, next thing they will discover Ackerman's corpse with two puncture marks in the throat, I wouldn't be surprised if Bowles didn't have him killed when he went back, lured him into the woods and sucked him dry.'

'Did Ackerman go back?'

'Yes.'

'Bangkok? Or Brisbane?'

'Bangkok, of course, I arranged a cheap return from Bangkok for him, it was just a quick visit, I should have asked him to stay longer, now I am responsible for sending him to his death, I should have put him up, I should have organised a visiting fellowship for him, I offered, but it is so much trouble and there was no money, if it wasn't for those bloody Maoists guerrillas he could have stayed in my house in the country and written his book. "You could still go there," I told him, "they may have moved on, they live in the jungle, if the house is occupied they won't seize it, it is only empty properties they are taking over," he would have been safer there and he would have saved the house.'

'But he didn't go.'

'No.'

'You're sure?'

'Of course I'm sure, I took him to the airport, I ordered his taxi and went with him to say goodbye, I shook his hand, probably for the last time, I shall never forgive myself.'

Plant chose to believe him. The alternative was to go to the summer residence and check out the Maoists. To make sure Ackerman wasn't holed up with them. Some other time, maybe. For the moment he would pass on that one

'Or Bowles,' Ghosh continued, 'I shall never forgive that red-haired little vampire, how could they appoint that horrid little boy as editor, I could kill him, I shall not be able to restrain myself, when Ackerman hears he will kill him for sure, you mark my words.'

17

'I think I would like to look at some of the books,' Plant said, when they had finished lunch.

'I have them in my house,' said Ghosh. 'I have preserved a complete run of the series.'

'Not the series,' said Plant.

Ghosh visibly bristled.

'I mean, yes, I would like to see the series too. That would be most interesting. But immediately I think I need to see what sort of publishing your old school friend does.'

'Dirty books,' said Ghosh. 'Filth in expensive editions.'

'That might be fun,' said Plant. 'But it's the rest of the operation I'm interested in. I'd like to see what the international list is like. There weren't any books on show. It seemed strange.'

'He is probably afraid people will come in and steal them.'

'Could be,' Plant agreed. 'I was just wondering whether they exist at all.'

'Probably not,' said Ghosh.

'You've seen copies.'

'I refuse to look.'

'Maybe you could ask him if I could look at them.'

'You can just go there,' he said.

'It would be better coming from you,' said Plant. 'And I'm not sure I could find the office on my own.'

Ghosh expressed exasperation. 'All right,' he agreed, 'but I shall not stay. Not after what has been done to my series. I could not guarantee my behaviour. You will have to look at them on your own.'

'That's all right,' said Plant.

'Mr Plant would like to look at your books,' said Ghosh. 'God knows why,' he added.

'A pleasure,' said the humble publisher. 'No problem at all, absolutely no problem, that is what we are here for. The only problem, alas, is that I have unfortunately absolutely no copies of Professor Ghosh's admirable series here.'

'What?' Ghosh exploded.

'They have not yet arrived from Australia.'

'That is all I need, all I need, now I have heard everything, that is it, that is the end.'

He stormed out of the building and disappeared amidst the crowds on the pavement.

'Always the man of feeling,' said the publisher.

'Actually,' said Plant, 'I should be interested in looking at your own titles. And those of your parent company.'

'Of course,' said the publisher. 'You are a writer yourself?'

'Not really,' said Plant.

'Some sort of journalist?"

'A researcher.'

'Ah, an investigative reporter.'

'At the moment just a researcher.'

'And what exactly are you researching?'

'At the moment I am researching the disappearance of Professor Ackerman.'

'Professor Ackerman has disappeared, well, well.'

'You know him?'

'Alas, only by repute.'

'Good repute?'

'Oh yes, good repute. A colleague of Professor Ghosh's.'

'And that is sufficient recommendation.'

The publisher smiled.

'Professor Ghosh is an emotional man, but he has a good heart. In the metaphorical sense. I hesitate to pronounce medically, you understand. As for Professor Ackerman, you think a study of our books will facilitate your search?'

'Maybe,' said Plant.

'In what way?'

'I don't know what way.'

'An intuition? A hunch, perhaps.'

'Maybe,' said Plant.

He led Plant into an inner office. A small table stood in the center with a couple of chairs. There were books in a bookshelf against the wall, others in a couple of glass-fronted bookcases.

'Unfortunately I have no copies for sale,' he said, unlocking the glass-fronted cases. 'This is our library, as I call it. The archives. If you want to buy any of them you will have to order them from our distributor.'

'No problem,' said Plant.

'Forgive me if I have to leave you with them. Alas, or should I say thankfully, I have work to do.'

He left but popped back in a moment later with an ashtray, which he put on the table beside Plant. He smiled knowingly. Plant smiled back, but knew enough to resist the temptation to light up.

They were solid looking books, bound in accord with American library standards of durability. They were without doubt expensive, the sort of expensive looking books lawyers like to have on the shelves behind their desks, lawyers who charge expensive fees and can afford expensive books with which to line their offices. Part reference, part décor. Image. And purchasing image never comes cheap. Highly priced books that needed constant updating, revised editions. Books on business law and tax law. South America, Europe, Asia. Books on art, painting, sculpture, both classic and contemporary. Again, highly priced. Art books always were. Décor for waiting rooms, like the legal books. Legal and Visual International. Lavi. As in lavabo, to wash, to launder? Could they be so blatant?

They might, because they didn't brandish the name around that much. The North American titles came out under the Legal and Visual imprint, but they were only a small part of the books there. The Kolkata company was called Artworld Orient. Other books bore the imprint of various libraries and cultural sounding organizations: The Academy Library of Australia, The All Asia Law Library, Editions EuroArt. Plant turned the title-pages and looked at the copyright information on the verso. The copyright credits were different from the publishing imprints. They tended to be foundations and institutes: © EuroArt Foundation, © The Pacific Rim Humanities' Center, © Siam Institute of History and Culture. They all sounded splendid, but they could all have been as ramshackle as Ackerman and Ghosh's South East Asian Library of Current Affairs. Plant had asked for a catalogue hoping to get an overview of the operation, but there were no catalogues.

The books were all clearly expensive. But how much revenue would they generate? He had never seen any of them in bookshops. Not that he any longer spent much time in bookshops. Perhaps they were sold by direct marketing. Or mainly went to library suppliers. With a small print run and a high mark-up, you could generate a profit. A substantial profit. But would it be substantial enough to sustain this international web of companies and foundations?

He noticed another pattern as he looked through the books. They were not printed in the country in which they were published. Perhaps that was the result of jobbing around for the cheapest printing rates. In that case you would imagine that a number of them would be printed in the same place, wherever was cheapest. India, for instance. But there was no apparent consistency. He noted printers in the Netherlands, Norway, Singapore and the Czech Republic. Each book seemed to involve two or three companies or institutions – publisher, foundation and printer – spread over two or three countries. It could be hard to follow through any inquiry about financial transactions, any inquiry about anything.

That was surely the point. Just to establish how many copies were printed would involve a different search for each title. Most publishers stuck with the same printer and negotiated special discounts for volume of business. Put all the jobs in one basket and get a kickback. So why were Legal and Visual International not doing that? To obscure the money trail? Was that why there were so many publishing imprints, and so many cultural and legal foundations credited as copyright holders? Any investigation would bog down in the tedious detail of partnerships and subsidiaries and trusts and foundations spreading from one continent to another, one tax system to another, one set of laws and reporting conventions to another.

The copyrights were never in the name of the authors. He remembered Prem's complaint about that, one of the many reasons he was not tempted to sell out to them. They had wanted all world rights in all world languages. It made sense. Not necessarily publishing sense. But in terms of moving money around from country to country, and laundering it on the way, it made a lot of sense. They could ship any of their products to any of their subsidiaries and affiliates anywhere. No matter if the books never sold, no matter how many or how few were ever printed, the invoices and consignment orders would be issued and duly paid, from one company in the group to another, round and round the globe, year after year. Law books, art books, they could cost huge amounts editorially, paying lawyers huge fees to research the law books, paying galleries and dealers and owners for reproduction rights, all of it endlessly negotiable and notional, vast sums of money transmitted round the world if necessary.

And maybe pallets of books were shipped around. Shrink-wrapped. Sealed. You could stow all sorts of substances in cartons of books. In hollowed out copies, in bindings without pages, in pages with bindings that looked like fine morocco leather but turned out to be compressed blocks of fine Morocco hashish, or pages of paper impregnated with LSD or amphetamines. Especially when your subsidiaries were in India and Thailand and Mexico and Amsterdam.

Plant conceded that it could all be his overheated imagination stimulated by the ganja. But it could all be true. The possibilities were, if not perhaps infinite, certainly numerous.

'Fascinating,' he assured the humble publisher.

'You have found what you want?'

'I'm not sure what I want,' said Plant.

'A clue, perhaps.'

'A clue?'

'To Professor Ackerman's disappearance.'

'Ah, Ackerman. You never met him, you said?'

'No, alas, we never met. My only dealings have been with Mr Starr.'

'Mr Starr?'

'The publisher of Legal and Visual International.'

'He came here?'

'Mr Starr is a frequent visitor, a frequent flyer, indeed. He likes to travel. And he loves our exotic art. He is a great collector.'

He smiled, it could have been knowingly.

'And did Mr Starr meet Professor Ackerman?'

'That I cannot say. It is possible.'

'But not with you.'

'Not with me, sir, no sir.'

He locked up the glass-fronted cases.

'I hope you find your man,' he said.

'Thank you,' said Plant.

18

Plant woke up in the night, his head throbbing, his face burning, his stomach seething. He was going to be sick. He hated the sensation, and the inevitability, knowing it was not going to go away. What he didn't know until later was how sick he was going to be, sicker than he had ever known.

In the intervening moments he wondered if it was the food at the hotel where Ghosh had taken him. So much for international, five star hotel restaurants. He never trusted them. Or had he been poisoned? Had someone at Legal and Visual laced the pink and green cakes with some toxic substance? The humble publisher? The nice Bengali girl in the sari? Or the emotional Professor Ghosh, had he been up to something? Without a doubt he was capable of being up to something, but whether it involved poisoning visiting private investigators, Plant was not sure. It was not an impossibility.

It was worse than lying in bed and hearing the bulldozers rend and devastate the bush outside, the great grunts and roars of the motors, the clanging of their blades, the crack of breaking limbs. It was more as if the bulldozers were inside, burrowing in his gut and bowels, shovelling shit and vomit in massive eructations and spasms. He would rush for the lavatory and vomit before reaching it, the vomit over his chest and stomach and feet, and then his bowels would open and the diarrhoea would start, and a convulsion at one end was matched by a convulsion at the other, vomiting and shitting simultaneously, and as a consequence covering lavatory and shower and bath and wash-basin with a diffuse spray of vomit and excreta, and he had to clean it up, he couldn't sleep there with the smells of shit and vomit wafting through, but as he tried to wipe down the walls he gagged again and vomited some more and the vomiting would be so severe he would have to lie down on the tiled floor, groaning as he lay there, the groans seeming to relieve something, pain or fear of pain or fear generally. When he was able he stood up again and tried having another shower. As the night went on the nausea and diarrhoea continued, the cleaning up and renewed befouling endlessly repeated, the smell of vomit and shit hanging in the air, permeating his sweat and skin and hair and tongue. He had never been so sick. By the morning he was utterly ravaged, sheets drenched in sweat, pajamas fouled, towels filthy, the bathroom a stables.

He lay there all day, smiling weakly when the chambermaid came in and cleaned up all his mess and brought him clean sheets. After that he rolled a smoke which settled his system enough to consider a cup of weak black tea. He took the lid off the electric kettle and made sure the water boiled at length.

After three days he emerged. Three days of continual vomiting and shitting. He made his way down to the lobby for another session with Professor Ghosh.

'Good, you are recovered,' said Ghosh. 'I was not worried about you. Anyway, I had more important things to worry about.'

Plant nodded. He had been too feeble to move until now, and in the presence of Ghosh he was beginning to feel feeble again.

Ghosh waved his stick in the air to attract attention. He attracted it. Attracting service took a little longer. Ghosh ordered a cappuccino and a cream bun. Plant looked the other way and stuck with weak black tea.

'It was probably from eating vegetables,' he assured Plant. 'You see, with meat there is a perceived danger, everyone is absolutely careful about meat, or fish, though I would never eat fish, of course, or sea food, not here, but with vegetables, you see, people are liable to think, ah, they are only vegetables, they are not a problem, people don't get vegetable poisoning, and they become careless about how they preserve them, they store them in the refrigerator and people don't order them very often so there isn't the turnover so perhaps they sit there longer than they strictly should and someone like you comes along, a delicate immune system, not adjusted to the natural bacteria of the city. And I am perfectly all right, you see. So I suspect vegetable poisoning. Beware of the vegetable, I say.'

Plant nodded, weakly.

'If I were to be a vegetarian, which I am not, at least in principle, I would be very careful in ordering vegetarian food in public places, particularly on aircraft, you can never be sure of it, it doesn't have the demand, you cannot be sure how fresh it is, and they mark it with your seat number on the container, what better way to poison you, assassinate you by your chosen dish, so I never specify, I take what comes, that is my advice.'

'Thank you,' said Plant.

'Meanwhile, I shall investigate,' said Ghosh.

'Don't worry,' said Plant, 'I'm sure it was just a stomach bug.'

'Oh that, of course.' Ghosh dismissed it.

Plant felt rather put out. It was not that dismissible. And who was to be sure that he hadn't been deliberately poisoned?

'I shall investigate Legal and Visual, I shall make inquiries, I still have contacts in this city, there are always relatives with some governmental connection, everybody knows somebody in government, or in the police, or security, someone will know, some journalist, when you attend a major university in a major city you cannot help making important contacts that at the time may seem nothing but that in the future bloom into a thousand blossoms.'

Plant nodded.

'I shall let you know, whatever I discover, I shall let you know.'

'You didn't investigate them before?'

'What would have been the point? Ackerman had made up his mind, whatever I might say.'

'You didn't want to confirm your suspicions?'

'Mr Plant, I did not have the strength, the bloody series was like a treadmill, it was like a parasite on a jungle tree, it had been sucking all my time and energy, like one of your Australian stag-horns in my throat, like a strangler vine. I wanted to start my own life, the little that was left of it, free of the university, free of the series, so how could I investigate?'

'But you're going to investigate now.'

'Too damn right I am,' said Professor Ghosh.

To Plant's distress he thumped his stick up and down on the floor. He could feel it vibrating through his frontal lobes.

19

Plant flew back to Bangkok and took the Royal Thai limousine service to the hotel. He felt he was beginning to find his way around. It had been Prem's advice to take the limousine, for sure. But finding your way around was in large part a matter of finding good advice and taking it. At the hotel reception he suggested the special Australian government rate and went straight to bed. He spent the next day lying there, in the hotel room, still fragile from Kolkata, dozing, watching television, going down to the restaurant for rice and a few vegetables and black tea. By happy hour he felt strong enough for a couple of beers, listened to a couple of sad songs, and made an early night of it.

In the morning he looked down from his window at the fish ponds, their golden carp floating restfully. After Kolkata he felt a sense of relieved familiarity, like being back home. Pity about the unsmoked ganja he had had to abandon. He had thought of offering it to Professor Ghosh to calm him down, but that might have been counter-effective and produced a terminal explosion, especially given Ghosh's authoritative assurance that it was no longer an available substance. So he didn't. He dropped it in a waste paper bin on his way out of the hotel. Maybe he should go back to the red-light district after happy hour and score a few more Thai sticks.

He picked up the complimentary *Bangkok Post* that had been left outside his door and leafed through it, despite himself. There was an article on how many foreign tourists were shipped back home dead each year: over a hundred Germans, eighty-something British. Dead from heart attacks after leaping into hotel swimming pools in the blazing sun, dead from abuse of over-the-counter medications, dead from unaccustomed sexual exertion, dead from too much alcohol in the heat. I will avoid all these dangers, Plant resolved. He turned to more cheerful fodder. Minister charged with corruption, Buddhist monk in massage-parlour scandal.

And then his stomach contracted in sudden shock. He felt himself sweating down his neck, under his arms, in his groin.

'Expat Aussie drowns in Canal. Body found floating by early morning boatmen. Contract lecturer Dr Roger Bowles, 35, was fished out …'

He put the paper down. His head was swirling, his vision blurring. He worked at calming himself, took slow, deep breaths, restored his equilibrium. He turned back to the paper but it had little more to report than was contained in the headlines. Just one more body to be freighted out. According to the article on tourist deaths, it would be an expensive business. Not all airlines were keen to carry corpses. It cost a lot more going back dead than alive.

'I could kill him,' he could hear Ghosh saying, 'I shall not be able to restrain myself, when Ackerman hears he will kill him for sure, you mark my words.'

He called Prem.

'You have heard the news,' said Prem.

'About Bowles?'

'Yes. Dr Bowels. Dead in a canal.'

'What happened?'

'I imagine he drowned.'

'You haven't heard anything?'

'No,' said Prem, 'there is no reason why I should. Only what I read in the paper. Do you want to know more?'

'It might be interesting,' said Plant.

'You want me to inquire?'

'Is that possible?'

'I could phone the embassy,' he said.

'Would they know anything?'
'Not that they would tell you.'
'No.'
'Would you like me to call the morgue? Do you want to see the body?'
'No,' said Plant. Emphatically.
'Perhaps I could inquire from someone in the press.'
'That might be good,' said Plant.
'I will see what I can do. You will be at your hotel?'
'Yes.'
'I will see what I can do and I will pick you up for lunch. Twelve-thirty.'
'Twelve-thirty,' Plant agreed.

Prem picked him up and drove to the Novotel. A French hotel chain in the Thai capital with a restaurant with Indian décor and Indian waiters, serving Chinese food. And inside the fortune cookies, what? Something in Arabic script? The mystery of the East?
'Yum cha,' said Prem, 'I hope that is all right.'
'There will be some vegetarian dishes,' said Plant.
'I will make sure. I will speak to the manager.'
The manager looked stricken. He spread his hands anxiously. He explained. Everything was cooked in pork fat.
Prem shared the anxiety.
'I had not realised. We can go somewhere else.'
'It's all right,' said Plant.
'No, no,' said Prem.
'Really,' said Plant.
The manager stood there; alarm, tragedy, resignation.
'It's no problem,' Plant insisted.
'Are you sure?'
'Sure,' said Plant. He was astounded at the manager's honesty. It was the sort of detail it might have been easy to forget. 'It's just that I don't want to eat large amounts of meat,' he explained.
'No problem,' Prem assured the manager.
He poured out the tea.
'You can cope with dead mammals in small amounts.'
Plant shrugged.
'That is admirably flexible. Death in homeopathic doses. Perhaps it will inure us to something greater.'

'I don't want to make a fuss.'

'No. We will forget it. Let us enjoy our lunch. While we talk about the late Dr Bowels.'

The food came in relays, dim sims filled with snow peas, dim sims filled with garlic spinach, plates of bok choy, crisp noodles in soy sauce, turnip cake, taro, little vegetable omelettes, and squid and prawns in rice noodles and prawn dim sims for Prem to eat and to tempt Plant with.

They enjoyed it.

'So what's the story?' Plant asked.

'The story? Or the truth?'

'Is there a discrepancy?'

Prem shrugged.

'What do the police think?'

'Oh, the police. They will no doubt say he was under the influence of narcotics and fell in a canal and drowned. It happens all the time.'

'And was he under the influence of narcotics?'

'I imagine so. He often was, I believe.'

'What about the press? Your journalistic contacts.'

'You make them sound very important. I simply work in public relations and place a few advertorial pieces. Nothing sensational, certainly not the crime pages. My clients would not like it if they appeared in them.'

'So nothing?'

'They say it gives a new definition to colonic irrigation. Dr Bowels in a sewage canal. But that is in very poor taste. I apologise.'

'They don't seem very concerned.'

'Not at all. Sadly. But that is the way it is. He was not universally loved.'

'But he was known.'

'Oh, he was known.'

'Why wasn't he liked?'

'He was not a very likable young man. He was very self-important. He pestered people.'

'What about?'

'Anything.'

'Why?'

'I think he liked to give the impression he was going about his father's business.'

'Is that what people thought?'

Prem shrugged again.

'I think people just thought he was big-noting himself.'

'Why would he do that?'

'To impress the girls, why else did he do anything?'

'But you don't think he was a government man.'

'Dr Bowels? No.'

'So why was he killed?'

'Who says he was killed?'

'So he just slipped and fell.'

'Why not? Or perhaps he tried to cheat some poor girl and she ran after him and he tripped into the canal trying to avoid paying her. Or perhaps her pimp gave him a push. Or perhaps someone sold him some cheap drugs and he stumbled. He liked to get things cheap. Or perhaps they had laced his drugs because he was being a nuisance. All these things happen. All the time. No one is going to bother too much. It is easier for everybody if he slipped and fell.'

'Were there any other symptoms?' Plant asked.

'Such as what?'

'Poisoning.'

'I have not heard. With narcotics, who is to say? An accidental overdose. An unsuspectedly pure quality heroin. A little strychnine. Really, people die from the most various and ambiguous means.'

'What are the symptoms of strychnine poisoning?'

'You think you have them?' Prem laughed.

'Could be. I was pretty sick in Kolkata.'

'You are not serious?'

'I hope not,' said Plant.

'I have no idea of the symptoms of strychnine poisoning,' said Prem. 'If you are worried, call a doctor at once. Or shall I drive you to the medical center?'

'If I don't improve,' said Plant.

'Don't leave it too long,' said Prem. 'Losing you as well as Dr Bowles and Professor Ackerman would look very careless. What is happening to your country's best and brightest?'

'You tell me,' said Plant.

'A manner of speaking,' said Prem. 'I understood from my grammatical studies that rhetorical questions did not expect an answer.'

'Always expect an answer,' said Plant.

'Is that your advice?'

'It doesn't mean you have to believe it,' said Plant.

'That is interesting,' said Prem.

'Isn't it?' Plant agreed.

'A flexible approach.'

'Absolutely.'

'How are you enjoying the food?' Prem asked.

'Excellent,' said Plant.

'No problem with the dead pig.'

'No,' said Plant. 'Only with Dr Bowles.'

'Even in death he does not leave us in peace,' said Prem.

'So it could have been murder, is that what you're saying?'

'It could have been an accident.'

'What do you think?'

'Oh me, I tried not to think about Dr Bowels while he was alive. I have few thoughts about him now he is dead. Poor fellow.'

'You haven't seen Ackerman?'

'No. Is he here?'

'I don't know. I just wondered if he might be.'

'You surely don't think Professor Ackerman might have administered the fatal push? Or hired someone to shove him in.'

'Is it likely?'

'It is just a matter of paying,' said Prem.

'How much?'

If Bowles had been right and Ackerman was running drugs, then he would have had the cash and the contacts.

'It is not necessarily expensive.'

'Did Ackerman have money?' Plant asked.

'He had a lump sum from his long service leave and his superannuation.'

Of course. Plant had not thought of them. A pension was being paid into Ackerman's account, enough to cover the direct debits on utilities. But he could have taken out half of it in a lump sum immediately he retired. And if he had never taken up any of his long service leave, there would be a sizable lump sum there. That could all add up to a substantial total. He could have invested the two amounts and be living off the income, living cheaply in Asia, without touching the half-pension coming in to Australia, assuming it was a half-pension. Or he might have another source of income anyway, if not Bowles' allegations of drug money, then maybe a secret service budget. One of those tax-free incomes people like Graham Greene had enjoyed. Careless work, Plant.

'Is it likely Ackerman would have killed him?'

'Alec was a kindly man,' said Prem. 'A man of peace. But Dr Bowels could be very trying.'

'Really?'

'You met him.'

'Yes.'

'And you didn't find him trying? Perhaps you are a man of great patience.'

Plant thought back to the evening in the bar.

'Yes,' he agreed. 'He could be trying.'

'When did you arrive back?' Prem asked.

'A couple of nights ago.'

'So just in time.'

'Just in time?'

'To push Dr Bowels into the canal.'

'Is that when he died?'

'The night of the thirtieth. And you arrived?'

'The thirtieth.'

'I hope you were not wandering around the red-light district.'

'I just checked in and went to bed.'

'Not even a meal?'

'I had been so ill in Kolkata.'

'So no alibi.'

'I guess not,' said Plant. 'Do I need one?'

Prem shrugged.

'Was he pushed? Is that what really happened?'

'Who can tell?'

'You think I might be a suspect?' Plant laughed. But he felt that the world was not laughing with him.

'A vegetarian assassin,' said Prem, 'although a flexible vegetarian, one willing to tolerate a little bit of death. It might serve to puzzle your authorities. Of course our authorities are more accustomed to the paradox of a Buddhist society with professional hit-men. However, I suspect that our authorities are going to be less concerned than yours.'

'Maybe I should move on,' said Plant.

'Maybe,' Prem agreed.

20

Never having met Ackerman, Plant found it hard to assess the likelihood of his being a killer. Not that meeting someone necessarily made it possible to tell. Undoubtedly there were many killers around who you would never suspect. There was no way of telling. There was no reason to suspect, either. Just that Ghosh's words kept running through his head. 'When Ackerman hears he will kill him for sure, you mark my words.'

He marked them. But what did they mean? Did academics take themselves so seriously? In Plant's observation, yes, they did. Seriously enough to kill over the editorship of a moribund series of books? Perhaps. But when it came to it would they do it? That was more problematical. When it came to it, would they ever do anything? He could hear Ghosh, shrill with emotion. 'I could kill him.' But would Ghosh ever actually do it? Prod Bowles with his walking-stick? Was it maybe a sword-stick? Or a gun for firing castor oil pellets?

He couldn't see Ghosh as a killer. Not an effective one. The wish, perhaps, but not the deed. Ackerman he had never seen at all. Was it possible he was involved in something, as Bowles had suggested? Perhaps. And knowing Bowles knew what he was up to, he arranged for someone to give him a hot-shot and drop him in the canal. And what would that achieve? If Bowles knew and Bowles had been working for some agency, any information he had would already be on file. And if Bowles were working for some agency, it was just as likely, more likely if Ghosh were to be believed, that he was up to his ears in the drug business himself. So his story about Ackerman being in Chiang Mai was the oldest story in the book. He might well have been in Chiang Mai. But smuggling opium, heroin, marijuana, Plant doubted it. It was far more likely that Bowles was fingering someone else for what he was involved in himself, wasn't that the secret agencies' specialty, the principle of black propaganda, indict the other for the activities you yourself are engaged in. The others are running drugs, sponsoring terror, using nuclear, biological, chemical weapons of mass destruction, we must impose sanctions, blockades, exterminate the brutes. And if Bowles had been in the business, then any number of people might have bumped him off: rival cartels, suppliers he had cheated, rival agencies, even his own agency, depending on how bent he or they were. Or maybe

Bowles wasn't a government man at all, but simply in the drug business. Or maybe he had been none of these things but just a language teacher with a penchant for prostitutes.

As for Plant himself being a possible suspect for involvement in Bowles' death, he could see the logic of that. Prem's logic. And if Prem could see it, no doubt others could see it too. And if a perpetrator had to be found, if the Australian authorities insisted and the Thai authorities cooperated, then he could well find himself accused of having been in the wrong place at the wrong time, and with no way to extricate himself. Of course suddenly departing might seem suspicious. But hanging around could be inviting trouble. There was no harm in putting some distance between himself and all this. But where should he go? The Ackerman trail had gone cold, had never been other than cold. Should he phone Mrs Ackerman for instructions? But what further instructions could she give? He already had his instructions. Look for her husband. But where?

He went down for happy hour and a couple of beers and the doleful laments of the sad-eyed singer. He was getting to like her semi-tone off-key delivery. It suited his mood.

A girl came over from reception with an envelope. She handed it to him and bowed. No stamp. Hand-delivered.

Plant took a mouthful of complimentary peanuts from the bowl on the table, washed them down with the draught Singha beer, and slit open the flat brown package. Inside was a postcard. One of those advertisement postcards you pick up for free. It had a photograph of a bookshop with rows of well-stocked shelves, another photograph of a conference room with bare table and empty chairs, and a scrolled design announcing the Asian Dawn Bookshop and Conference Center: Manila's international literary marketplace.

Plant turned it over. It was addressed to Prem. There were a couple of lines of scrawled handwriting: 'I talked to Johnny about stocking your books. Try him. Alec.' The card was dated the twenty-fifth. The bookshop address and phone numbers and fax number and email were printed at the bottom. He looked at the postmark. The date was indecipherable. He shook the envelope. There was nothing else inside. He walked over to a phone booth and called Prem. No answer.

He had his second beer before going to reception and inquiring about a flight. It gave him time to think. But he didn't need to think.

The singer in the foyer sang 'Nice Work If You Can Get It.' She didn't make it sound cheerful.

He was heading for the lifts when the girl from reception came over to him again. She cupped her hands together and bowed in the namaskara gesture.

'Sorry,' she said, 'I forget. There is also a package for you.'

'A package?'

This is it. This is the bomb.

He must have sounded anxious.

'A bag,' she said.

He went back to reception with her. She gave him a plastic bag, strong plastic, department store insignia. It weighed heavy. He peered inside it. There were a dozen books and a couple of sheets of paper protruding from between them. He read the top sheet. 'If you go to that Manila bookshop, perhaps you could ask if they would take these on sale or return. Many thanks. P.' There was a postscript. 'I am unavoidably out of town for the next couple of weeks.'

The second sheet was an invoice and consignment note.

He carried the bag up to his room, dumped it on the table.

What a nerve, he thought.

But later, when he had finished packing and organised himself for a mid-morning departure, he realised it would provide an effective entrée to the shop. Plant the commercial traveller. Plant the book rep. A reason to speak to the owner, or manager, or whoever was there. Johnny. A way of asking about Ackerman. He wondered if Prem had worked all that out. Almost certainly he had. As well as seeing the opportunity to move a few more of his books.

21

Plant settled himself into the window seat and prayed that no one would arrive for the aisle seat. Then he could sit by himself alone with his own thoughts. Not bugged by anyone next to him. It was a futile thought, he knew. Why were so many of this thoughts futile thoughts? Think positive, he told himself. Think absence, think emptiness, think Eastern. Freedom from toil, freedom from care, freedom from the revolving wheel. Think nothing. It seemed to be working. The aisles were still. The hostesses paraded past shutting the overhead lockers. Everyone was seated. And then it happened.

He didn't look. If he didn't look it mightn't be anybody. The overhead locker was opened and shut. Some great bandbox, hatbox was stuffed in. An oversize carry bag was pushed in front of the seat beside him. So much for one piece of cabin baggage only. How do some people get away with it? A flurry of fabric and she had edged her way in. Plant practised detachment. He avoided looking at her. He wanted to be alone. He fastened his seatbelt and closed his eyes.

The hostess woke him with a meal he didn't want. She stood there holding it over him till he folded down his tray. Then she served the girl in the aisle seat. He shouldn't have looked. Easily said. But he did.

He heard himself saying hello. The surprise. But he knew her.

She smiled professionally. With the lips. Mouth closed. No words.

'How amazing,' he said. 'Only last night I was listening to you singing.'

'Only last night?' she said. 'And the nights before, I think.'

'I didn't mean only in that sense,' he said. 'I meant …'

'I understand,' she said impatiently.

'You do?'

'I speakee zee English,' she said, in theatrical pidgin.

He looked doubtful. It was exactly what he hadn't wanted. A fraught conversation. Even if it was exactly what he had wanted in some other idiotic part of himself. If it has to be anybody sitting beside me, let it be some beautiful woman, some exotic Mata Hari, he had found himself thinking before he had cancelled the thought, a Mata Hari being the last thing he wanted. But too late. The thought had gone out. The Mata Hari of the atrium. Close encounter with a cabaret artiste. And she had registered him there, night after night.

'I'm surprised you notice the clientele.'

'There's not a lot else to notice,' she said.

'I guess not. I guess you know the songs backwards.'

She gave him the closed lips smile.

'Yes,' she said. 'But sometimes I manage to sing them forwards.'

'You were good,' he said. 'Are good,' he added quickly.

'I'm not really.'

'Yes you are.'

'No I'm not. I can hold a tune. Just about. That's all they want.'

'You're putting yourself down.'

'You reckon?' She laughed. 'No, I'm not good. I may not be wicked but I know my limitations. I don't have any illusions about my singing. All you gotta do is wear a low-cut dress and a low-cut bra and bend over a bit. That gets them in. They love it. All the old men. They say East and West never meet. Bullshit. They meet around me. All they want to do is look at your tits. Two for the price of one. Businessmen. Tourists. Businesswomen. You could sing any old shit in any young voice.'

'I guess so,' said Plant.

'I guess you'd know,' she said. 'Happy hour.' She laughed again. Too pointedly, Plant felt.

'Anyway, you've got a break now,' he said.

'Like shit I have,' she said. 'I've got another gig, that's what I've got.'

'In Manila?'

'In Manila. What about you?'

'Yes, Manila,' he said. 'Not a gig. But that's where I'm going.'

'Which hotel?'

'I haven't booked anywhere yet.'

'Here, hold this,' she said. She passed her food tray across and pushed up the folding table and reached into the handbag on top of the carry-bag. She took out a business card. A hotel card.

'Mention my name and they'll give you the special rate.'

'Thanks,' he said.

'No problem,' she said. 'You get the special rate and I get the finder's fee.'

'The only thing is,' said Plant, 'I don't know your name.'

'Really? You're kidding.'

It was a mistake. To tell a performer her name was not known was bad strategy. Blown it in one. The laborious courtesies of not seeming to be making a pick-up, the scrupulous non-inquiry, and now he had offended the essence of the artistic spirit. It doesn't matter what you say as long as you spell my name right.

'I'm sorry,' he said.

'You amaze me,' she said. 'And you're supposed to be an inquiry agent.'

'How did you know that?'

'Everybody in the hotel knew that,' she said. 'It's the sort of thing you gotta know when you work some place.'

'I guess it is.'

'So you weren't inquiring about me?' she said sweetly.

'No.'

'I am shattered.'

She put her hand to her heart, her breast, somewhere round there.

'Should I have been?'

'When I heard you were an agent I thought maybe you were a theatrical agent, so I hoped you were, natch.'

He could have said, but I often thought about you.

'Don't tell me I'm losing my fatal charm,' she said.

'No,' he assured her, 'not at all.'

'Well, that's something,' she said.

'So what is your name?' he asked.

'In Bangkok I am Miss Anna. You know, Anna and the king.'

'Yes,' he said.

'In Manila, I am Miss Imelda. In Hong Kong I am something else.'

She gave him a winning, professional smile.

'Just three names?'

'They'll do for now,' she said. 'For the old men, you know. Names from the past.'

'So you're singing in Manila.'

'Sure, in the hotel, same as before. Why don't you come and listen to me? It's demoralizing singing to an empty space.'

'I might just do that,' he said.

'Why not?' she said. 'Live dangerously.'

The hostess collected their trays.

'Don't think I'm rude,' said Anna-Imelda. 'I gotta get some rest. I'm on tonight.'

'Tonight?' said Plant.

'Be there if you don't believe me,' she said.

'Oh, I believe you.'

'You can still be there,' she said.

He offered her the window seat so she could lean against the fuselage and sleep. She took it.

Plant the chivalrous.

22

Plant checked in at the hotel, gave Imelda's name, asked for the special rate.

'Artist's rate. You are an artist then, sir.'

'I've written the odd piece or two,' said Plant.

'Ah, less the singer than the songwriter.'

'More a journalist manqué,' said Plant.

'A journalist monkey. Very good, sir. Very good indeed.'

He laughed with appreciation as he keyed in the details.

A boy came over and took Plant's luggage. Plant followed him to the lift and up to his room, tipped him, locked the door, turned on the television and the air-conditioning and lay down on the bed. When he awoke it was dark outside. The television was quacking away. Valley girl talk. He switched it off. He thought of going down to hear Miss Imelda. Out of sheer politeness, if nothing else. But he felt chilled from the air-conditioning, his limbs aching. He took a block of chocolate from the mini-bar and ate it while he tried to wake up. The effort required to wake seemed too great. He undressed and climbed into bed.

The Asian Dawn Bookshop and Conference Center was a two-storey concrete building. It stood between a travel agency and Jemima's Bakehouse. A security guard with an automatic rifle sat on a chair outside a bank on the other side of the road.

Plant took his bag of books to the cash register and asked to see the manager.

'What is the nature of your business?' asked the girl at the counter.

Plant said he had some books the manager might care to stock.

'He does not see publishers' representatives in the morning,' she said. 'Except by appointment.'

'Tell him I have a sort of appointment,' said Plant. 'Professor Ackerman suggested I call in. I have come all the way from Australia.'

'Ah, boomerang,' she said, as if to suggest he might promptly go all the way back.

'That's right,' said Plant.

'Didgeridoo,' she added.

'Spot on.'

'Detention Centres,' she said. 'Refugee camps.'

'Yes, well,' said Plant.

He was unsure whether this was a series of code words or the result of a Foreign Affairs campaign. Get to Know Australia.

'Come upstairs,' she said. She took him through a door at the back and up a wooden staircase. A wood and glass partition ran across the length of the building. She pointed to a metal and vinyl stacking-chair.

'You wait, please.'

'Thank you.'

She tapped on a door marked seminar room and went in. Inside two men were talking loudly, almost shouting, one high-pitched, the other deep and throaty.

'And if I am CIA what are you, al-Qa'eda this week, is that it?' said the high pitched one, a rapid, excitable delivery.

'One thing you can say about me,' said the other, low and slow and considered, 'is I have never allied myself with the forces of reaction.'

'And your mayor? What is he but walking reaction? No, I withdraw that. Waddling reaction.'

'I have to earn a living.'

'And I don't?'

'You call crawling on your hands and knees for American subsidies earning a living?'

'I crawl? I crawl? At least I am not a collaborator.'

'And who do I collaborate with?'

'Everybody. Your grandfather collaborated with the Spanish. Your parents collaborated with the Japanese. And you collaborated with the Russians and Red China till they stopped throwing money away. Now no doubt you collaborate with the fundamentalists.'

'How could anyone collaborate with the Russians and the Chinese at the same time?'

'Did I say at the same time? A serial collaborator, that is what you are.'

The girl must finally have made her presence known for the voices stopped. Plant could not hear what she said. But he heard the high-pitched voice call out 'Send him in, send him in.'

She came out into the corridor and beckoned. Plant went in.

A short, bald chubby man sat in a cane chair, a cup of a coffee beside him on a long conference table. At the other end of the table a moustached, aquiline, long-haired, slightly younger man sat smoking a cheroot. They were the length of the table apart, which perhaps explained their raised voices. The walls of the conference room were lined with bamboo. There were no posters, no photographs, no indications of any kind, cultural, spiritual, ideological.

'Come in, come in, any friend of Professor Ackerman is welcome here, this is open house to Australians, isn't that so Alfredo?' said the chubby man with the high, excitable voice.

'Huh,' the moustached man grunted.

'Alfredo here cannot forget the White Australia Policy of his youthful years. He would have liked to have deserted us but they would not admit him.'

'At least I didn't get bought off with a writer's fellowship to the States,' said Alfredo.

'But you would have,' said the chubby man. 'You were all set to. I wrote you a reference.'

'Huh,' said Alfredo again. 'Then that volcano wiped out their air base and they didn't need to bribe us any more. No more writers' fellowships. Bye-bye, Iowa.'

'Bye-bye, Iowa?' said the chubby man interrogatively. 'I should have thought you would be celebrating bye-bye Subic Bay. Freedom from the imperialist oppressor.'

'So now we have ten thousand prostitutes with no clients and no work for anyone.'

'There are always Australian tourists,' said the chubby man. 'They will be the new clients. Isn't that true, Mr ...?'

He waited for the name.

'Plant,' said Plant.

'And I am Johnny,' said the chubby man. 'And this is Alfredo. Alfredo is our enduring revolutionary, as you no doubt heard. He sings his slogans from the rooftops, don't you, Fred.'

'Better than croaking down the line to Uncle Sam's listening posts.'

'Fetch Mr Plant a drink,' Johnny said to the girl who was still standing in the doorway. 'A coffee. Or do you want a beer? An Aussie beer, maybe.'

'A coffee,' said Plant.

'And Professor Ackerman has sent some of his inimitable books, I see,' said Johnny, reaching an arm towards Plant's package.

'Not exactly,' said Plant.

'Let me see.'

Plant pushed the carrier bag down the table. Alfredo took out a copy as he helped it on its way.

'It's by a friend of Professor Ackerman's,' said Plant.

'I have heard of him,' said Johnny, looking at the cover, turning to the back of the title page to look at the copyright and publishing and printing and cataloguing information, the way everyone in the book industry seemed to, the only page they ever showed much interest in.

'Professor Ackerman suggested you might be interested in selling them.'

'Of course.'

'The paperwork is there,' said Plant.

'I am always interested in selling anything.'

'Self especially,' said Alfredo.

'But more often I merely hold stock,' Johnny said. Sadly.

'Don't believe him,' said Alfredo. 'He says that to everyone. "Yes, I will stock your book but I do not expect to sell it. So don't expect to be paid." Then one day you come to collect the unsold copies and take them back and they've all gone.'

'Shoplifters,' said Johnny. 'People are so untrustworthy nowadays.'

'This is the place to come to learn untrustworthiness,' said Alfredo.

'Alfredo here was once an up-and-coming short story writer,' said Johnny. 'Never quite a novelist. Never quite got that far. His talents were too marketable. His mayor bought him and now he never looks back, do you Fred?'

'One more year,' said Alfredo. 'I give him one more year, then I quit.'

'And then you write your magnum opus, of course.'

'You will see.'

'I don't think so,' said Johnny. 'You have left it too late. The times have passed you by. Who would want to read the ramblings of a discredited Maoist now? The pathetic wheezings of the flower power generation as they die of emphysema. Let a hundred flowers wilt. Would you read them, Mr Plant?'

Plant shrugged.

'I don't know. I might.'

'You see,' said Johnny, 'not even a firm order of one. How could I even stock such a book? Assuming it will ever be written. Which as you know I sincerely doubt. How can I agree to publish something that doesn't exist and probably never will? Anyway, I am giving up publishing, I am selling out.'

'Wise move,' said Alfredo. 'It's what you've always been best at, selling out.'

The girl came in with Plant's coffee.

'I got to go,' said Alfredo. 'Some of us have to work.'

'Write more lying speeches for your embezzling mayor,' said Johnny.

'I should just sit on my ass all day on the payroll of the CIA?'

'You could afford to. They must pay you well enough to play your ultra-radical comedy out.'

'Nice to meet you, Mr Plant,' said Alfredo. He handed across a business card. 'Feel like a drink or anything, give me a call. We'll have dinner some time.'

'Thanks,' said Plant.

Alfredo left. In the silence that fell, Plant could hear the two ceiling fans revolving gently.

23

'Was that all serious?' Plant asked.

'Just a little game we play,' said Johnny, 'just a traditional Filipino pastime.'

'Ah,' said Plant.

'It's called politics.'

'I see.'

'I am not sure you do. The aim is to discredit your opponent. Besmirch the opposition. Tell enough lies so no one believes in anyone. In that regard it is serious enough.'

'I am familiar with that,' said Plant.

'It is not unique to our tragic country? Supplier of housemaids to the world.'

'No,' said Plant.

'I do not know whether to rejoice or despair,' said Johnny.

'Is there any truth in any of it?' Plant asked. Just to jog him out of his comfortable melancholia. Just to make a play for the upper hand.

'I will tell you a story,' said Johnny. 'Other people will be rushing to tell you, so it is better I tell you my version. The true version.' He looked up as if for approval.

Plant delivered it. 'Yes, of course.'

'Many years ago I established a magazine. *The Asian Dawn*. You may not have heard of it. But in this tragic country it was something new. Something positive. A ray of hope. A platform for democratic reform. I have always believed in democracy. I have always opposed totalitarianism. Of every shade. Of left or right. Of church or army. I published the best of our writers and thinkers in *The Asian Dawn*. I published the young Alfredo, promising stories, though he likes to forget that. And then?'

He waited expectantly.

'I don't know,' said Plant.

'You do,' said Johnny.

'You ran out of money.'

'You see, you knew. Of course. I ran out of money. What should I do?

Should I abandon our hopes for democratic reform? Should I surrender to the dark forces? Or should I seek out subsidy?'

'You sought out subsidy and surrendered to the dark forces,' said Plant.

Johnny chuckled.

'In those days there was an international organization whose avowed aims were our aims. It supported intellectuals throughout the world. Organised conferences. Sponsored magazines. They were very generous. They came to our aid. *The Asian Dawn* was saved from premature nightfall. They held seminars in this very room where you sit even now. They flew in intellectuals from all round the world.'

'Cultural Freedom.'

'Exactly. And then one day it was revealed that all along they had been secretly funded. You know by whom. I was devastated. I was a shattered man. I could not face myself in the mirror. I went unshaven. I dared not answer the phone. I refused to read the papers. I would be pilloried in the press. Besmirched. I stayed in my room, afraid to be seen in public. And then, Mr Plant, something amazing happened. There was a hammering at the door. I thought it was the mob come to tear me apart. Burning American flags and waving banners of poor Che Guevara. Brandishing little red schoolbooks. The thoughts of Chairman Mao. You know the sort of thing. The hammering persisted. I put my head beneath the pillow, like your Australian ostrich. It did no good. I could hear voices. My wife answered the door. It was my assistant. He was breathless with excitement. There was a queue all around the block waiting for the bookshop to open. Not a mob, Mr Plant, but a queue. An orderly queue, excitable, but orderly. Waiting for me, waiting for my help, my aid, my support. They had read the revelations. The so-called radical press had castigated me: a tool of the CIA, a running dog of Uncle Sam, a lackey of the State Department. And now all these people were queuing for my help. They wanted me to help them get American visas. They wanted me to help arrange subsidies for their theatre groups. They begged me to use my contacts to get them published in America. They implored me to bring out American writers to lecture in their universities. Well, Mr Plant, what do you think?'

'Amazing,' said Plant.

'Amazing indeed. I never looked back. It put my shop on the map. People came and bought American books. Poets came to organise poetry readings. The seminar room was always occupied. Always some activity.'

'And the magazine?'

'Ah, the magazine. Because of the revelations the funds had ceased. The magazine could not survive. We limped along for a few issues. But in the end we had to close down. I began publishing books. The bookshop thrived and the profits supported the publishing. The bookshop became a beacon of light. A beacon of light in a darkened world.'

He smiled, with satisfaction in his mission.

'The important thing, Mr Plant, is to remain true to one's principles.'

'Whatever they are,' Plant said, it could have been in agreement, or interrogation.

'I am a democrat, Mr Plant.'

'Whatever that means.'

'And you, Mr Plant, sound to me like a cynic.'

Plant neither confirmed nor denied.

'Cynicism is no answer, Mr Plant. Nor, necessarily, is simple-minded commitment. I was approached by the NPA. You know the NPA? The New People's Army. The successor to the Huks. They were fighting a guerrilla war against the dictatorship. There was a lot of support for them. They wanted to extend their appeal. Come in from the heat. Take the reins of government. They offered to make me a general. But I refused. I said, "You have support but you are losing sympathy. What is the point of raids on village police stations and army outposts? All you do is kill a few young men, young men just like your own young men, from the same villages, from the same poverty. These young policemen, these young soldiers, they are not your enemy, they are no one's enemy, except perhaps their own. What choice do they have? The landowners exploit the villagers. The politicians and the big businessmen live off the profits of exploitation. They own the land or the landowners bribe them to prevent reform. What can these young people do? The girls can go overseas as housemaids; the boys can become policemen or soldiers or guerrillas. What other choices are there? They all share the same poverty, the same hopelessness. You must work for a political solution." "That is why we are approaching you," they said. But I could not become a general in an army that killed poor young villagers. Young men without shoes. The world laughed at Imelda Marcos's shoes. They do not ask why she had so many shoes. To reassure herself she was no longer a poverty-stricken villager who had to walk barefoot. Shoes, Mr Plant. You remember Van Gogh's painting of the sabots. The symbol of the poor peasant. The sign of poverty. The image of oppression. Our poor do not even have sabots, Mr Plant. Our poor have only their calluses. And even calluses do not protect you from snake-bites.

'So. The reactionaries say I am a communist agent. The communists say I work for the CIA. What do you think, Mr Plant?'

Plant smiled back. As much as he could. He couldn't get his eyes to smile any more persuasively than Johnny's.

'Hey?' said Johnny.

'I think I'd prefer not to speculate.'

'A wise man, Mr Plant. Sit on the fence and no harm will come to you, perhaps. Nor anything else. Tell me, what brings you here?'

'I am trying to find Professor Ackerman.'

'You mean he is lost?'

'It appears so.'

'Missing?'

'Missing.'

'How tragic.'

'I hope not.'

'Of course, of course. But when someone goes missing in this violent country, we have to prepare ourselves for tragedy. Did he go missing here?'

'He was last heard of here.'

'That is not quite the same.'

'No.'

'So we can hold out hope.'

'I hope so.'

'And why are you looking for him? Did he owe you money?'

'His wife hired me.'

'To do what?'

'To find him.'

'And then what?'

'She hadn't heard from him. She was worried.'

'She has not hired you to kill him? Or to deliver divorce papers to him?'

'No.'

'These things happen. But perhaps not in Australia.'

'They happen in Australia.'

'There we are then. Nowhere is safe. No man is an island.'

'He sent this postcard,' said Plant. He handed it over.

'Ah, my shop. I see why you have come here. I thought at first that

Professor Ackerman had sent you.'

'Not exactly. But if you read the other side.'

Johnny read it.

'He suggested you might sell his friend's books.'

'So bringing them seemed as good an entrée as any.'

'That's right.'

'So how can I help?'

'I thought he might have seen you recently. Given the postcard.'

'He could have acquired these postcards at any time. We have been giving them away for years. People like things that are free. Even small things.'

'The date.'

Johnny looked back at the card.

'He could have written the date at any time. And the postmark is unclear.'

'I know.'

'Clutching at straws, Mr Plant.'

'It is all I have to clutch at.'

Johnny made a tut-tutting noise. He looked at his watch.

'So he wasn't here in the last couple of months?' Plant persisted.

'No.'

'And you haven't seen him?'

'No.'

'Is there anyone else he might have visited? Or who might know if he's around.'

Johnny scratched his bald head.

'You want me to give you a call if I hear anything?'

'I'd appreciate it,' said Plant. He gave him the name of the hotel.

'Rely on me, Mr Plant,' said Johnny, standing, the interview at an end.

Somehow Plant was not sure that he could.

24

Plant walked aimlessly down the boulevard away from the hotel. Hoping an idea would seize him. Wondering what he was doing in Manila. Amidst the roar and hooting of the trucks and the buses and the jeepneys and the cabs, a particularly insistent horn on the road beside him forced itself in on his attention. A huge American convertible was crawling at walking pace beside him. The girl in the front passenger seat looked at him dispassionately. The driver waved.

'Hey,' called the driver.

It was Alfredo.

Plant came out of his reverie, waved, returned the greeting.

'Where you going?'

'Nowhere.'

'Want some lunch?'

He had not long ago had breakfast, but why not?

The car stopped.

'Hop in, man.'

He hopped in beside the girl. She gave him a gracious smile and moved closer to Alfredo to give Plant room.

'My secretary,' said Alfredo.

'Pleased to meet you,' said Plant.

'One of the perks of office,' said Alfredo.

She slapped him affectionately. Playfully, anyway.

'I thought we might see you,' said Alfredo. 'You finished for the morning?'

'I haven't even begun,' said Plant.

'Great, man,' said Alfredo. 'That's how it should be. Life's a holiday. Come and have lunch. Come and celebrate.'

'Celebrate what?'

'Anything,' said Alfredo. 'Whatever you like. Just being alive. That's enough in itself.'

He pulled out into the traffic flow to a chorus of complaining horns. How fragile a state, Plant reflected, is just being alive.

'First some sightseeing. We go to the zoo. It's on the way.'

'The zoo?' said Plant.

'You like zoos?'

'Not really,' said Plant. 'I don't like to see caged animals.'

'Depends on the animals,' said Alfredo. 'Some deserve to be caged.'

'I don't know,' said Plant.

'I do,' said Alfredo. 'Wait till you see these savage beasts. Cages are too good for them. When the revolution comes we turn this zoo into a slaughterhouse.' He laughed. 'You'll like it, don't worry.'

They saw it. The Batasang Pambansa, the Legislative Assembly.

Alfredo roared with delight, slapping and stroking his secretary enthusiastically on the thigh.

'Alfredo,' she said. Sharply.

'OK, OK,' he said, 'save it till later, hey?'

She slapped him back.

'That's our zoo, man,' said Alfredo. 'I thought you would've known that, being a monkey journalist.'

'No, I didn't know that,' said Plant.

'Far out,' said Alfredo.

'How did you know I was a monkey journalist?' said Plant.

'Word gets around the jungle.'

'Actually, what I said was journalist manqué.'

'To me,' said Alfredo, 'all journalists are monkeys. You feed them peanuts and they jerk off for you. Cheap man, cheap.'

Plant nodded agreement.

'You don't seem like a real journalist to me.'

'No,' said Plant. 'Not any more.'

'That's good,' said Alfredo. 'So we can have a relaxing lunch. None of this off the record business.'

'Sure,' said Plant.

'So what are you?' asked Alfredo. 'Don't tell me you're just a tourist. Even tourists got to eat.'

'I do investigations,' said Plant.

'Just so we know,' said Alfredo.

'Word hadn't got around?' said Plant.

Alfredo gave his deep, satisfied laugh.

'Is that a yes or a no?' Plant asked.

Alfredo laughed some more.

He pulled into an empty parking lot in front of a low, windowless building. A neon sign ran across the roof. NON-STOP GIRLS. SEVEN DAYS. SEVEN LIVELY SINS. Another sign in the shape of a huge black bat with blood dripping from its mouth announced ETERNAL NIGHT CLUB. The motto beneath declared 'A sin a day keeps the light at bay.'

Alfredo tapped on the door. They were led to a table in the dimly lit interior. Matt black walls. A raised stage at one end of the room and a set-up for musicians. Black drapes behind it. A couple of men were drinking beers in a corner. One was in police uniform, a huge revolver at his belt. The other stood up and came across. He was in formal attire, pressed dark trousers and the traditional frilled white shirt with long, cuffed sleeves, the barong Tagalog, sheer gauzy nearly transparent cloth embroidered in the front, the lower part outside the trousers, because in colonial times the Spanish had decreed that the shirt should be tucked in so that men couldn't hide any bladed weapons. Gold bracelet, gold rings, gold chain round his neck, gold teeth when he smiled. Plant thought of Mrs Ackerman.

'My friend,' he said, embracing Alfredo.

'My new friend,' he said embracing the secretary.

Plant stood at the ready, but was offered merely a vigorous handshake. He waited while the two men had a dialogue in Tagalog.

'Maybe fish,' said Alfredo.

'Sure,' said Plant. It didn't seem a place to insist on the vegetarian. Probably fish was considered vegetarian enough. 'Are they open?'

'For me,' Alfredo smiled. 'I told them I have a distinguished foreign visitor.'

'That's very cooperative of him.'

'We were in gaol together,' said Alfredo.

'I see,' said Plant.

Alfredo laughed. 'I see, too,' he said. 'You are a gentleman.' He turned to the secretary. 'The definition of a gentleman is someone who never asks why you were in gaol. He waits politely till he is told. Or makes private inquiries afterwards. So, I will tell him.' He turned to Plant. 'Beer to begin with?'

'Sure,' said Plant.

Alfredo called out. A waiter appeared with a couple of bottles of San Miguel and a mineral water.

'She has to work this afternoon,' said Alfredo.

She gave him a disdainful flip with the back of her hand.

'We are gentlemen. We shall not ask the nature of her work,' said Alfredo.

She flipped him again.

'In the emergency,' said Alfredo, 'I was rounded up. We were all rounded up. Students, politicals, writers, everyone, all locked away.'

'Johnny too?'

'No, not Johnny.'

He took a long swig of beer.

'Best thing that ever happened,' he said, and gave his satisfied, throaty laugh. 'That's where I made my most valuable contacts. They didn't distinguish between politicals and others. It was all political, anyway. Everything's political. Nightclub owners, gangsters, hit men, anyone who hadn't come up with enough protection money. Put us all in together. That was a mistake. On their part. How long do you think you would survive in gaol, heh, Mr Plant?'

'I don't know,' said Plant. 'Not long, probably.'

'Six months,' said Alfredo. 'I was in six months. I made all these contacts. All the bar owners. Friends for life. You want a girl, you want drugs, you want a hit-man, you want it, I know where I can get it. No problem. It was an education. Friends for life.'

'Amazing,' said Plant.

The fish came. Alfredo dissected it expertly, taking out the spine and bones in one deft action.

'You know the Chinese superstition?' he asked. 'You must take the bones out like this. You must never turn the fish over, otherwise you capsize the boat. Everyone drowns. Interesting, heh? You like to hear sayings? All travellers like to hear local proverbs. It makes them feel they are acquiring information. The purpose of travel, to gather wisdom.'

'True,' Plant agreed.

'And what information have you acquired?'

'Not much.'

'But you are looking?'

'Is it so obvious?'

'You said you do investigations.'

'Ah, yes,' said Plant.

Alfredo patted Plant reassuringly on the arm. 'In my business everyone always wants some information. But perhaps you are just here for the filthy climate.'

'I'm looking for someone who disappeared,' said Plant. 'His wife hired me to find him. His name is Ackerman.'

'Alec,' said Alfredo, 'where's he disappeared to?'

'That's what I'm trying to find out.'

'So how can I help?'

Did I ask him to help? Plant asked himself.

'Did you know him?'

'Sure.'

'You knew him well?'

'Average. I wasn't in gaol with him.'

He gave his throaty laugh again.

'You see,' Alfredo said, 'we get a lot of Australians through here.

Some are tourists. Some are criminals. Some are missionaries. Some are paedophiles. Some are doing the Americans' dirty business. They come across as friendly people. Not a super power. Not the world's policemen, like Americans. Not colonialists, like Europeans. People who won't talk to Americans will talk to Australians. I guess some smart bastard figured out people would take a while to figure out they're under contract to Uncle Sam.'

'You're saying Ackerman was one of them?'

'One of which? He was a friendly guy. Always had time for a beer. Regular Aussie bloke. Not like the Americans. He'd go round to Johnny's, sit up in that seminar room, sit and talk for hours. As long as he had a beer in his hand. Or on the table.'

'You're saying he was on to Johnny?'

'Hard to imagine why,' Alfredo chuckled. 'But maybe. Certainly it suits Johnny to let people think he's under suspicion. Gives him some much needed credibility.'

He ordered a couple more beers. The secretary declined another mineral water.

'And of course you should also consider the possibility Johnny could have been on to him. Johnny the-nearly-a-general in the NPA, very impressive.' He gave a throaty laugh. 'You can never be sure with you Australians. So many of you were not born in Australia. You come from Britain, or Europe, even Asia, now. You are not all of you necessarily Uncle Sam's underpants. You maybe have other commitments. Maybe the Australian authorities themselves might like to know. They might like you to talk to people overseas. People you think are oppositional. Share subversive thoughts. Which are sent back to Canberra. Or Washington. Who knows?'

He took a swig of San Miguel.

'Or it could be he was just your classic liberal.' He grinned. 'Poor man. Or maybe they were up to something, together. Some secret cell of surveillance. Or subversion. Or both. It can get very confusing. Even for the people in the middle of it. Not sure where they really stand or who they are really working for, so much deception, so many lies. They get lost.'

'Did you see much of him?' Plant asked.

'Alec? Sure. Once in a while. We'd have a drink, watch a bit of music, look at the girls. He'd ask about city politics. Slum conditions. Usual stuff. I could steer him in the right direction. He was some sort of academic, right? The sort who write earnest articles about what needs to be done. Or say they're going to.'

He laughed, as deep and throaty a laugh as ever, but without much humour.

'We all know what needs to be done.'

'Was he here recently?'

'Could've been. Why don't you ask at the hotel?'

'Which hotel?'

'The one you're staying in, man.'

'Is that where he stayed?'

'Sure.'

Plant gave a grunt.

'Ask the manager,' said Alfredo. 'Tell him I told you. He's a good friend of mine. We were in gaol together.'

'Was he a political or a criminal?'

Alfredo slapped him on the back. Another throaty laugh.

'You're not as dumb as you act.'

He called out in Tagalog and the waiter came with the bill. Plant reached for his wallet.

'No, no,' said Alfredo. 'You're my guest.'

'Really,' Plant tried.

'No, I've just been with a friend of the mayor.'

Alfredo took a plain brown envelope from his briefcase. Sealed. A Manila envelope, of course, Plant registered. He registered its thickness too, and the way Alfredo ripped it open at the end, and the thick wad of banknotes inside and the way he peeled some off and stuffed them in the waiter's hand and the way the waiter smiled.

'Thank you,' said Plant.

'My pleasure,' said Alfredo.

He patted his secretary on the rump.

'Now we drive our friend back to his hotel and then more pleasure.' He laughed. A sinister, satisfied laugh. It was the same laugh he gave when he pressed another sealed brown envelope into Plant's hands as they pulled up outside the hotel. 'Open it in your room,' he said. 'Not here.'

25

Plant turned into the hotel and went up to his room. He could have asked to see the manager and the guest records and tried to establish when

Ackerman had last visited. But he didn't. It would keep. Immediately after lunch was not a good time to pursue inquiries. And he had a few things to think over in the privacy of his room. More than a few. And Alfredo's parting gift to open.

He took off his shoes and socks, splashed water on his face. Then he opened the package.

Plant sat in his hotel room smoking Alfredo's gift and thinking about things. It had even come with a couple of packets of rolling papers. A thoughtful gesture. Saved him from having to go down to reception and ask for a tobacconist. A thoughtfulness meriting considered thought.

So how had Alfredo known such a gift would be welcome? More than welcome, almost necessary. It was no secret in the circles in which Plant moved. Back home. Small circles, getting smaller by the year. But no secret. But he wasn't back home. He was in a country he had never visited before, with people he had never met before.

Except for one. He took a long slow drag and thought. So much to think about. Where to begin? He could begin with Anna-Imelda, the sad chanteuse, the one person in the Philippines he had ever encountered before. Yet would she know he smoked? She knew he was a private investigator. So much for the private. If she knew that from the hotel management, or the hotel staff, maybe she knew from one of the chambermaids that his room had reeked of the sweet smell of marijuana. Maybe hotel security had been nosing around. If that was how she knew. Unless she heard from the bar-girl he had bought from. Hardly from the taxi-driver in Kolkata. Or did she sing there? Under what name? Kali Minogue perhaps.

Or did Alfredo have his Australian sources? Had he already been checking up on him? He certainly knew a few things. The journalist monkey business, that had to have come from the receptionist on duty when he had checked in. Directly, or filtered though management. And the manager, of course, was Alfredo's chum from gaol. The man he was due to ask about Ackerman's last stay. The extraordinary convenience of it, staying in the hotel Ackerman always stayed in. Just like Bangkok. Except that he had made the decision himself, on his own information, in Bangkok. And here: here it was the sad-eyed singer of the islands who had suggested where he should stay. So fortuitously where Ackerman stayed. Or was said to stay. Still to be checked out.

Am I being played games with, or am I being steered? he asked himself. Am I being monitored, or am I being diverted, distracted? And more to the point, am I getting anywhere?

He reflected. Perhaps he should make a list. A list of what he had established. Or perhaps it was better just to list it all in his head, rather than committing it to paper, which might turn up in one of Alfredo's Manila envelopes.

He wasn't sure he had established anything. He wasn't sure whether Ackerman was dead or alive, whether he was attempting to disappear or simply visiting old friends, old haunts. He couldn't get a fix on the man. Was he a crook, smuggling heroin from the Golden Triangle? Or a low-rent academic, recycling the same lecture round the world in return for free advance-booking discount economy-class airfares? Was he the kindly, generous protector of his former students, or was he going round the world killing them? Was he a covert radical, being entrapped by assets of the world's policeman; or was he a professional agent working under cover to maintain a free world fit for free trade? Was he the classic freeloader with his free insurance and his tax-deductible travel, paddling around the fleshpots of the east? Or the disciplined ideologue, sponsoring self-help schemes for the betterment of the exploited of the third world, subverting post-industrial capitalism's late imperialist phase? Or was he the global entrepreneur, with his contacts in global publishing and money-laundering? Or was he simply running away from the Ackerwoman? Or was she the Lady Macbeth of the Gold Coast, the Mrs Thatcher of the sunshine state, sending her spouse out to kill and conquer? Or had she sent him out to be killed and conquered, to collect on the life insurance payout? She had said that there wasn't any life insurance, but she would say that, wouldn't she?

Plant sat there, reflecting on the wisdom of the great philosophers. The first thing we know is that we know nothing.

It was a pleasant enough afternoon. Extraordinarily pleasant. He put on the television a couple of times and turned it off after a scroll through the channels. It seemed pallid in comparison with his own reflections. He drank a couple of small mineral waters from the mini-bar. He savoured Alfredo's gift. He hoped it wasn't laced with some fearful mind-altering psychotropic substance. It seemed not to be, but who could tell? Reality seemed weird beyond chemical possibility.

In the end he dragged himself out of his room to go and see the manager. He could have phoned no doubt, but he didn't want the manager coming up to visit. Once again the windows didn't open. He put the air-conditioning on to its highest and floated out to the lifts.

The manager was unavailable, which was a relief. As he'd figured, subconsciously, it was happy hour time. The afternoon had passed in a delightful dream. He ordered a San Miguel. Miss Imelda wasn't due on for another hour. He waited, chewing peanuts like a monkey in a zoo.

He didn't see her enter. She came up behind him, spoke in his ear.

'You get your special rate?'

'Artists' rate,' he said.

'Is that what they call it?'

'So the man said.'

'So you're happily settled in? Got everything you need? Happy apart from happy hour?'

He nodded.

'Can I buy you a drink?' he offered.

'Not now,' she said. 'Not before I go on. Buy me one later. When I finish.'

'When is that?'

'Twelve, twelve-thirty.'

'I don't know if I'll still be awake.'

'Poor fellow. Have a nap now,' she said. 'Come back down later. I'll still be here.' She squeezed his arm. 'Be seeing you.'

She had walked away before he could say no.

He sat through a handful of numbers and then he dutifully followed her instructions. He gave a friendly wave and headed for the lifts. Found his room. Turned down the air-conditioning. Set the bedside alarm. Had a smoke or two. And a nap.

He sat nursing a beer till she finished her set. It seemed to go on and on. He would offer his hearty applause, hearty enough to mark the end of her evening's performance, and she would launch off into something else. Perhaps Alfredo's gift had extended time, slowed things down. Perhaps she was taking a feminine pleasure in stringing him along. Perhaps it was a good audience and she sensed they wanted more. It didn't look like a good audience to Plant. Not even a substantial one. Just a few lost souls sitting around the foyer, waiting to be picked up, by arrangement or serendipity, waiting for the late flights or early flights out, catching up on the newspapers, killing time. But she sang for them. With all the perverse generosity of the unseen, the unheard, the unacknowledged.

'I'll get you a drink, what'll it be?' he said when she finally came over and the electric keyboardist was packing up his electric keyboard.

'Not here,' she said.

That hadn't been his expectation. He had dragged himself down from the security and comfort of his smoke-filled room to the plangent emptiness of the soaring atrium, and now she wanted to drag him off somewhere further. Still, he was, if not on holiday, here for the varieties of Asian experience. Treat it as a holiday. It wasn't getting far as an investigation. He might never get a job again. He might never be able to afford holidays any more.

The doorman hailed a cab for them.

'What's he writing down in that little book?' Plant asked.

'The cab numbers. Then if you don't come back and your body is found floating in a canal and your Rolex and your wallet have been stolen, they know to ask the cab driver if he did it. There used to be lots of phoney cabs that kidnapped tourists.'

'Are there still?' Plant asked.

'Why should it have changed?'

She told him which colour cabs to get and which not. He didn't find it reassuring. He wasn't sure when it came to it he would remember which was which.

'You better not go out alone then,' she said. 'Or with strange women.'

'You're not strange are you?' Plant asked.

She smiled at him. More enigmatically than reassuringly.

'Why would you think I was strange?'

'I was just asking,' said Plant, 'not thinking anything.'

'Would I tell you if I was?'

'You might.'

'And you'd still get into a cab with me?'

'I might.'

'You like adventure, is that it, Mr Plant?'

'I don't know about that,' he said.

'Then we shall have to find out, shan't we?' she said.

26

He entered the Eternal Night Club with at least an initial feeling of familiarity. I have been here before. It was busier than at lunchtime, but not greatly. A line of more or less naked young ladies danced around on stage to the music of a trio of musicians. A few Australians and American sat at a few tables. Tourists. Ex-servicemen revisiting the site of their youth. Expatriates. Gangsters. Who knew? Certainly not Plant.

'We meet again, so soon,' said the manager. 'You like it here. Very good. Excellent.'

They ordered drinks and talked about this and that for a while.

There was some sort of light show going on, unless they were picking out the dancers with coloured spots. But it was more swirling than spots, swirling like the coloured oils they used in ancient light shows in prehistoric times before the end of history to simulate the effects of acid or psilocybin, that was what it was like, sixties, seventies retro, slowly shifting and dissolving streaks of colour, swirling, viscous, serpentine, some dislodged herpetic presence rising up through the throat and eyes, not necessarily menacing, though with its edge of menace hanging there with the voices and the music, the voices discordant with the music which was discordant enough in itself, discrepant rather than discordant perhaps, wafting in and out of audibility, not at all clear what they wanted, questions about identity, philosophical issues he had always preferred to pass by, sidestep them so they slid past and round in their greens and golds and reds, metaphysical questions about why are you here and who sent you here, as if the will of the creator could be known and the purposes of creation could be revealed and the name of the demiurge disclosed, questions about purpose and intention and understanding, who are you working for, who do you report to, who do you know here, what do you know? Knowing yourself is what it's all about, he tried to explain, the message of the oracle guarded by the serpents, the serpents again, writhing through him till they caught up with their own tails, tales out of school, he told them, that would be telling. That was when they slapped him, though not a hard slap, more a slap and a tickle and he responded to the tickle quite positively, smart guy, no, he assured them, my achievements are very modest, I had academic ambitions but I surrendered them. As for Professor Ackerman, I know less about him than anyone, less probably than everyone here, which produced another slap and tickle, and another glass of liquid, much of which he managed to drink but a fair amount he managed to spill, it had the heaviness of oil, the drops on his chin and throat beaded like gelatin, unpleasant stuff. The girl asking him could have been the singer though the singing was still going on, her little sister maybe, there were two of them unless he was seeing double, which he might have been, or maybe a whole line up of them, singing to him, ministering to him, releasing his constricting clothes, fondling his body, asking him questions, as scantily clad as the singing showgirls. He tried to answer, he wanted to be cooperative, they were nice girls, perhaps not nice girls in the sense of nice, but they seemed pretty nice, especially in their state of undress, their mutual state of undress, how could he not try to be as nice as possible in such circumstances, they sang to him and he sang back, short sad songs because he didn't know the tunes or the lyrics very well, he tried to get the rhymes but that didn't seem to satisfy them, if anything it seemed to annoy them and they were back at his academic attainments, wise guy, though uttered in a rather contemptuous and dismissive way, I'm just a guy who can't say no, he told them, not attempting the tune, the sentiments not the song, a sentimental journey, that's what it was, he explained, he wanted to hear the temple bells and explore the mysteries of the east, and my, is it mysterious, he was amazed at the mysteriousness of it, bemused, astonished, astounded, stoned beyond the bounds and leaps of time and fortune. I don't like needles, he told them, never have, always preferred a smoke, one last smoke, permit me that, he begged, and they gave it him and he smoked it and then bang.

Plant woke up with that terror that accompanies total amnesia. That absolute inability to recognise where he was. He was in a bed. In a room. He felt appalling. He felt nauseous and the terror of the unknown multiplied the unease of his stomach. He tried to think back and slowly pieces returned. Manila. That was it. The hotel. But it wasn't. It wasn't his hotel room. It was a room he had never been in before in his life. But he was in it now. Naked. In bed. A double bed. He raised himself up and looked around. It was furnished like a hotel room but it wasn't his hotel room. He looked at the pillow beside him. It held the impression of a head, as if someone had slept there. Someone other than himself, someone beside himself. He groaned. He swore. He blasphemed. He looked up at the ceiling and saw himself reflected in the mirror. He groaned some more. No doubt one-way glass, a video camera recording everything. Nothing of which he could remember. Maybe there was nothing to remember. Maybe he had slept on both pillows. He felt a momentary relief in his stomach. He got out of bed. Cautiously. His head felt awful. His clothes were in a heap on the floor. No sign of anyone else's clothes. No discarded underwear. No abandoned shoe. No trail of silk or chiffon leading to the door or window. He went into the bathroom. His face in the mirror didn't look good, but it might have been a bad mirror. He turned to the bath. A couple of towels had been tossed into it. Used. He looked back at the mirror. His face looked worse. Pallid with shock, dark bags beneath the eyes from liver stress. Round the edges of the mirror traces of condensation clung to the glass. If he had had a bath or shower he would have remembered, surely. He told himself he might have showered in the night and forgotten it. But he didn't believe himself.

He went back into the bedroom. He re-examined the pillows. Both indented. He sat down on one side. His side. Should he strip the bed, look for stains? Or should he get dressed and get out as quickly as possible? Or have a shower and try and recall where he was, how he got there?

He sat there and tried to recall. The hotel. A few joints. Miss Imelda. He could remember the songs. You're just a no account. You let me down. It's a sin to tell a lie. Then the taxi ride. The Eternal Night Club. Oblivion.

'You have arisen, splendid,' said the manager of the Eternal Night Club. 'A happy miracle. What a relief.'

'Was I that bad?'

'Not bad. I would never say bad,' said the manager, 'not when you have seen the bad as I have seen the bad. But still, it is good to have you with us, nonetheless.'

'Was I about to die?'

'You feel like you are about to die? I have the perfect answer,' said the manager. He called out in Tagalog. 'Any moment now and you will come back to life. Fully resurrected. All systems go.'

'You said it was good to have me with you as if I was about to croak.'

'As a guest, of course. It is good to have you with us as a guest. Complimentary, naturally.'

'What was I doing here?'

'You are having a pick-me-up. Any moment now.'

'Last night.'

'Ah, last night. I would not say you were bad, but not really good enough to be returned to your hotel. In those circumstances it was more discreet to accommodate you here. You know how things are.'

'I have no idea how things are. I've no idea how anything was.'

'An admirable state, a fortunate characteristic, like your dear President Reagan and his dear friend Mrs Thatcher in their latter years, unable to remember anything troublesome, or anything at all at the end.'

'I am not an American. Nor British.'

'Nor am I,' said the manager. 'But we are all allies, of course. We all have our American friends. Let us never forget that.'

The waiter arrived with an evil looking concoction. Plant eyed it balefully.

'Quite safe, quite safe. Nothing to fear. Tomato juice, Worcestershire sauce, a few hairs of the dog. And vitamin C. Very important. Cuts the drug effect.'

'What drug effect?'

The manager laughed.

'Always a joke. I like it. What a comedian you are.'

Plant eyed him as steadily as he could.

'Quite innocuous. This time.'

'And last time?'

'Ah, last time.' The manager laughed. 'And the time before. And the time before that. What a time you had.'

'Was I …?'

'Not at all,' the manager said rapidly.

'What do you mean?'

'Well, up to a point.'

'Up to a point what?'

'Up to a point below par, perhaps. Under the weather you might say.'

'Who was with me?'

'Who was with you?'

'In my room.'

'Oh, your room. Ah, discretion, of course. No one will speak. We see nothing. You are assured of our discretion. You are perfectly safe.'

'I don't feel safe.'

'Perhaps another pick-me-up?'

'I haven't drunk this one yet. I need to know.'

'No need,' said the manager. 'Everything taken care of.'

'Including me.'

The manager laughed. 'Oh yes, you were taken care of.'

'What was her name?'

'I never ask names,' said the manager. 'I am sure if she was there she will tell you herself.'

'So there was someone there.'

'If you say so. We, of course, saw nothing. Heard nothing. We shall say nothing. Monkeys, you know, wise monkeys. Not journalists.'

The manager left him with his pick-me-up. Plant drank it and felt no better. He sat alone at a table for a while in the black-walled room. When he went looking for the manager, the manager had gone.

'Where is he?' Plant asked.

The waiter shrugged. 'Gone.'

The Eternal Night stretched around him desolate. No non-stop dancing girls. No strobing lights. Except the flashes within his head. No one singing sad songs. Or happy ones.

'You go,' the waiter said.

It could have been a question or an order.

'Sure,' said Plant.

He opened the door into the blinding light of the remorseless sun. Traffic roared down the boulevard. Trucks. Taxis. Police cars. Jeepneys. Great American convertibles. Mercedes with darkened glass. Military personnel carriers. Ambulances. Taxis. Taxis. Taxis.

He hailed them.

In the end one stopped. It could have been any colour or every colour. He no longer cared. But it got him back to his hotel. And when he took out his wallet to pay there was still money in it. He hadn't been robbed and dumped in a canal.

But he felt shocking. Awful. Appalling. Terrible. He seemed to be able to stumble through a thesaurus of synonyms. His mental capacity was not totally erased. But he still felt bad. The thing to be said for drugs was that they didn't have to torture you to get the answers to their questions any longer. They didn't need to waterboard you or put electrodes to your testicles or brandish bolt-cutters at your toes or red-hot wires at your nostrils. That was all strictly for the sadists and not necessary at all. But drugs still left you feeling pretty shaken. Who knew what they used? Shellfish toxin and ugly-looking mushrooms and synthesised cactus extract and artificial ergot. And who knew the effects of combining them? They must do terrible things to your system. Especially to a system you had already done terrible things to, by previous exotic combinations, just recreationally. The thing to do was to look at it as recreation and not get upset. Lie back and enjoy it. What I did on my Asian holiday. But positive thinking didn't prevent the spasms in the stomach and the recurrent flashes of fear discharging through his consciousness. Wherever consciousness was hiding out, displaced and dug down deep. Bastards. Why couldn't they just have asked? Politely. Formally. He would have told them. Suitably threatened. No need to put the threats into practice. Whatever it was they wanted to know. He had no secrets. He knew practically nothing, why did they have to probe around like that? What did they think he knew? What were they looking for? And for that matter, did they find it? Was there something he knew that he didn't know he knew? Something whose significance eluded him but which they had been pursuing. Could be. Could be indeed. And how would he ever know?

The phone rang and Plant answered it before he could think not to. His reflexes were still operating, all too readily. Out of the control of the conscious mind.

It was the hotel manager.

'You asked to see me.'

Plant conceded that he had, way back before the dark ages.

'I'll come down now,' said Plant.

He went down.

'How are you this morning?' the manager asked.

'Shocking,' said Plant.

'You had a good evening? Nightclubbing? Very good.' He laughed and rubbed his hands. 'You like to go sightseeing this morning? The American war cemetery? Walk round the old town?'

Plant shook his head. Not a wise move. He could hear the detached retinas rattling against the sides of his skull as the electro-chemical light bounced between them.

'Work,' he said.

'Ah, work, not tourist,' said the manager in tones of great sadness and understanding.

'I need to ask you a few questions, if that's all right. Confidential. About one of your guests who seems to have gone missing. I was wondering if you could tell me if he stayed here recently.'

'Is this a police matter?'

'Not a police matter, not at all,' Plant assured him. 'He hasn't done anything wrong.'

'Except disappear.'

'Yes. Well, that may not be wrong. It may be totally explicable. But …'

Plant left it there.

The manager left it there, too.

'Alfredo suggested you might be able to help.'

'Ah Alfredo, of course,' said the manager. 'I remember now. Professor Ackerman.'

He opened a drawer and took out a Manila envelope. A large one, but slim, flat. Not bulky like the ones Alfredo seemed to specialise in. He handed it across to Plant and stood up. Meeting over.

'Anything else you need?'

'Thank you,' said Plant, 'I don't think so.'

He went back to his room and opened the envelope. According to the records, or the records as printed out, Ackerman had stayed from the thirteenth to the eighteenth. Plant checked his watch for the date. As he thought. He was still functioning. The eighteenth. Ackerman had checked out four hours earlier.

27

'Johnny of the Asian Dawn speaking, Mr Plant. You remember me, I remember you. You keeping in good health, I hope so, that's good. Mr Plant, I have in my shop now even as I speak on the telephone someone you might like to meet.'

'Ackerman,' said Plant.

'No, not Professor Ackerman as it happens, so sorry, no, I have Mr Starr of Lavi, no less, Legal and Visual International, the publishers of your Professor Ackerman's series of books. So close yet not close enough. Perhaps Mr Starr will be a guiding star.'

'Is that likely?' said Plant.

'We three kings of Orient are,' said Johnny. 'Who could say if we put our heads together?'

'You're saying I should come over.'

'Only if it interests you, Mr Plant, only if it interests you.'

'And you think it will?'

'Who can speak for other people?' said Johnny. 'But if I could, I would say yes, possibly.'

'I'll be over,' said Plant.

Starr was a tall, nervous, uncomfortable man in a light grey business suit, highly polished black shoes, and a lavender shirt without a tie. He spoke with an American accent, though it might have been one learned in Europe. He was in his fifties, give or take ten years. Johnny directed them to the Asian Dawn seminar room and then discreetly withdrew. Plant assumed it was probably wired for sound.

'You were asking about me,' said Starr.

'No,' said Plant.

'Making inquiries.'

'Not at all,' said Plant.

'That's not what I heard. I heard you were in our Kolkata office, asking questions.'

'I was asking questions about the whereabouts of Professor Ackerman.'

'Is he gone missing?'

'Yes.'

'Well, fancy that,' said Starr in a flat, unmelodious voice.

'Do you know where he is?'

'Do I know? Why should I?'

'No special reason.'

'I didn't even know he'd gone missing.'

'Why would you?'

'Exactly,' said Starr.

'And you have no idea where he might be?'

'Can't say I do.'

Plant grunted.

'See, this is what I mean about you going around asking questions. You sure ask a lot.'

'It's my job,' said Plant.

'And what is your job?'

'Research and investigation.'

'So you go around researching and investigating.'

'That's right.'

'Why were you researching and investigating me?'

'I told you. I wasn't.'

'Not what I heard.'

'I am employed to look for Professor Ackerman. Since you acquired the publishing programme he established, it seemed reasonable to inquire if he had been in contact recently. As a way of attempting to trace him. I have not been inquiring about you or your company.'

'Not you and Professor Ghosh?'

'No.'

'If I didn't know Professor Ghosh, I might not believe you. And since I don't know you, I'm still not sure I believe you.' He opened his briefcase and passed a newspaper cutting across to Plant. Plant looked at the grainy photograph of Ghosh and the accompanying text. It was in an indecipherable script. Indecipherable to Plant, anyway. Bengali, presumably.

'Sorry, can't read it.'

Starr took out a couple of typed sheets of A4. He handed them across to Plant, too.

'What's it from?'

'Some disreputable radical gutter press that fortunately no one reads.'

'But you got a copy.'

'I get copies of everything.'

'You must have an excellent cuttings service,' said Plant. He looked at the A4 sheets. 'Translators, too.'

Starr ignored him.

It was an interview Ghosh had given. He had gone to town. He had held forth about globalised media and how it was the destruction of independent national publishing in India. And worldwide. Many of the global companies were simply fronts for money-laundering and the drug trade. An Australian investigator recently in Bangkok and Kolkata had assured him that the trade was organised at the highest levels of the air force, military, intelligence agencies and government, and used multinational businesses as fronts for its activities.

'I didn't assure him of that,' said Plant. 'He told me all that.'

Starr laughed. It was not a laugh of expansive humour or relaxed bonhomie. Plant had not expected it to be.

'You saying he pulled the old stunt? Attribute something you're not game to put your name to to someone else.'

'Yes,' said Plant.

'Why should I believe you?' Starr asked.

'These are threats to editorial diversity and independence,' Ghosh thundered. 'Global group Lavi recently unilaterally appointed a new editor to the formerly prestigious Asian studies list it had acquired, dismissing the previous board of editors without warning. One has to ask about the growth and expansion of groups like this, the private investigator told me.'

'What does one have to ask, Mr Plant?' Starr asked.

'Come again,' said Plant.

'I assume you have finished reading and have encountered your urgent utterance.'

'Not mine,' said Plant.

'So you have nothing to ask.'

'I didn't,' said Plant. 'But you've succeeded in arousing my curiosity.'

'Arousal can get you into all sorts of trouble,' said Starr. 'So, I believe, can curiosity.'

'I am not looking for trouble,' Plant said.

'That's wise. Leave it to the professionals.'

'I am simply looking for Professor Ackerman.'

'That could be trouble.'

'It's beginning to look that way. You know him?'

'I can't say I know him,' said Starr. 'No, I wouldn't say I know him. Our paths have crossed.'

'How's that?'

'In Asia all paths seem to cross.'

'Is that so?'

'You doubt me?'

'Not at all.'

'You sound sceptical.'

'It goes with the job.'

'How unfortunate,' said Starr. 'It must put people off.'

'Better than putting people on.'

Starr made a noise. Plant took it as a laugh, though it didn't sound much like a laugh.

'So you didn't know Ackerman but you took over his series.'

'Business deal,' said Starr. 'You don't have to get personal to do a business deal.'

'Why did you take it over?'

'He just wanted out. He didn't care who took the books as long as he didn't have to bother with them any more.'

'And he didn't object to Dr Bowles becoming series editor?'

'He suggested him. He didn't want to do it himself.'

'You invited him to stay on?'

'It was never an issue. He wanted out.'

'And you wanted the books?'

'Within reason. It's a respectable series. Respectable people respect it. Within reason. I wouldn't have gone begging for it.'

'You go begging for anything?'

'Not a lot. There's enough product around. It gets harder to keep these hobbies alive. People come to us to bail them out. We can afford to be selective. We don't want to take on stuff nobody wants. We don't want to carry a burden of debt. But if you know your business you can make it work. Niche publishing. Make sure there's a niche there. If there is, stick with it.'

'And you have niches throughout Asia?'

'You see, you are asking about me.'

Plant said nothing. It was true, he did seem to be asking questions. Not the ones he would have liked to have asked. He couldn't work out how to ask those without giving offence. And Starr exuded the sense that he was a man best not offended.

'Niches throughout the world, not just Asia,' Starr said. A touch of the pride of megalomania there, perhaps, Plant inferred.

'It must keep you busy.'

'As long as it doesn't keep *you* busy, you've no need to worry about that,' said Starr.

Plant gave a wise nod.

'So if you have no questions about Lavi …'

'I never did,' said Plant.

'So you say. And you are not proposing to trouble us with further inquiries or further unfortunate statements to the press.'

He picked up the cutting of Ghosh's interview and the translation and returned them to his briefcase.

'I'm only concerned with finding Ackerman,' said Plant.

'In which case I will take up no more of your time,' said Starr. He got up to leave.

'Where did you see Ackerman?' Plant inquired.

'Always another question.'

'Yes.'

He waited.

'In Bangkok.'

'And that was when?'

'Not so long ago,' said Starr, going through the door. He didn't wave good-bye.

28

Johnny came into the conference room bearing coffee and biscuits.

'Mr Starr has gone,' he said. 'I thought you might like some refreshment.'

'To regain my strength and equanimity?' said Plant.

Johnny chuckled.

'A friend of yours?' Plant asked.

'More of a business acquaintance,' said Johnny.

'What sort of business?'

'He is a publisher.'

'You sell lots of his books?'

'Not really,' said Johnny. 'They are far too expensive for my customers.'

'Even Ackerman's series?'

'You don't buy books like that in bookshops. Not even my bookshop. Too specialised.'

'Never?'

'Sometimes a library might order one through me. But usually they buy direct. Or through library suppliers.'

'So what business do you do with Starr? Is he offering to buy you out?'

Johnny laughed.

'Alas, not a chance. My little publishing operation publishes fiction, which is not for him. And my bookshop is even less to his taste. '

'You suggested it?'

'I suggest it to anyone I think could afford it. But it is not his sort of thing.'

'I thought he was into books.'

'As a publisher, not as a retailer. A select number. Not that many. A few titles at high prices. But my stock, masses of books at low prices, it overwhelms him. I see him recoil from the shelves as he enters the shop. He rushes up here away from the books.'

'To do business?'

'Oh, Mr Plant, you are so persistent. When I say business acquaintance, I use business in the loosest possible sense. I mean no more than Mr Starr and I inhabit the same world. Different regions of it, perhaps. But the same world of communications. Publishing, selling, writing, editing. So inevitably we meet. Trade fairs. Receptions.'

'Diplomatic receptions?'

'I cannot recall. But if, for instance, some visiting writer or artist or scholar on a world tour came to Manila, it would be quite normal for me to be invited to a reception at some embassy. Of course. And similarly, as an international publisher with companies in so many countries, it is conceivable that Mr Starr might similarly be invited. And it is possible that in such a way we might sometimes meet. These things happen all the time.'

'But you don't remember if you did.'

'Of course we did. We have met many times. But over the years I forget the details of where and when. I have been in the book business for nearly fifty years. One way and another. I have travelled around the region, attended conferences, festivals, symposia. I meet people at all these gatherings. That is why I go to them.'

'Why?'

'Why? Why, to discuss issues of literature and culture. To meet old friends. To do business.'

'But Starr is more a business acquaintance than a friend.'

'Yes.'

'Except that you don't do business with him.'

'Oh, Mr Plant, you make my head reel. I merely try to help. I knew you had an interest in Lavi.'

'How did you know?'

'You told me yourself.'

'I don't think so.'

'How else could I have known?'

'That's what I'm asking.'

'Perhaps your interest in Professor Ackerman suggested it. Implied it. I know he was certainly interested.'

'Interested enough to hand over his publishing to them.'

'Oh, more than that, I think. Before he did that. He was always interested in global corporations operating through Asia. It was one of his research areas.'

'So he knew about Lavi before they took over his books?'

'I would imagine so. He might have believed he would know more if he went into partnership with them.'

'Is that what he was up to?'

'Merely a speculation,' said Johnny. 'But if I had been in his shoes …'

Plant looked at Johnny's white shoes. He could not imagine an academic in them. Not even a retired Queensland academic. But then, never having seen Ackerman, he had no idea what sort of shoes he wore.

'You do not get information by asking questions,' said Johnny. 'You need to get in there, get close to your quarry, get inside.'

'I see,' said Plant.

Johnny nodded appreciatively.

'You're suggesting there's no point my asking any more questions.'

'Not a lot.'

'But how can I get close to my quarry?'

'What exactly is your quarry?'

'Professor Ackerman, what else?'

'Who knows what else?' said Johnny. 'There are so many fronts and feints and subterfuges in this part of the world.'

'Just Ackerman,' said Plant. 'But since I don't know where he is, it's kind of hard to get close to him.'

'Perhaps you need a rest,' said Johnny. 'Relaxation. Take your mind off the case. Let your imagination roam free. Have a brief holiday. Then things often become clearer with an amazing rapidity.'

'You reckon?'

'Listen, Mr Plant, I was thinking, you might like to visit my place in Baguio City. I have a little cahute up in the mountains.'

'A cahute?'

'A little hut.'

'Is that Tagalog?'

'No, French-American. As in cahoots.'

'And who would I be in cahoots with up there?'

Johnny laughed.

'Whoever you choose. It would be a change of climate. You could do some writing up there, maybe. Many people have borrowed it. I like to encourage people to write about my country.'

'Do some writing?' said Plant.

'Journalism, maybe; it is still writing.'

'I'm not exactly a journalist. Any more,' said Plant.

'I know, I know, a journalist monkey. You ever try monkey stew? Lots of monkeys up there.'

'I'm a vegetarian.'

'Like the monkeys,' Johnny said. 'Think about it. Maybe you'd like to spend a few days and write your memoirs.'

'Memoirs?' said Plant, startled. Was this a threat? Your days are numbered: write a confession now. Or a dismissive assessment of the emptiness of his life: they will only take a few days to write.

'Like Professor Ackerman. It is one of Alec's favourite places. He likes to go there and write his memoirs. Or think about writing them.'

'Go where?'

'I told you, Baguio City. It is the summer capital.'

'Is he there now?'

'He might be. Who can say? He comes and goes. It has two bedrooms, anyway. So there would be room.'

'You only just thought of this,' said Plant. It sounded ungracious.

'I should have offered it you before, I know,' said Johnny.

He gestured with his hands, open wide, whatever that meant.

'No, no, you're very generous. I meant, you only just thought that Ackerman might be up there.'

'I have no idea if he's up there now,' said Johnny. 'But it might help you, who knows? Pick up a scent, perhaps.'

'A scent?' Plant asked. 'What sort of scent?'

Johnny chuckled, a contented chuckle, almost a fat man's chuckle.

'You are very sharp, Mr Plant, sharp as a razor. Maybe just the scent of aftershave, but maybe some sweeter fragrance, who knows?'

'Did you say Ackerman was writing his memoirs?'

'So he said.'

'What sort of memoirs?'

'Memoirs. The sort of thing we old men often talk about doing.'

'About Asia?'

'Oh yes.'

'They could be quite interesting.'

'Indeed. If he writes them.'

'Political?'

'Isn't everything political, Mr Plant? One way or another.'

'So there might be some interest in the memoirs.'

'Depending on what he puts in, of course.'

'Interest before publication?'

'It is not impossible, I'm sure,' said Johnny. 'He has met some interesting people. Lived in some interesting times. He picked up the gossip when he travelled. He was a great gossip.'

'What I'm getting at,' said Plant, 'is whether there's a connection between his writing his memoirs and his disappearance.'

'If he has disappeared,' said Johnny.

'And if he is writing his memoirs,' said Plant.

They both chuckled. Neither very convincingly.

'I will leave that to you to establish,' said Johnny.

29

Plant took the bus together with assorted locals and their market produce, piglets, fighting cocks, children and backpackers. He had never been so terrified. The bus hurtled round hairpin bends, above precipitous drops, unfenced roads winding round impassable mountains. He resolved to fly back. The lush greenery, the louring clouds dropping down onto the mountains, the wisps of cloud rising up to join them from the valleys, the roadside stalls, he accepted that it was all amazing. But the roads were terrifying, the traffic suicidal, homicidal. No doubt the driver knew his job, no doubt he was familiar with every bend and climb, with every crumbling road edge and every rickety bridge. But Plant was not. He had taken up Johnny's offer because it seemed like a good idea to get out of Manila. Check out of his hotel. See some of the countryside. Experience nature. He did not feel happy enough to venture down to happy hour again. He did not know whether it was fear or anger or embarrassment that the sad singer would produce. He was happy not to know. He was not ready for another evening of drugs and amnesia at the Eternal Night Club. He was not sure that Starr was not threatening him. It was all becoming a nightmare. And the bus ride continued it. Where were the temple bells of yesteryear?

At Baguio City he took a taxi. Johnny had said the house was only a ten minute walk. Which no doubt meant twenty if not thirty. Assuming you didn't get lost. He had had enough excitement on the bus.

Johnny had given him a key and instructions on how to turn on the power. Neither was needed. The lights were on in the house and the door open. He stood at the entrance and called out 'Knock, knock.'

The sad singer came to the door.

'You come for happy hour, huh?'

He could have said fancy seeing you or what are you doing here? But it required no vast time of reflection to realise that he was neither surprised nor in doubt. It was all rather obvious. He had picked up the scent and it was a familiar one.

'Who is it?' a voice called from inside. A male voice.

Plant let her explain.

‘That private investigator who’s been asking after you.’

He rather liked that. Respectable. Polite. Certainly better than the monkey journalist. Or the Ozzie dick. Or the gumshoe from Gondwanaland.

‘What’s he want?’ the voice called out.

‘I want you, Professor Ackerman,’ said Plant.

‘Really?’

‘Yes, really.’

‘Well, you’ve come to the right place.’

Ackerman came down the hallway with a knife in one hand and a bottle in the other. Plant braced himself. The girl stepped aside. Ackerman came out to the doorway.

‘Good timing,’ he said. ‘Just cooking dinner. Have you eaten?’

Plant said no, he hadn’t eaten.

‘You must stay for a bite, then,’ said Ackerman.

He looked at Plant’s travel bag.

‘It looks like you were planning to stay anyway.’

‘Johnny said I could have the place for a few days,’ said Plant.

‘Did he now?’

‘Yes.’

‘Jolly nice of him,’ said Ackerman.

‘I thought so.’

‘Generous fellow.’

‘Yes.’

‘Well, come on in,’ said Ackerman.

He walked back down the hallway. Plant followed. The passage opened out into a kitchen that doubled as a living-room. Sink, stove, fridge, table, small table, cane chairs, newspapers, magazines.

‘Would you like a drink?’

Plant looked at the San Miguel in Ackerman’s hand.

‘A beer would be good.’

‘Darling,’ Ackerman called out.

‘I heard,’ she said.

She took a couple of bottles from the fridge and placed them on the small cane table beside the chairs.

‘Happy hour,’ she said. ‘Buy one, get one free.’

Then she went to the CD player and put on a disc. The songs she sang. Unhappy ones.

‘So what can I do for you?’ Professor Ackerman asked, chopping up onions and sniffing back the tears.

Plant took out the photograph Mrs Ackerman had given him and compared it with the man in front of him.

'I suppose it is you,' he said.

Ackerman took a look at it.

'Hard to say,' he said.

He was a tall, slightly stooped figure, suntanned, with brushed-back, crinkled, grey hair. It was short and neat, not shaggy. He had bare feet, off-white cotton trousers and a light fawn bush-shirt complete with epaulettes. The whole ensemble was of the casual but distinguished look, with a suggestion of the colonial office or military mufti. It went with the stoop, the sort of stoop that came from looking down benevolently but firmly on shorter peoples and students. He seemed fit and alert. No signs that he'd gone troppo.

Plant sipped at his beer. And wondered. Now he'd found him, what next? He couldn't recall being given any instructions regarding that. Just find him. No mention of what to do then. No orders to order him back, coerce him, kidnap him. It was as if she hadn't expected Plant to find him. Or hoped he wouldn't. Not alive.

'I don't know,' said Plant.

'I thought you said you wanted me.'

'I did, didn't I?' said Plant.

'You did.'

'That's right.'

'But not for anything you can bring to mind.'

'I was just sent to find you.'

'Who sent you?'

'Your wife.'

'My wife,' said Ackerman. His eyes wandered across to the girl.

'Mrs Ackerman,' said Plant.

'Yes, I know her name.'

'She said she hadn't heard from you.'

'No.'

'But now I've found you I guess that's it.'

'No message?'

'You could call her, maybe.'

'Is that what she instructed?'

'No. She didn't give any instructions beyond just find you.'

'And now you have.'

'Seems so.'

'Good,' said Ackerman, giving up on his onion chopping and sitting down in one of the chairs. 'Well, now that's over and done with we can relax and have a drink.'

'I guess we can,' said Plant. 'I guess I'm already doing that.'

'Wise man,' said Professor Ackerman.

The girl sang along with Billie Holiday, stir-frying over a hot stove while the men sat back with their beers.

'I didn't know you two knew each other,' Plant said to Anna-Imelda, not keeping the annoyance out of his voice.

'You never asked.'

'I never thought of it.'

'There you are, then.'

'But you knew I was looking for Professor Ackerman.'

'Did I?'

'And you never said where he was.'

'It wasn't my business to say,' she said. 'It was up to Alec.'

'Absolutely,' said Alec. 'You did very well.'

'Very well?' said Plant.

'In saying nothing. You can never be sure who's asking questions and why. As we say in Ireland, Whatever you say, say nothing.'

'You're not Irish, are you?' Plant asked.

'No,' said Ackerman.

'But you just said you were.'

'No.'

'Didn't you say, "As we say in Ireland"?'

'Indeed I did,' said Ackerman. 'When in Rome, do as Rome does. Doesn't make me Italian.'

'Just an avid reader of Brewer's *Dictionary of Phrase and Fable.*'

'It pays to increase your word power,' said Professor Ackerman.

'So you knew I was looking for you.'

'True.'

'But you didn't respond.'

'I didn't know you. I had no idea why you were asking around.'

'Your wife hired me to find out where you were, if you were still alive.'

'So you said.'

'You might have guessed she would be concerned.'

'I might have. But there again, I might not.'

'Are there a lot of other people interested in you?'
'Who can tell? Until they come asking.'
'Have they come asking?'
'Not as unambiguously as you.'
'Is that a yes or a no?'
'An ambiguity. Things are never that clear-cut.'

30

After a dinner of stir-fried noodles and vegetables Anna-Imelda produced a bag of dope and rolled a few joints. It got Ackerman going in full flow. Maybe he didn't need much to get him going, Plant reflected. Firm, mellow, patrician tones, the sort of voice that was used to holding forth, and rather enjoyed the experience. All those years of being the lecturer and everyone just sitting there having to listen to him, rank upon serried rank. The habit of a lifetime. And the dope. Maybe two habits of a lifetime.

'I took that bus once,' Ackerman said. 'The first time I came up here. I'd been in Manila and called in on Johnny's bookshop. I didn't know it at the time but in those days everybody called in at Johnny's shop.'

'They still seem to,' said Plant.

'Maybe,' said Ackerman. He had the academic's skill of absorbing and overriding interruptions. 'But when I say everybody I mean everybody. I was in my hotel when Johnny called me up. "You want to meet Nino," he said, "come over now, he's in the shop."'

Ackerman took a long drag on the joint he'd been Bogarting. Another bad habit of a lifetime.

'That was how I met Nino.'

'Nino?' said Plant.

'Benigno Aquino,' said Ackerman. 'The senator.'

'The one they shot?'

'The one they shot.'

'What was he like?' said Plant.

Why not? Why not ask, why not show polite interest? He had found Ackerman, the job was done, why not relax into idle gossip, encourage an old man's maunderings?

Ackerman required little encouragement.

'One of the most amazing characters I ever met,' he said. 'Brilliant mind. Sharp. Incisive. He had all the figures off pat. Production, population, profits.'

'The man who knew too much,' said Anna-Imelda.

'And open. Forthright.'

'So they killed him,' said Anna-Imelda. 'Take warning, Plant. Never be open and forthright.' She passed him a newly rolled joint. 'Not that I think you ever would be.'

'He invited me to visit him on his estate. His wife's estate really. She had the money. The land. "You must call in," he said, "on your way to Baguio City." So we did.'

'We?' said Plant.

'I was travelling with a colleague.'

'What sort of colleague.'

Ackerman laughed.

'Yes, well, I have wondered since. At the time he just seemed like a fellow academic. He had all the contacts. We met some newspaper owner. "You can't go by bus up there," he told us, "you'll be killed by bandits. I'll fly you up." So he got his pilot to fly us up. One of those four-seater light planes. A Cessna or a Piper or something. "See those nicks in the wing," the pilot said. "Bullets. Fly too low and the Huks shoot at you."

'You know about the Huks, I suppose,' said Ackerman, holding forth in academic mode, whether Plant knew or not he was going to tell him. 'They were communist guerrillas. The Hukbalahap. The communists won a dozen seats in the 1950 elections but Macarthur had them declared illegal. So they took to the hills. Now they call them terrorists or insurgents. Back then they were called guerrillas. Carried on the war from where they'd left off fighting the Japanese.'

'Did you get shot at?' Plant asked.

'We didn't fly low. Then we landed at Nino's private airstrip. He came out to meet us. He was hopping mad. The commander-in-chief of the American airbase at Clark Field had flown in earlier in the week in a jet helicopter and the jet engines had scorched the grass on his golf course. He was real mad about that grass, I remember. Then we had lunch. Just the two of us and Nino and his wife and his bodyguard. I don't recall his wife said anything. Or the bodyguard. Seemed like the usual set up: submissive wife, dominant husband. But she was the one who became president. I remember the maids kept sticking their heads round the door and giggling at us. "Beatles," they said. We had long hair like they weren't used to in the Philippines in those days. I don't know whether they thought we really were the Beatles. And Nino talked. He was an amazing talker. That was the beginning of my political education. How things are done. He'd been in Marcos's party and left it. That was normal. People left parties if they didn't get the deal they wanted. Then Marcos came up there electioneering. "You know what we did?" Nino told us. "We put on a special reception for him. A celebration. He didn't expect it, but we did it. Free rum and pineapple juice for everyone. All the voters. All the villagers. They loved it. They'd never seen ice before. So they drink rum and pineapple juice by the gallon. Glug, glug, glug. Slurp, slurp, slurp. By the time Marcos arrives they're all drunk. All asleep or vomiting in the ditches. No one there to hear him. Empty hall. He was furious." Another time they infiltrated the Marcos party and fixed it so the dumbest candidate got pre-selection. Or the least popular one. Anyway, the one no one was going to vote for. He was amazing, Nino. We just flew in from nowhere and he told us all this stuff.'

'Amazing,' said Miss Anna-Imelda. 'And look where it got him.'

'I asked him about the Huks. Were they around? "Sure," said Nino, "out in the sticks." "Do you ever see any of them?" I asked. "See them?" he said. "Of course I see them. I lecture to them." "Lecture to them?" I said, "what on?" "On dialectical materialism, what else?" he said. "I try to keep them ideologically correct. Otherwise they will just become bandits in the pay of some rich landlord."'

Ackerman sat back, shaking his head reflectively.

'I'll never forget it. Here was this man playing golf with the American commander-in-chief one day and lecturing on dialectical materialism to the Huks on another.'

'Amazing,' said Plant.

'How to get yourself assassinated,' said Anna-Imelda.

'Who assassinated him?' Plant asked.

'He'd been in exile in the USA after Marcos declared the emergency. He flew back to contest the presidential election. A security man shot him as he got off the plane at the airport. Then they shot the security man.'

'Convenient,' said Plant. 'So who was behind it?'

'I've a theory on that,' said Ackerman.

'A prescription for suicide,' said Anna-Imelda. 'You go around telling everyone your theories, you'll end up like Nino. You talk as much as him, you'll go the same way. Save it for the book.'

'The book?' Plant asked.

'My memoirs,' said Ackerman. Proudly, it seemed to Plant. As if he thought he was a national icon handing down the word to his public.

'Is that what you're writing about here?'

'Working on them,' said Ackerman.

'And you tell this Nino story?'

'Amongst others.'

'Couldn't that be kind of dangerous?'

'Not till they're published.'

'I'd have thought it would be more dangerous before they were published,' said Plant. 'Say if someone didn't want your theories to appear in print.'

'Could be,' said Ackerman. 'But they might find it informative. Could be they would prefer to wait until I finish to see what I have to say. So there is every incentive to ensure that it will be a long book. Take a long time to finish. Not completing it could be my insurance. The recipe for a long and happy life.'

He laughed, contentedly. It seemed to give him satisfaction that he might be a target, that his memoirs might be explosive. Academic delusions of grandeur? Plant wondered. Identification with the subjects he studied? An old man's imaginings that it had all been important? Pipe dreams of the sixties? Or was there something in it?

'Do you have a publisher?' Plant asked.

'Oh no,' said Ackerman. 'I don't want to tie myself down. Not till I've finished. I don't need that sort of pressure.'

'What sort of pressure?'

'Having to deliver by some set date. I had enough of that having to teach. Preparing classes every week. Those days have gone.'

'They certainly seem to,' said Plant.

'Unregretted, unlamented,' said Ackerman.

Outside were the sounds of the equatorial night. Frogs or cicadas or geckos or whatever they were, croaking and trilling, choruses rising and falling like the breathing of the universe. Smoke hung idly beneath the roof. The San Miguel glistened. Anna-Imelda sang softly in the shadows.

'And you have to be careful,' Ackerman went on. 'You could sign a contract and hand the book over and find it never came out. You get the wrong publisher with the wrong connections and they might buy it just to suppress it.'

'Does that happen?'

'It could.'

'Is it likely?'

'Could be. With something sensitive.'

'And are your memoirs sensitive?"

'Alec is a very sensitive man,' said Anna-Imelda.

'I've known some interesting people in my time,' said Ackerman. 'People I taught became important in their fields.'

'Foreign students?'

'Foreign students. And Australian.'

'You kept in touch with them?'

'They kept in touch with me,' said Ackerman.

'Kept you up to date on the gossip.'

'A bit more than gossip.'

'Kill and tell,' Plant suggested.

'What makes you say that?'

'Were you involved in operations?'

'Operations? What sort of operations?'

'Covert action. Foreign affairs. Security.'

'Me? No.'

'Though if you were you would have signed an agreement not to say anything.'

'I imagine so.'

'Neither confirm nor deny.'

'Presumably. Why do you ask?'

'I thought it might be why you disappeared.'

'Disappeared?' said Ackerman. 'I haven't disappeared. You're talking to me now.'

'Your wife thought you had disappeared.'

'Ah, my wife.'

'So you're not on the run. Not a maverick agent being pursued by the intelligence services of the world.'

'Do I look like one?'

Plant gave no answer.

'I am here. I haven't disappeared. I'm not running away. I am simply a retired academic writing his memoirs.'

'Without a publisher.'

'I do have my own series.'

'I thought you'd handed that over.'

'The running of it, yes.'

'But you still have an interest.'

'Shall we say the press still has an interest in what I write.'

'Lavi.'

'Yes.'

'So you'll publish with them.'

'Not necessarily. But it does mean that if no one else bites they're always there. I may not have a contract but I am not bereft.'

'You'd be happy with them?'

'Happy? Yes and no. Solves one problem. But they're not much of a trade publisher. Never hit the bestseller list.'

'Do you want to? Is it the sort of book that could?'

'It would be nice,' said Ackerman.

'I guess it would,' said Plant.

He looked at Ackerman, sitting back there. How many professorial memoirs ever made the bestseller list? Was this just the craziness of senility, or the calculation of experience? Was the guy mad or cunning? Had he flipped, or had he finally found contentment? He seemed pretty contented. And Anna-Imelda sure sang a soothing, siren's song.

'And you're happy with Lavi.'

'Of course.'

'Unlike Professor Ghosh.'

'Oh, Ghosh. He isn't happy with anything. He kept saying we could have got a better deal. But he never did anything about it. If it had been left to him we wouldn't have had a deal at all.'

'So you don't object to Lavi as such?'

'Why should I? Successful global enterprise.'

'You're researching them?'

'I'm retired. I'm not researching anything any more.'

'You didn't mind Dr Bowles becoming general editor of the series you established.'

'No, not at all. Someone had to do it. It's no big deal. Just shuffling the odd manuscript around. A drag, to be honest. There's no point in doing it unless you get some academic pay-off. Some sort of editorial credit that helps get you promoted. I'd promoted myself out of the place, why should I want to keep on with it?'

'Power.'

Ackerman shrugged. 'Not really. You're more likely to get resentment for what you don't publish than power from what you do.'

'You know Bowles is dead.'

'Yes, terrible business. Imelda told me. Silly bugger, playing around like that.'

'Playing around?'

'Bar girls. Risky business.'

'You don't call this playing around?' said Plant.

'This?'

Plant gestured towards Anna-Imelda.

'We're not playing around.'

'Serious stuff,' said Plant.

'Absolutely.'

'And Mrs Ackerman?'

'I haven't been with my wife for years.'

'How many years?'

'Hundreds,' said Anna-Imelda.

'And how long have you two known each other?'

'Longer than that,' said Anna-Imelda. 'A thousand lifetimes.'

'In this lifetime,' Plant specified.

'I cannot remember the time before I knew Alec. To me it is not worth remembering,' she said.

Plant turned to Ackerman.

'Couldn't agree more,' Ackerman agreed.

All very jolly, Plant reflected. He tried to get the narrative back on track.

'You were saying you got the bus to Baguio City one time.'

'Oh yes,' said Ackerman. 'I forgot. After lunch Nino got his bodyguard to drive us down to the highway. No more private aircraft. That's when we picked up the bus to here.'

'You didn't get attacked by bandits?'

'No,' said Ackerman.

'Nor kidnapped by Huks?'

'I lived to tell the tale,' he said.

'How much longer?' said Anna-Imelda.

'You'll alarm our young friend saying things like that,' said Ackerman. 'He won't be able to sleep.'

'That so, Plant?' she asked.

'I don't know,' said Plant.

'Here,' she said, handing across a jumbo joint, 'this'll put you to sleep.'

Plant took a couple of drags and handed it back.

'Keep it,' she smiled. 'Specially for you.'

31

Plant awoke in deep pain across the eyes. And behind them. And above them. His mouth was dry. His gums were numb. His tongue was furry and swollen. His throat was sore. His tonsils felt infected. Beyond that he did not care to explore. His stomach was indescribable. He hated vomiting. But he was probably going to have to.

He was not tied to a chair. He was not handcuffed to the bed. There was nothing preventing him from moving except fear of the pain and nausea that movement would almost certainly induce. It was a beautiful morning out there. Noon even. The sun beat down. Far too brightly, far too strongly. In the distance a dog barked. Otherwise it was quiet. Peaceful.

Anna-Imelda and Ackerman had gone, of course. He did not have to get out of bed to confirm that. But he got out of bed all the same. There was no farewell note. No sign of them at all. No scattered clothes. No manuscripts in progress. No suitcases or travel bags. The washing-up had all been done and put away, which was considerate of them. The bed had been made. They hadn't stripped off the sheets and put them in the laundry to wash, so it was possible they planned to return and sleep there again. But unlikely, Plant felt. He didn't expect to see them back there. He wondered if he would ever see them again. He wondered what he was going to report to Mrs Ackerman. Of course, having seen them and lost them might mean he was still employed, till he found Ackerman again. Unless Ackerman had called his wife. If he had then it was all over and Plant would be flying back to his bush retreat. He felt he would rather like that. For the moment he had no idea what he was going to do. Go into town and buy some aspirin, maybe. If he could make it that far in the blazing sun.

Of course, they might have felt that by being in residence when Johnny had loaned him the house, they were intruding on his space. They might politely have moved into a hotel in town. Somehow he doubted it. He was not going to go round the hotels to find out. Not even at happy hour. For a while he was not going to do anything at all. Except go back to bed and lie down and groan. He wasn't sure that groaning made him feel any better. But it suited his mood. He lay there groaning for a long time.

He fell into a half-sleep but it did not help him recover. He thought of drinking some water but he was unsure whether it was safe, so boiled a kettle to make tea but there wasn't any tea that he could find. He waited for the water to cool down, which it didn't. Not appreciably. He went back and lay on the bed and began to make a list in his notebook. He tried making it in his head but it proved impossible to remember what he had just thought, so he had to use a notebook, even though it hurt his eyes. A list of possible explanations. Like number one, Ackerman disappeared because he had run off with a singer. Like two, that was too obviously the plot of *The Blue Angel* so it had to be a subterfuge. Though three, it could be an archetype and so eternally valid, or at least valid for a couple of centuries. So four, he disappeared in order to write his memoirs which were politically sensitive and people might want to stop him from writing them. But five, he seemed to be happily telling Johnny that he was writing them, which was like making a public announcement of the fact and, six, he was happily recounting episodes that might be sensitive to Plant whom he had never met before and whom he knew was a private investigator, even if a not very efficient one on current showing. So that didn't add up. So perhaps, possibility seven, he had met the Huks years ago through Nino and was carrying on Nino's good work of keeping them ideologically correct as they mutated into the New People's Army and then into Muslim fundamentalists. Or eight, under the guise of lecturing to them on Marxist ideology, he was reporting back on them to someone, as Graham Greene allegedly did to MI6 about the leftist political leaders he met. Though that story might have been MI6's way of discrediting Greene, if he happened to have been an authentic leftist. Which he might have been, though it was difficult to tell. Anyway, Greene wasn't the issue right now. Or nine, Ackerman might have been investigating Starr and Legal and Visual, or might have been in the past before he retired. Or ten, he might have turned up something on Lavi and been running away from Starr, who seemed a person worth running away from. Or he might, number eleven, having been buying a dope crop, as Bowles implied; for Starr maybe. Or he might have been hanging out to murder Bowles and now be in hiding. Not that he looked like a hit-man, but if Bowles's allegations were true it might have provoked Ackerman to silence him. That was number twelve, and number thirteen, he might have wanted to silence Bowles because the allegations were untrue. Fair enough. What would it have taken to murder Bowles? He was not an especially appealing person. Not to Plant. Anyway, he could have hired someone to do it for him. Make that fourteen. And fifteen, he could have been investigating Bowles. Or, sixteen, Prem. Or, seventeen, Johnny. Assuming he was working for someone under his academic cover. Though eighteen, he had retired and he might not have wanted to work at all, which was certainly the impression he gave. Maybe, nineteen, he was just on holiday and wanted to be left alone. Or just wanted to run off with a cabaret singer and spend the rest of his life, or at least a few weeks, with Miss Anna-Imelda. Which rather than being possibility twenty came round to the first speculation again.

Dear Mrs Ackerman, I found your hubby. Here is a list of nineteen or twenty reasons why he might have been in hiding. Indeed why he is still in hiding. Since having found him I then lost him. What shall I do now? Yrs, &c.

No, it wouldn't do. That was the one thing about which there was no doubt, no doubt at all. It wouldn't do. None of it would do. The truth might be there but he didn't know which of the possibilities it might be. Or it might not be there, it might be something else. Anyway, he had no proof for any of it. And furthermore, he had no Professor Ackerman, either.

It was at that point that a man walked through the doorway of the room with a gun in his hand.

'Hands up and off the bed.'

It was not an easy manoeuvre. It is surprising how many things hands are a help for. And it is surprising how holding your hands up in the air affects the rest of your movements. Plant concentrated on doing it without falling over. He didn't want to make things worse than they already were. The way they were seemed bad enough.

'Hands behind the back, face the wall, spread your legs,' said the gunman.

Plant did it.

He tried to think what the gunman was like, as he faced the wall. He didn't have a clue. Motorcycle helmet, jacket, he hadn't noticed if it was denim or leather or synthetic. Jeans. Boots. He hadn't noticed. Could have been boots. Could have been trainers.

His hands were handcuffed behind his back.

Handcuffs. That put a different complexion on it. Or did it? Law enforcement rather than banditry. Was there a difference? Was there any difference between bandits and ideologically correct bandits, or between bandits and law enforcement? Maverick law enforcement and ideologically correct law enforcement, did it make any difference? It could just as well be criminal elements as national security. To imagine they were distinguishable or separate might just be naivety.

It was something to think about, anyway, while a pillowcase was put over his head.

'Outside.'

He was held by the arm and walked out of the house, beneath the blazing sun that he could not see.

'Inside.'

He was pushed into the back of a vehicle. There was a roof, because he banged his head on it. A van. There were no seats. There were crates that could be holding fighting cocks or ravenous piglets or hungry hunting dogs. The van took off and he rolled around the floor. He rolled around the floor whenever the van swerved or took sharp turns or braked. He should never have thought that about the bus trip to Baguio City. It was not the worst experience of his life. It never does to formulate extremes. 'Tis not the worst when we can say this is the worst. Something worse soon follows. Like this van trip. He concentrated on wedging himself into the corner at the back of the cab. With his hands still handcuffed behind his back, it was hard to stay in any position.

The drive seemed interminable. He had no idea where they were going. It was dark. A closed van. And he still had the pillowslip over his head. It was hot. It was painful, being bounced on the metal floor. At some point he fell asleep with the heat, the stuffiness, the monotonous rumble of engine and road noise reverberating round the metal sides and roof. It did nothing for his headache. He had no idea how long he slept, how long they drove. He had no idea whether they were headed further out into the country or back to Manila, whether they were destined for a city or hacienda, or some jungle hideaway or police outpost or rebel stronghold or military camp.

32

In the end they stopped. Then they walked him out of the van, into a building, onto a chair.

'Your name.'

Plant gave it.

'Your name, please.'

He told them again.

'Professor Ackerman, do not play games with us.'

'I'm not playing games with you. Who are you, anyway?'

'Who we are is not the question. The question is who you are.'

'I've told you who I am.'

'I do not think so, Professor Ackerman.'

'I am not Professor Ackerman.'

'Why do you deny it?'

'Because I'm not him.'

'We know who you are. There is no point in lying to us.'

'If you know who I am, what's the point in asking? Especially if you refuse the answer. Anyway, I'm not who you think I am.'

'What are you doing here?'

'I am a private investigator looking for Professor Ackerman.'

'Oh yes.'

'His wife hired me to find him. He had not been heard from for three months.'

'Who are you working for?'

'I told you, Professor Ackerman's wife.'

'What is the true nature of your business?'

'I told you, I am a private investigator.'

'No, Professor Ackerman, just tell us the truth.'

They would not accept that he was not Ackerman. They were determined that he was Ackerman. They seemed to be searching for Ackerman as eagerly and assiduously as had Plant. They must have been staking Ackerman out. And closed in just as Plant arrived on his own search. Was that a coincidence? He could not tell. Generally he disbelieved in coincidence. But he couldn't tell. He was numb from the drive and the futile interrogation and from being knocked around when they got exasperated with him as he kept on denying that he was Ackerman. They slapped him around the head, punched him in the stomach and kidneys, marched him down a corridor and threw him in a cell. He assumed it was a cell. He couldn't tell. His arms were still handcuffed behind his back and the pillowslip remained on his head.

He sat on the floor for a while and tried to think. The floor seemed to be concrete, the walls some rough brick or breezeblock. He sat there a long time. At some point a couple of men came in and released his handcuffs. He took off the pillowslip. The men wore balaclava style head gear. One had a gun, the other a bowl with some noodles in a soupy liquid, and a spoon.

Plant ate.

After he had eaten he said 'I want to make a statement. Get me a pen and paper and I will make a statement.'

The guards put his handcuffs and pillowslip back on and left without saying anything.

After a long time they came back and unlocked the handcuffs and gave him a pen and a notepad. They stood there while he wrote, guns out. He did not find the circumstances an aid to spontaneous composition.

'My name is Keith Plant,' he wrote. 'I am a private inquiry agent employed to search for Professor Alec Ackerman at the request of his wife, Mrs Alice Ackerman.

'Professor Ackerman has been missing for three months. I was directed to Baguio City in my inquiries where I encountered Professor Ackerman, together with his travelling companion, a singer known variously as Ms Anna, Ms Imelda and so on.

'I had dinner with them and they drugged me. When I awoke the next day there was no sign of them. I had no time to go in pursuit when I was seized at gunpoint and brought here.

'You can confirm my identity from my passport, driver's licence, credit cards and other ID in your possession.

'I am willing to discuss ways of collaboration in our search for Professor Ackerman.

'Yrs, &c.'

Being willing to discuss ways of collaboration didn't commit him to running the man down and killing him. If that was what they intended. Probably they didn't. Otherwise Plant would be dead already. Shot first. Identification later. This hadn't been a search and destroy mission.

The statement seemed very flat and banal. But he could think of no other way to express it. He just wanted to get out. Get them to accept that he was who he said he was. And let him go. He wasn't sure how far he wanted to collaborate in the search for Ackerman. He rather felt he might phone Mrs Ackerman, report that her beloved was still alive, and sign off. If he could. He didn't think it would be as easy as that, any of it, but he would try. He would certainly try.

He handed the note over and they put the handcuffs and the pillowslip back on and slammed the door.

After that they left him alone. It was better than being knocked around. Shouted at. Roughed up. Punched. He preferred it when they left him alone. That said, it still wasn't much fun. The small bare room. Rough-cast walls. No view. No bed. No pillows. He sat propped against the wall, hands cuffed behind him, and contemplated the long day and the long night. They were both very long. And no one to share them with. No nightclub owners. No political writers. No bar girls. No drug dealers. No drugs.

How long do you think you would survive in gaol, heh, Mr Plant?

Footsteps came along the corridor. One set, maybe two sets. The door was opened and his pillowslip pulled off. Three men in balaclavas and army-issue fatigues stood in front of Plant.

'Horse's ass,' said one of them, and turned on his heel and walked out. The pillowslip was replaced and the door slammed shut.

An American accent. Ass pronounced the American way. Some British pronounced it that way, too. Regional British. But it didn't sound British. It was a North American expression. It sounded like Starr. But that might have been Plant's paranoid imaginings.

The footsteps went away. Nothing else was said. Just the one phrase. Someone's response to seeing Plant there. An enraged response. The voice sounded considerably enraged. The silence as the footsteps went back along the corridor suggested heavy menace.

It sounded like Starr. But were two words enough to go on? Didn't one American sound much like another? It was Starr's build. Tall. But it was only a momentary impression. The country was probably swarming with tall Americans.

If it was Starr then he would have known Plant was not Ackerman. But in that case why had he not just said 'Sorry, all a mistake,' and let him out? So it didn't work like that. But all the same, now they realised he was not Ackerman it should mean that he would be released. Unless they bumped him off in annoyance. Every minute in which nothing happened added to his alarm. The fear that they were going to hold on to him anyway, that they were not going to let him go.

In the end they came for him, for all Plant knew it could have been for execution. Against the wall, firing squad. Or along the corridor, bullet in the back of the head.

They led him out of the room, the cell, the barracks, whatever it was.

He never saw. He was walked along corridors, through doorways, down steps, along paths, and then he was pushed up into the back-seat of a vehicle. In a seat this time. A rise in status, a mark of courtesy. Perhaps. They still left the pillowslip and the handcuffs on. Wouldn't it look odd to passers by, to motorists looking in? Presumably they had tinted glass so no one could look in. But no doubt since he could look out through tinted glass, he was kept effectively blindfolded. Maybe that suggested there was something in the surroundings that he might recognise. And given his limited acquaintance with the Philippines, that meant a limited number of places. But perhaps it didn't mean that. Perhaps it meant they didn't want him recognizing the place in the future. Which suggested it was the sort of place he might encounter. Or maybe they just didn't want him recognizing the driver. All in all it told him nothing. But it passed some of the time of the drive trying to think the possibilities through. It was a long drive. No one spoke to him. The driver and his co-driver or back-up or bodyguard or whatever he was spoke to each other in Tagalog occasionally. At least Plant supposed it was Tagalog. It could have been Arabic or Russian or Bengali for all he knew. He had no idea if they were driving him into Manila or back to Baguio City, he had no idea where he had spent the last few days. This was the way to see Asia, the authentic experience. The rough roads, hairpin bends, hooting coaches: blindfold, maximum physical experience, nausea, vomiting, bruising, blackouts, minimal visual stimulation, zero comprehension. He dozed. As through so much of his life.

The vehicle stopped and they got him out, hardly helped, but not quite manhandled. They led him up a pathway and onto a porch. One of them rang the doorbell. The other removed the handcuffs.

'Move before we've gone and we shoot you,' one of them said.

Then they left. Plant heard them drive away. The door opened.

33

Alfredo stood there, a cheroot in one hand, the other reaching out to take the pillowslip.

'Hey, good to see you, man,' he said. 'Come in. Johnny said he'd told you you could stay up here. But then you kind of disappeared. But now you've reappeared and' – he looked at Plant appraisingly – 'seem to be in good shape, so it looks like there is no problem.'

Alfredo put the pillowslip over the back of a kitchen chair. Return politely accepted, no issue of theft. No problem.

'Did you know those two guys?'

'Which two guys was that?'

'The two who delivered me here.'

'I didn't see any two guys.'

'Really.'

'That's the way it is.'

Plant told his story. Such as it was. Pillowslip, handcuffs, closed vehicle, imprisonment, interrogation, release. Motive: presumably mistaken identity. Or maybe not. Maybe just to give him a fright. Give him a warning. A warning about what? A warning about everything.

'I don't know who they were. Police? Military? Guerrillas? Terrorists? Private army? Drug dealers? Security?'

'Who knows?' said Alfredo. 'There are so many possibilities.'

'So how did you get into the act?' Plant asked.

'We were worried about you. We heard things. Like you were missing. Someone makes a call. Pick you up here. It's good to see you, man.'

He got up and slapped his hand on Plant's shoulder.

'You never know when they say to pick someone up quite what they mean. Like what state you might be picking them up in. Decomposed. But see, nothing to worry about, no decomposition. All is well.'

'If you say so,' said Plant. 'I've just been kidnapped. Knocked around. I could have done without it.'

'Anything broken? Ribs cracked?'

'I don't think so.'

'You'd know,' said Alfredo. 'So why didn't they break your ribs? Weren't they really trying? I thought you said you'd been tortured.'

'Interrogated.'

'So what's the difference?'

'Quite a lot, I would have thought.'

'And you had it. Quite a lot. The difference.'

'I didn't get any ribs broken.'

'Isn't that nice they were gentle with you,' said Alfredo. Surprised. Or mocking. Or puzzled. Or knowing, for that matter.

'I was fucking locked up,' said Plant.

'You didn't enjoy it?'

'I can't say I did.'

'No fun, imprisonment.' He laughed. 'But you get used to it.'

'You speak from experience.'

Alfredo laughed.

'Ah, experience,' he said. 'What an interesting concept that is.'

Somewhere in the hills dogs barked. Insects hurled themselves against the screens on the window, circled suicidally around the light globe in the kitchen.

'So what was it all about?'

'I think they thought I was Ackerman. Except Ackerman is twenty years older than me, at least. He was staying here when I got here.'

'So where is he now?'

'I've no idea,' said Plant. 'He was here a few days ago.'

'So he is alive. He isn't missing.'

'Yes. Well, he's still missing.'

'He was alive when you saw him?'

'Yes. But he disappeared the next morning. Then I was kidnapped.'

'Tell me,' said Alfredo, 'what exactly is your interest in Professor Ackerman?'

'I was hired by his wife to find him.'

'Have you told her you found him?'

'I've been kidnapped, how could I tell her anything?'

Alfredo held out his mobile phone.

'Give me a break,' said Plant.

'Anyway, looks like you will have to report you have since lost him.'

'Could be,' agreed Plant.

'Why did she want you to find Professor Ackerman?'

'Because he had disappeared.'

'Is that all?'

'Isn't it enough?'

'Why didn't she go to the authorities?'

'She didn't know who to go to.'

'Really? So she went to you?'

'That's about it,' said Plant. He could see how it might seem strange. It was beginning to seem strange to him.

'Did you talk to Ackerman?'

'Yes.'

'What about?'

'Mainly he rambled on. He was telling stories of the rich and famous he had known. He is writing his memoirs.'

'Is that so?'

'I thought everyone knew.'

'Perhaps they do. Why would he be writing his memoirs?'

'Maybe he dreams he can write a bestseller in his retirement.'

'Did it sound like a bestseller?'

'I guess if you put in political assassinations and the drug trade and the security services and guerrillas and terrorists, it could be.'

'Could be,' said Alfredo.

'I don't know whether he knew any guerrillas or drug barons or secret operatives or terrorists.'

'Oh yes,' said Alfredo.

'Oh yes, what?'

'Oh yes, he knew them.'

'You know that for sure?' asked Plant.

'Sure.'

'How?'

'It is the easiest thing to know for sure. As soon as anyone makes contact with anyone in that sort of world, it is known. Even if he didn't know that is what they were. He knew them and they knew him.'

'So who did he know?'

Alfredo shook his head.

'You're not saying?'

He shook it some more.

'Best not to,' he said.

'Let me ask you something,' said Plant.

Alfredo nodded. There was no flamboyant 'of course,' no chummy 'sure.'

'Could someone think Ackerman's memoirs were sensitive? And want to grab him? Is that why he's hiding out?'

'Has he been hiding out?'

'I think so. It's hard to say.'

'Could be,' said Alfredo. 'Or it could be it's something else he's writing, not his memoirs.'

'About Legal and Visual?' said Plant.

'Why do you say that?'

'It seemed the obvious thing to say,' said Plant. It had been what Johnny seemed to have been hinting, that Ackerman had been trying to get close to Starr.

'And what is Legal and Visual?' Alfredo asked.

'You don't know?'

'Why would I know?'
Plant shrugged.
'They're a company that took over his publishing programme.'
'So?'
'So maybe he came out here to investigate them.'
'Here?' said Alfredo.
'They're all over Asia.'
'Why would he want to investigate them?'
'Maybe he thought they were dodgy.'
'Are they dodgy?'
'I don't know,' said Plant.
'I thought you were an investigator.'
'I'm not investigating them.'
'Aren't you?'
'I thought I already made that clear. No.'
'Not to me you didn't,' said Alfredo.
'I'm not,' said Plant.
'And Ackerman? What you reckon he was doing here? Writing? Or investigating?'
'Could have been either, or both.'
'Who do you think he was working for?' Alfredo asked.
'Ackerman? I don't know. He could just have been working for himself.'
'Or your secret service. Or our secret service. Their secret service.'
'Theirs? Whose?'
'Take your pick.'
'I see.'
'Or the terrorists.'
'You reckon?' said Plant. 'Lecturing them to keep them ideologically correct?'
'Something like that, perhaps,' said Alfredo. 'It is well known that your mutual friend is connected to the leadership.'
'Which mutual friend?'
'Your little singing friend.'
'Anna-Imelda?'
Alfredo chuckled. Fondly. Maybe he liked her voice.
'You're saying she's a terrorist?'
'Just well connected. An agent of influence. A sympathiser. A collaborator. A conduit.'
'Well, well,' said Plant. 'How do you get to know that?'

'You get to hear these things.'

'Tell me about Anna-Imelda,' said Plant.

'Anna-Imelda,' said Alfredo. 'What is there to tell?'

'I don't know. That's why I'm asking you.'

'You fancy her?' said Alfredo. 'You into songs?'

'Just tell me about the singer.'

'Beautiful body. Dubious morals. Passable voice. Had a high-grade boyfriend for a while. He goes off into the hills. Big guerrilla chief. She stays behind. Indoctrinated. Though there are others who say she indoctrinated him. And sent him off to fight for the cause while she hung out with the low-life of Manila.'

'Which cause?'

'Good question. What does it matter? Marxists, Muslims.'

'They're rather different.'

'I wouldn't worry too much about the particular ideology,' said Alfredo. 'It's the fire-power that counts.'

'Does her boy friend have fire-power?'

'He certainly does.'

'Where from?'

Alfredo laughed.

'A lot of people are working on that one,' he said. 'Some are trying to dig up the truth and some are trying to bury it.'

'So lots of disinformation.'

'Sometimes you get to think that's all there ever is.'

'An amazing story,' said Plant.

'You like it?'

Plant shrugged.

'Or you like her?'

'Some lady,' said Plant.

'True,' said Alfredo. 'There's even been the suggestion she might be like a plant.'

'A plant?' said Plant.

'You don't know what a plant is, Plant?'

'Sure I know.'

'Sure you do. Takes one to know one.'

'Are you saying you think I'm one? Why would I be?'

'Who knows?' said Alfredo. 'Someone figured if they planted you here it might stir things up a bit, maybe. Get a bit of action going. Speed things along.'

Plant thought about it. He didn't like the thoughts he had. He returned his attention to the topic of Anna-Imelda.

'So what sort of plant is she supposed to be?'

'A poisonous one,' said Alfredo. 'Best you keep away.'

'Cosying up to the guerrillas like Guevara's girlfriend? Who turned out to be CIA.'

'Who can tell? Just warning you in case you were getting too romantically inclined.'

'Or you could be feeding me disinformation because she's the real thing.'

'The real thing,' Alfredo reflected. 'What would that be? That make her more appealing or less appealing to you?'

'It's hard to say,' said Plant. 'I guess basically I like to know where I am.'

'You're in the Philippines, man,' said Alfredo. 'But you'll be leaving shortly.'

'Is that so?'

'Don't worry, I'll make sure of it,' said Alfredo.

Plant looked across at him. Alfredo had the amiable look of someone trying to suppress a smile, whether a smile of satisfaction or amusement Plant's skills in physiognomy were not sufficiently advanced to detect. He might have been the political officer of a Maoist guerrilla army walked in from the hills, or he might have been a local businessman. A drug dealer or a journalist, or the mayor's speechwriter. As any of which he could have been working for the government, any government, Philippines, American, Chinese, or Australian. Or he could just be a guardian angel. Or Anna-Imelda's secret lover, come to that. There was no point in worrying. Whatever people said they were, they were probably something else as well, not even necessarily instead of. Whatever they claimed or implied. Was it a matter of inscrutability, or inflexibility? The traditional mystery of the orient? Or the flexibility of the future, all flexitime, flexicards, blow and bend with the wind? There was an Austrian verb that expressed it: lavieren. Moving in an undulating way, avoiding commitment, bending with the wind. Maybe that was the root of Lavi.

34

'What you like to do tonight?' asked Alfredo. 'Cock-fighting? You like to go to a cock-fight?'

Plant shuddered inwardly. Outwardly, too, probably.

'No.'

'Sightseeing?'

'No thanks.'

'Gambling?'

'Not for me.'

'You want a woman? I know this girl, she only goes with foreigners, a knockout, I can phone her madam.'

'No thanks,' said Plant. 'I've already been knocked out.'

'You already got a woman? Where've you stashed her?'

'No.'

'I heard there was one around.'

'The only woman around was Anna-Imelda.'

'And she wouldn't share her favours?'

'I didn't ask.'

'Not usually a matter of asking,' said Alfredo. 'You want a boy?'

'No.'

Alfredo shrugged.

'So just tell me anything else you might have forgotten, and we can get this all wrapped up before you leave the country.'

'Am I leaving the country?'

'If I was you, I would,' said Alfredo.

Plant phoned Mrs Ackerman from the airport after he had checked in. Alfredo waited beside him as he called.

'Plant,' she said. 'I've been trying to reach you. Where've you been?'

He tried to tell her he had been kidnapped. Knocked around, incarcerated and deported but she cut across him.

'My husband called me. He's not lost. I've been trying to phone you to tell you to come back.'

'I know. I found him.'

'He didn't mention you,' she said doubtfully. 'When did you find him?'

'A couple of days ago.'

'Why didn't you tell me? He called me himself a couple of days ago.'

'That's because I spoke to him,' said Plant.

'So why didn't you call then?' she asked.

He tried to tell her again but she cut across him as before.

'Anyway, the point is, he's not lost.'

'I know. I found him.'

'He didn't mention you at all.'

'It's because I found him that he phoned.'

'He didn't say that.'

'He didn't?'

'No.'

Bastard, thought Plant. He was finally getting a fix on the man. Amiable, adulterous academic, genial general editor, rabid ratbag.

'I'll settle our account now. Just return the credit card in the mail,' she said. 'You might as well come back right away. Unless you want to stay on for a holiday. Do you want to do some sightseeing?'

She'd be offering him a girl next.

'I'm leaving now,' said Plant. 'Did he having anything to say?'

'What do you mean?'

'Did he say why he's been missing?'

'He's not missing.'

'I know. I found him.'

'There's a terrible lot of noise on this line,' she said.

'I'm at the airport. Did he say why he vanished? If he did?'

'I'm sorry, I'm not hearing you, Plant.'

The line went dead. No goodbye, no thank you, nothing like that. Presumably she wanted it to seem like they had been cut off.

The good thing, he told himself as he waited in the departure lounge, was that he wasn't expected to bring Ackerman back. How would he have done that? In chains? Narcotised by a blowdart to the neck? It was a very good thing. The other good thing was he didn't have to explain he had lost Ackerman as soon as he had found him. Ackerman had phoned her, which got him off having to deal with that embarrassment. At least there were some good things.

He felt better once he was on the aircraft. At least she hadn't cancelled his ticket. Would that have been possible? Just refused to bring him back and refused to pay him, leaving him stranded there, washing glasses in the Eternal Night Club, while Miss Anna-Imelda sang her sad songs interminably through the endless night.

Yes, it was possible. Everything was possible. But at least he was on the aircraft. One thing he knew for certain, he was taking no risks until he got back. Whoever sat beside him, he wasn't going to speak to them.

He called in on Mrs Ackerman. Get it over with and start a new life. The Gold Coast glimmered in the gentle light, the high rises shimmered and shone, reflecting the sun, reflected themselves in the Nerang River and the Broadwater and the creeks and canals. Some thought it a place of crime and corruption, development scams and gambling and prostitution and the no doubt nameless vices as well, the towers of Vanity Fair with a hinterland of canal development abhorrent to greenies. To Plant, returned, it was a haven of peace.

He returned the company Amex card to Mrs Ackerman.

'I said just put it in the mail,' she said.

'Security,' he said, 'you never know.'

'Well, if you don't …' she said.

'There are a lot of things I don't know.'

'There are, aren't there?' she said. Meaningfully. All too meaningfully.

'I did find him.'

'If you say so.'

'Even if I lost him again.'

'That was careless.'

'Yes, well, they got away.'

'They?'

'They,' he said.

He felt no obligation to cover for Ackerman. Or his singing friend. Once someone had drugged you unsolicitedly, the conventions of loyalty and confidentiality no longer applied. Not as far as Plant was concerned.

'Who were "they"?'

'He and his friend.'

'And does this friend have a name?'

'She has several.'

'Go on.'

'Anna-Imelda.'

'I see.'

'Sorry about that,' said Plant.

'You don't seem at all sorry.'

'I was after I'd been drugged and kidnapped.'

'I'd have thought that was the sort of thing you would have liked.'

'Not me.

'Or at least been used to.'

'I don't think it's something you get used to,' he said.

She didn't offer him a drink.

35

Plant sweated on his property. The man of the land. It was early morning, six-thirty, but still he sweated. He was ripping out lantana from the creek bed. Dragging out fallen branches from the camphor laurels. 'Eradicate all toxic camphor laurels' declared the green graffiti around the district. He wasn't about to start that. Lantana was one thing, camphor laurels were huge. And he rather liked them. He confined himself to collecting their fallen branches for firewood. The greens opposed that, too. Leave fallen branches for native fauna to live in. But he didn't. He wanted to clear his creek. Obsession.

By nine-thirty it would be too hot to do any more. Too hot for Plant. He thought of the labourers in Manila and Kolkata and Bangkok. On building sites. Hauling loads. And here he was saying he couldn't work after nine-thirty. Well, after ten. After ten it became a labour. A toil. But the first early hours, the first two or three, were a delight. You could lose yourself in nature. That early morning clarity.

He could have been refurbishing his skills as a one-time research scholar or a one-time journalist and tried writing a piece on travelling in Asia. He lit a joint first thing in the morning and considered it. Then he strolled round his estate. It was more fun than writing. His five acres. Imperial Adam. He looked across at his neighbour's block. The bulldozers had gone. They had left a wake of destruction, trees and bush cleared down to a creek. Ready for lawns to roll down to an excavated lily pond.

It had given him ideas. Not of bulldozing out trees. He was appalled at that. But the creek. He had a creek. He looked for it, overgrown with grass beneath a cover of lantana, saplings clustering beneath the huge camphor laurels that rose above it sucking up the water, lantana and creepers reaching up into the leaf cover.

Learn from the enemy. It sounded like another of those pieces of wisdom people tended to give him. In our country we have a saying. Steal your enemy's ideas. It certainly worked for political parties. So, he would steal the idea of clearing the banks of his creek. His dried-up stream. In flood times it was a torrent, impassable. He had been cut off from the world more than once. For a couple of days at a time. He had stocked up with a loaf and wine beforehand. And bought Blundstone Weatherseal Wellington boots afterwards. For the next time. He rather liked the sense of isolation.

Now he sweated in his Wellingtons and Akubra hat and cleared the undergrowth by hand. It wasn't that hard. You just did it, piece by piece. You hacked away at it and it was preferable to hacking out journalism or a PhD. As long as you kept a look out for snakes and spiders and ticks and leeches it was less risky than wandering around Asia looking for lost academics. At least you were on your own property. Private. For a fragile moment, at least.

Fighting the lantana was like fighting enemies. He had a lot of lantana. Some he could tug out by the roots. When the lantana had become old and thick and substantial, cascades of creepers issuing forth, it was quite easy to pull the root out. Sometimes it would break off, old and rotten. The bigger, the more vulnerable. The very young, they were easily pulled out too. But some in vigorous growth required the saw. Secateurs at other times. Shears. His arsenal of weaponry. The activity filled his consciousness. He speculated on political analogies, the vulnerability of old, over-extended empires, or youthful nation states. Sometimes he turned to more personal comparisons and fought a composite of resistant lantana briars and wily elusive forces like Professor Ghosh and Ackerman and Starr. To say nothing of Mrs Ackerman. Nature, clients and quarry merged in a satisfying identity of the irritating to be extirpated. He sweated and swore and felt sick on the stomach with wrenching and tugging, his hands and arms scratched sore and itching. There was a satisfying physicality to it. Not that Asia had lacked the physical, the night at the Eternal Night Club, the abduction from Baguio City. But he could grasp the lantana in a way he could not have grabbed Ghosh's greasy professorial locks, tug at its twisted limbs in a way he could hardly have twisted Ackerman's beastly bare ankles.

There were other paradoxes worthy of possible political application. When you had ripped out the lantana you had to put it somewhere. He had seven huge heaps of lantana stacked at different points, like the tumuli of dead warrior kings. He needed space to put the rubbish, space to burn it. The logistics were fascinating. He brooded on them for hours, the hours after 9.30 when it became preferable to brood than to labour, to meditate on labour-saving strategies rather than to apply them. So you rip out your political enemies, you still have to do something with them, dead or alive. Great funeral pyres? They were reputed to have dropped them into the jungle from helicopters in Thailand. Demonstrators. Unionists. Communists. Back here the helicopters were mainly looking for dope plantations. As far as Plant knew. Though you never knew anywhere for sure, did you?

He had a good bonfire going when the first intruders came. It was not that easy to get a good bonfire going, Plant discovered. You need to make sure it isn't a total fire-ban time. He assumed it wasn't. It wasn't summer. It felt cold, damp even. Which was not good for burning. Heaps of damp lantana. And the lantana was green, most of it, though there were a few dead, dried strands. He should have left it all to dry out for six months. But by then it would probably be total fire-ban season.

He kindled fire and it went out. He scoured the house for newspapers to start again. In one way it was satisfying how few newspapers he could find. He missed them. In the past he had enjoyed reading a good newspaper. Now they didn't seem so good, and he didn't want them in the house. Intruding over the breakfast marmalade. Not the sort of consciousness you wanted to let in. Telling lies as you fried an egg. And generally as uninformative and unnutritional as a breakfast cereal packet. He reminded himself to make a point of picking up the local give-away papers if he was planning to start a lot of fires. He knew of seven he was planning. That seemed a lot.

He got the fire going and blazing away to a certain degree. He took a break for a smoke and a glass of ginger beer, wiping the sweat from his brow. Honest labour as opposed to useless toil. He sat on his canvas chair outside the door and composed a homily on its virtues. The virtues of honest labour. The virtues of canvas too, cannabis, canvas, hemp, all the same word, give or take a bit of consonantal drift. He examined the Bundaberg ginger beer bottle. It declared its contents were naturally brewed to be better, and from a genuine old recipe. He relished the natural and old. And the better.

This was when the car drove up his driveway and parked on his grass. A ten-year-old Laser. There was a silence for a while. A stasis. Then both doors opened. Two women got out. One seemed in her fifties or sixties, the other in her seventies. The older one struggled out of the passenger seat with two aluminium walking-aids, not exactly walking-sticks nor precisely crutches. Maybe the components for assembly into a machine-gun. They wore hats like hats out of an English rural murder mystery as costumed to sell to American public television. They began to approach him. Slowly. Up his driveway.

Plant sat paralysed. He had not expected this. He had not expected anyone, had not known what to expect. He felt their heavy menace as they came closer. It was like the slow, inexorable approach of volcanic lava.

The older one with the machine-gun components said they were Jehovah's Witnesses. The other who had been driving produced a magazine. A printed one.

Plant said he knew the literature, thank you, but he had to take care of the fire he had burning. He finished the ginger beer, cupped the joint in his hand and seized a fork. He was able to keep a good twenty metres distance from them, smiling genially and striding purposefully away as they turned toward him. He felt the Wellington boots contributed to the purposefulness. He splashed some more methylated spirits on the fire and it blazed up with a satisfying roar.

He stood behind the smoke and flames till they drove off. It took them a while. An inordinate while. They moved slowly and cumbersomely. The one with the aluminium shooting-sticks moved with difficulty, like a moonwalk vehicle. There was a long silence after they had got into the car and slammed the doors. As if they were putting out a radio call for back-up. Plant waited till they drove off. He heard them drive up the driveway of the desecrated neighbouring bulldozed plot, and drive out again. He really did need to keep a supply of hash cookies to feed to them. It had been done to Jehovah's Witnesses before. If they were Jehovah's Witnesses. And if they weren't, it still might calm them down. Make them giggle. Delay their assembling the shooting-sticks into a machine-gun. Put them off their shot.

The car drove away down the road. Plant listened to the sound of it, receding through the valley. As it faded he became aware of some other presence. The wallaby was chewing leaves some ten feet away and watching him speculatively. Its ears revolved individually. A sophisticated early-warning system.

The following evening Plant wandered around his grounds collecting fallen branches. Much of the clearing up was just clearing up, menial tasks of dragging out fallen limbs, collecting handfuls of long slender twigs. It was actually quite easy. As long as you took care not to pick up a black snake by mistake. Once you had adopted the slow plod of the peasant, that determined not to be hurried trudge of the country worker, you settled into a gentle rhythm. Yet at first Plant had resented it. He slashed into the lantana, wrestled with its roots, lacerated his arms and hands and face with deep satisfaction. There was much more machismo in ripping out things, the epic archetype of tearing out Thessalian pines by the roots. You could wrench your stomach muscles or back or shoulder as you grappled with the long networks of briars, and it gave a satisfaction which just picking up fallen timber could not at first equal. Plant puzzled over the nature of satisfaction. He was not a man to whom laziness had no appeals. He could sidestep obligation as readily as the best and brightest. Why didn't he enjoy picking up branches and dragging them to the woodheap in the same way as ripping out lantana by the roots? He ascribed it to being conditioned to value the exertions of the great jungle explorers. The Empire builders. Glamour, honour, as the native bearers slashed their way through for the burdened white man. While back at home the old woman who gathered sticks for her fire on a Sunday was sent up to the moon. A proverb we have in our country.

A strident voice broke in on his easy philosophizing. A female voice. An American female voice.

'There's no privacy,' it called out in anguish. 'There's a house there and a house there.'

'I won't come then,' said another voice, female, American, younger, a daughter, a lesbian lover, intruders all.

Maybe, thought Plant with a sudden, eager, wild surmise, the block desecrators were selling their desecrated block. And here was someone who wanted privacy looking at it. Should he encourage her to buy it?

He trampled round amongst his twigs, wondering whether to call out in assurance, 'Oh, it's private enough here,' which of course would have assured her that it certainly was not, which would drive her away. Was that a good thing or a bad thing? He wasn't sure he wanted an American woman on the next block. He didn't want anyone. That was his basic position. And anyway, a desire for privacy might not go along with a desire for quiet. She might want to be private so she could make a lot of noise all day and night. Drumming. Carpentry. Listening to Barbra Streisand at full volume.

In the end he decided not to say anything. He just stood there in his

Akubra hat and King Gee work shirt and trousers and his Blundstone Wellington boots. He imagined that might seem menacing to an American woman. If she saw him. At the gate she turned, fixed him in view. If she had good sight.

He watched her walk around the neighbouring block, the other woman standing by the car at the entrance. A bright red Jeep, one of the fancy ones, a Jeep recreational vehicle, but its military paternity clearly evident in its military styling. After they had driven away he walked down to where they had been. There was no For Sale sign.

36

The clearing up was looking good when the limo arrived. Plant was not surprised to see it. The third intrusion. Two surveillance teams then the real thing. Everything went in threes. Except five-fold things. Like the Pentagon. Or sixes and sevens. And tens. And dozens. And scores. And hundreds and thousands. And battalions. Rarely a single spy.

It was a grotesquely out of place vehicle. A long black stretch limo on Plant's rutted track. A pity he hadn't got the lantana piles burning. It would have looked like *Götterdämmerung* with the bonfires and this black menacing limo. Where would it have come from? It wasn't even a white stretch limo from the Gold Coast with tinted windows and a driver in a Hawaiian shirt. No, this was strictly a big city, heavy, inappropriate, out of place, threatening with menaces, GBH sort of car. Plant was not surprised when Starr stepped out.

Starr was annoyed. Maybe angry expressed it better. Enraged. He strode in an enraged manner.

'You told me you were not investigating me,' he said, without any prefatory greeting, no social niceties.

Plant sat in his canvas chair on the deck. Paralysed again. Not even able to rise politely.

'I'm not,' he said.

'But you have been.'

'Not at all.'

'So you lie to me again.'

'I haven't lied to you,' said Plant with extraordinary self-confidence. He could not have said he felt it. Confidence. Rather, he tried it on to see what it felt like. It felt tolerably good.

Starr was in his dark suit and blue shirt. Ever the businessman. He opened his businessman's briefcase and produced a folder of print-outs and A4 sheets. He brandished them at the camphor laurels.

'Word gets back to me,' he said. 'People tell me you've been phoning up my affiliates. Wasting their time. Requests for information. Shareholdings. Directors. Trading names. I could have given you all this is in a moment. For free. If you had said it was what you wanted.'

'I didn't ask for it. It's not something I ever wanted,' said Plant. It sounded curt, almost offensive. He tried something more mellow. 'Fascinating as I'm sure it all is.'

'As I'm sure you know, Mr Plant.'

'No, I don't. Let me have a look.'

Starr held back.

'Since you said you'd have given me them if I'd asked for them. Whatever they are.'

'Requested in your name,' said Starr, still not handing them over.

'My name, maybe, but not me.'

'Billed to your credit card,' said Starr.

'Not me,' said Plant.

'And how would that be?'

'I haven't requested anything. Or paid for anything.'

'Billed to your Amex card.'

'I don't have an Amex card.'

'Not what it says here.'

'Mrs Ackerman had an Amex card issued in my name on her company account. She wanted it that way. So she'd know what the expenses were for. And so she could claim it as gallery business. Claim it against tax, you know. I turned it in when I finished the job. Maybe she handed it over to someone else. Or used it herself.'

'Have you finished the job?'

'Yes. Certainly have.'

'So why are you still conducting the search?'

'I'm not conducting it. I haven't called anyone. It's not my card. I'm not using it.'

'You saying someone else is doing it in your name?'

'Obviously.'

'It's not that fucking obvious to me,' said Starr.

'It's billed to Mrs Ackerman's gallery account. I'd check with her.'

Surely Starr would have done that. It wouldn't tax his resources to check back on account names to find the names behind the names. It was the way Starr operated himself, behind foundations and institutes and corporations and partnerships. Plant didn't feel he had sacrificed Mrs Ackerman. Not a lot. Not anything Starr would not have known.

'Why don't you come and sit down?' Plant suggested.

Starr advanced on the house. The gunman driver stayed in the front seat, the door and window open. Nothing to impede a shot.

'We can sit out on the deck,' said Plant.

He didn't want these people inside any more than he wanted newspapers getting in.

'A drink?' Plant offered.

'No.'

'Tea, coffee?'

'I just want to get down to business,' said Starr.

'Business,' said Plant.

'Yes, business.'

'Your driver?'

'He just wants to drive back. So cut it out, Plant. Stop flapping around like you're playing the host.'

'This is more a home invasion than a friendly visit, you mean,' said Plant.

'It's up to you how you want to play it.'

'The friendly way,' said Plant. 'Without a doubt.'

'So we do it the friendly way,' said Starr. 'OK, Mr Plant, what are you up to?'

He raised an admonitory hand. Almost papal.

'And don't say nothing. Cut the cackle this time and say just exactly, and I mean exactly, what you've been doing. Then we'll see about going away.'

'I've been clearing out the lantana,' said Plant.

'Do you deny you've been investigating my companies?'

'Absolutely,' said Plant. 'Neither you nor your company nor the company you keep. I was hired by Mrs Ackerman to find her husband. I found him. End of story.'

'Not quite end of story,' said Starr. 'I heard you lost him again.'

'I wasn't hired to bring him in,' said Plant. 'I'm not a bounty hunter.'

'I never imagined you were,' said Starr. He seemed to find the concept amusing. He showed his teeth when he laughed. They were white and faultless and American.

'So.'

'So, someone is nosing through my company records. Phoning people up. Asking for information here, copies of certificates there. All in your name. Which you say is being used not by you but by someone else.'

'Correct.'

'And you suggest the someone is Mrs Ackerman.'

'Could be. Or someone she employed to do it for her.'

'So why is she investigating me?'

'I have no idea.'

'I don't believe you.'

'Truly,' said Plant.

'When did you say you quit working for Mrs Ackerman?'

Plant told him.

'You can prove it?'

'I can show you the final invoice I sent. She paid it. Should be on my bank statement.'

'When did you get back?'

'The same time. Day before, I guess. I phoned her the next day. End of employment. That was it.'

'Prove it?'

'I can show you my passport.'

'Boarding card. Passports don't record incoming residents' dates of arrival.'

'Ticket?'

'Ticket means nothing. Boarding card.'

'I don't think I kept it.'

'Of course you did. You kept it so if there's any dispute with Mrs Ackerman you can prove you were on the flight. So if the taxation people query your business expenses you have evidence you were on that flight. If you want to query your frequent flyer points, it's the only evidence that will do. You know that. You kept it. Just go and bring it to me. And the passport, and the invoice, and your bank statements and your credit card statements, too, while you're at it.'

'You want a herbal tea while I look for them? Ginger beer? Spelt bread sandwich?'

'Don't waste time fucking around,' said Starr. 'Just go get them.'

Plant went.

'I hope my cooperation will save me a further incarceration,' said Plant when he returned.

'What do you mean?'

'The time you had me abducted.'

'I never had you abducted.'

'From Baguio City.'

'Why would I want to abduct you?'

'Why would you want to visit me, for that matter?'

'Not for pleasure, that's for sure,' said Starr.

'You don't seem very surprised I was abducted.'

'Neither surprised nor interested.'

'You don't want me to tell you how I was held in a cell and visited by someone sounding like you.'

'Horseshit,' said Starr.

'Got it in one,' said Plant. 'The language of the new world rather than the language of Shakespeare.'

'Schmuck,' said Starr.

'The language of the old world, if you prefer,' said Plant. 'But still not the language of Shakespeare.'

'Just give me the paperwork,' said Starr.

He leafed through it all. The secret of Rockefeller's early success was said to be the thorough, methodical way he worked through the bookkeeping. Starr worked methodically through the passport, the invoices, the bank statements, the boarding card, the ticket. That was how you became rich. That and having some money to start with. Plant was always on the lookout for tips on how to become rich. He watched Starr's meticulousness with fascination.

Starr handed it all back, all except the passport. He kept that, tapped it against his knee thoughtfully, as if to implant the suggestion that he might just not return it. Plant found it an unacceptable suggestion. It was theft. He stood up, reached over, and took it from Starr's hand. Starr offered no resistance, no recognition of anything remarkable. This, Plant decided, could only be the behaviour of someone who was a trained psy-ops expert. Like his old headmaster. Or the head-boy. Either of them. Customs officers he had encountered. It was not incompatible with being a publisher. Not at all. It got to Plant. It was designed to make you feel uncomfortable. It succeeded. But Plant was no stranger to discomfort. It was a familiar sensation. Almost comfortable.

'So what's the problem?' he asked. 'Why shouldn't Mrs Ackerman or someone go through your company records? It's all public information. Why shouldn't she phone up and ask? What have you got to hide?'

Starr gave Plant his malevolent grin.

'There is nothing to hide. She is perfectly entitled to go through the company records available to the public.'

'Such as they are,' said Plant.

'I just want to know why it is being done.'

'I can't help you on that,' said Plant. 'Why don't you go and ask her?'

'What a brilliant suggestion,' said Starr. 'How you cut through all this confusion and complexity and reach right to the heart of the matter.'

'Thank you,' said Plant.

Three black cockatoos flew overhead, shrieking.

'You know her, don't you?'

Starr shrugged.

'So there you are.'

'You make it sound so simple, Mr Plant.'

'Isn't it?'

'If it were do you think I would have driven out here?'

'A day in the country,' said Plant.

'You're welcome to it.' said Starr ungraciously. 'So why did her husband go missing?' he asked. 'If he did.'

'No idea,' said Plant. 'That wasn't my business. I just had to find him. As it happened, I never got to ask him. They slipped me a Mickey Finn and vanished. That was the last I saw of him. And the first, for that matter. That was when you had me abducted. Were you trying for me or for Ackerman?'

Starr shook his head in disgust or distaste or despair.

'Maybe Mrs Ackerman thinks he's on your payroll and wants to track him down again.'

'He never was on my payroll,' said Starr.

'Involved with the series.'

'He is not involved.'

'So it all remains a mystery,' said Plant. Brightly.

Down near the creek a whip bird cracked the whip.

'What the fuck was that?' Starr asked.

'A whip bird.'

'A whip bird? Thought it wasn't like any gunshot I'd ever heard.'

'You've heard a lot of gunshots?'

'Plenty. But I've never seen a whip bird. Show me.'

'They're very hard to see.'

'You're holding out again.'

'Truly,' said Plant.

'Truly?' said Starr. 'That's not a word I've heard in a while.'

Plant could have said, 'It's the company you keep.' But he didn't. He chose a less combative mode. More self-deprecatory.

'There are all sorts of linguistic survivals in these forgotten valleys,' he said.

'You don't say,' said Starr.

The whip bird cracked the lash again.

'Actually, it's two birds,' said Plant. 'The one gives the long hissing noise, and the other comes in with the crack. That's why it sounds stereophonic.'

Cerrraaaack.

'Unbelievable,' said Starr.

From up in the bush came the sound of beating. Four heavy thumps, as if someone were beating a carpet, or punching a punch bag. Starr looked round.

'Wallaby,' said Plant.

'Amazing creatures you got round here,' said Starr.

Plant smiled, the smile of the contented man of the land.

37

'What sort of things was Mrs Ackerman looking up?' Plant asked.

'If it was Mrs Ackerman,' said Starr.

'It wasn't me,' said Plant.

'Maybe not,' said Starr. 'You still ask too many questions.'

'What's with the string of companies?' Plant asked, asking another one.

'Tax minimization.'

'Tax minimization?'

'I am a child of my generation,' said Starr. 'I do not deny it.'

'What generation would that have been?' Plant asked.

The black stretch limo looked very seventies, parked there.

'I was against war and for peace,' said Starr. 'My parents insisted I became a lawyer. Get a safe job. People always need lawyers and accountants and doctors. I fought off the doctor bit. No mama, it's not that I don't like the sight of blood, I think I could get to like it too much. I just don't like sick people. Let the sick hang out with the sick. I'd be a terrible doctor. I didn't want to be a terrible doctor. I didn't want to be a terrible lawyer, either. But what were the choices? I could drop out, there was no money in it. I could become an anti-war protester and get beaten up. None of it appealed to me. So I came upon the solution. I would specialise in tax law and find ways of avoiding funding war and oppression by finding ways to avoid paying governments their taxes. International tax law. My parents begged me, do criminal law and prosecute some of the murderers and rapists. I did not want to prosecute anyone, nor did I want to defend villains. I just wanted to make enough money to get out of the law. Make a lot of money and on moral principle pay none of it out in taxes. That is the way to get rich. Simple. That, Plant, has been my life story. No less, no more. A simple, honourable, moral crusade, designed to lead to wealth. Which it did. An all-American story.

'So first of all I'm advising clients on international tax law. Then I figure there are these missing information sources here, so I start publishing books on international tax law. Fill the need. Updates every year. New editions with the very latest information. Soon I am maximizing my knowledge of international tax law in order to run an international tax law book publishing company, without paying tax. Neat, eh?'

'Elegant,' said Plant.

'It is mandatory to avoid paying taxes in these times, Plant. You know that. It is one's moral duty not to fund corrupt regimes and military solutions. Not to fund the travesty that passes for education that ensures no one questions whatever the state does. So I do not imagine you are going to be sniffy about creative accounting across international frontiers. Why should you be? It's crime prevention, Plant, double crime prevention, in fact. The taxes are not paid, which is one crime prevented, since tax-collection is institutionalised robbery, as we all agree. And since the taxes are not paid they cannot be used to wage war, maim women and children, create orphans, produce chemical malformations, and desecrate the environment, which is another crime prevented.'

'When you put it like that,' said Plant, 'it sounds good.'

'How else can you put it? Since the 1950s government has spread corporate welfare amongst the munitions manufacturers and the aviation industry and the computer industry, and violence and destruction through the rest of the world.'

'Which government?'

‘All governments,’ said Starr.

‘So you were just doing your duty.’

‘That’s how I see it,’ said Starr.

‘And the art books,’ said Plant. ‘Where do they fit in?’

‘I love art. I wanted to be an artist. My parents insisted, a doctor, a lawyer, or an accountant. My dream was to sit around all day with a room full of naked models and works of art hanging on the walls. Life class. And there I was in law school. Can you imagine?’

He emanated deeply felt tragedy as he sat on Plant’s deck. Little birds flew in and out of the grevillea and bottlebrush flowers. Honeyeaters, finches, firetails, blue and scarlet wrens. But Starr was blind to the present. Dreams of draping naked bodies with diaphanous, vaporous drapes, and then the click of a camera, floated before his eyes.

‘And did you achieve it?’

‘Achieve what?’

‘Your dream.’

‘Yes, I did. I am a very fulfilled man, Plant. Very fulfilled. With no need to pry into other peoples’ business.’

‘I assure you I have not been prying into yours.’

‘If you had pried efficiently, anyway, you would know I began art publishing very early. Very early. I knew of course that the art market was a way of moving money around the world and facilitating the moral aim of not paying tax to oppressive regimes. There seemed after all a synergy between tax books and art books. I fulfilled my dream very early.’

‘So what is left? Just keeping it all going?’

‘What a jaded way of putting it. I positively enjoy keeping it all going. I intend to live to a hundred. A hundred and twenty. And keep it all going.’

‘That’s good,’ said Plant.

The driver sat chewing indigestion mints. Perhaps he wasn’t Starr’s bodyguard. Perhaps he just came from the limousine service.

‘So for the last time, you are not investigating my companies.’

‘No.’

‘You say Mrs Ackerman is. Why?’

‘No idea,’ said Plant. ‘Maybe she admires you.’

‘Admires me,’ said Starr. He sounded startled at the concept.

‘You’re not that despicable,’ said Plant. ‘As publishers go.’

‘Why would she admire me?’ Starr asked.

‘Imitation,’ Plant suggested. ‘The sincerest form of flattery. Maybe she wanted to copy your business practices and become rich and fulfilled too. She's into art. She has a shop on the Gold Coast.'

'She would love to hear it called a shop,' said Starr.

'Gallery, then.' It did sound immediately more impressive. But was it? 'Maybe she's having trouble with her tax bill and is looking for ways to minimise it. Had a look to see how you do it.'

'I don't think so.'

'You think she's making money.'

Starr shrugged.

'I wouldn't know.'

'You don't deal in art.'

'Only personally.'

'What does that mean?'

'It means like personally.'

'You have an individual entity as well as a corporate one?'

'I am a company, too, if that is what you mean,' said Starr. 'Aren't you?'

'No.'

'No, you're not. You should be. You'd pay less tax.'

'Maybe I should consult you.'

'I don't take on individual clients these days. Get yourself a good accountant. It would be worth your while.'

He looked round Plant's estate.

'You could run this jungle on it. Mad not too. A tax loss farm if ever I saw one. Why else would you want it?'

He shook his head.

'You worry me, Plant. I don't think you've got it all together. In your personal life. In your accounts. You really should be a company. A string of them, really, if you're going to work offshore.'

'I'll think about it.'

'Maybe you will, maybe you won't,' said Starr. 'One thing is certain, you'll never do fuck-all about it.'

He stood up.

'I gotta be going.'

He shook Plant's hand.

'See ya, mate,' said the driver, nodding and chewing.

Starr took a long, last meditative, malevolent look at Plant's five acres.

'So much destruction, so many rubbish heaps, so much killing. You should get into growing, Plant, it is so much more positive and profitable.'

The limo lumbered gently down the driveway. Plant jotted down the registration number on the shopping list he kept by the phone. Just for the record. He added a couple of items after it, toothpaste, shampoo, so it didn't stand out, in case anyone came to look. Anyone else. Toothpaste. Shampoo. Innocuous enough. Didn't give away some terrible vices. Everybody used toothpaste and shampoo. Everybody who still had teeth and hair.

A wonderful peace descended. Plant rolled a smoke and reflected. He found there were things about Starr he quite liked. A child of that generation. It was nice to have someone open up to you, offer you his innermost philosophy.

Plant did not believe a word of it. If everything was so innocuous Starr would not have flown into the country and driven down for a visit. Of course, he might have had business in Australia. Other business. But to make a personal visit to Plant suggested that intimidating Plant was high on his list of business priorities. Starr was not a man who enjoyed country drives. You could sense that.

It had turned out genial enough but it might not have done. He did not like the thought of Starr and his driver having located his country retreat. Not one bit. It was not going to help him sleep sounder at night.

He sat on the deck and thoughts formed in his head. What was Starr up to? Hadn't he better check him out? And receive another stretch limo visit? Have someone else check him out? But if Starr were into really serious stuff, then phone inquiries were clearly out of the question. Email similarly. Let alone mail. They were all routinely monitored anyway, and if Starr were in any way sensitive his name would be a keyword to trigger interception, whether he was a person of interest to or a covert operative employed by any of the three letter organizations, or two letters and a numeral, or even four letter organizations, let alone any of the unknown ones that didn't even have acronyms. And there was every reason to believe he was into serious stuff. Like the expensive way he dressed and hired limos and the way he delivered menaces, politely done as it was, surprisingly done in person rather than by deputies. That might suggest he was not that big but in no way diminished the seriousness. Could be thought to increase it.

Serious stuff could be tax evasion, money-laundering, drug trafficking, gun trafficking, or intelligence. Or all five. You did not make careless, unconsidered, casual inquiries about intelligence or drugs or guns or money-laundering or tax evasion. If you were wise you never even thought about it, any of it. But since Starr had visited, Plant felt the need to know what he was up against. He would have to make a personal visit of inquiry. Not unlike Starr. But without the menace.

He wondered whether Starr had driven up from Sydney. Or Canberra. More likely he had flown into Brisbane. And there were lots of smaller airports an hour or less away. Coolangatta, Ballina, Lismore, Casino. Though not all with stretch limo hire services on hand.

The thought of the road from Sydney congealed with the thought that he wasn't sure that he wanted to spend the night alone at his retreat. He felt he had cleared enough lantana for a while. Now he would like to spend some time installing a security fence and surveillance equipment. He felt uneasy. Unnerved, even. There was no point in denying the feeling. That would be idiocy, to persuade himself there was nothing to worry about. There was everything to worry about. Worry settled over his five acres like a magician's fog.

He took out his travel bag and threw in a few clothes. He wasn't planning a long visit. He made himself an avocado and tomato sandwich on spelt, and set off. He would drive as far as he could, or felt like, and then stop in a motel if he felt tired. If he didn't, he would do it in one go. Ten or eleven hours. He would arrive some time after midnight. The preferred time to consult his old friend Fullalove. The man who knew more than you ever wanted to know about things you would be wise to be afraid to ask about.

38

'Hell, man, you advertise the investigative reporting and research assistance, you should know how to find out things like that,' said Fullalove.

'But I don't want it traced back to me.'

'You want to use my computer so the smart bomb strikes here.'

'I was thinking you might know a way round.'

Fullalove laughed.

'Run it past me again.'

'There's something fishy about him,' said Plant. 'It's a matter of seeing who his connections are.'

'Go through his catalogues, see who and what he's published,' Fullalove suggested.

'He doesn't seem to have a catalogue.'

'Distinctly fishy. He must have a stock list for getting orders.'

'Maybe,' said Plant, 'but I don't have one. And I don't want to ask for one. Not now.'

'Company records?'

'The Ackerwoman's obviously done that and he claims they're clean. They probably are. I could always get them from her.'

'But.'

'Yeah, but I'd rather not. And I don't think that's the way to go. I need more personal stuff. Where he was at college and when. Who with. Get his degree transcript and see if there are any missing years.'

'Sure,' said Fullalove. 'So how do we do that?'

'Do you know anyone in admissions at one of the universities?'

'Can't say I do.'

'Nor do I. If I could find someone, they could just put through the request. They ask for student transcripts from around the world all the time. No one need notice we're looking.'

'We?'

'A manner of speaking. If we can't find anyone in admissions, we print a letterhead, say Starr's applied for a job, and ask for his record.'

'A splendid letterhead, I assume. He wouldn't be applying for any old job.'

'I'll work out something,' said Plant.

'And when you find the missing years, assuming they exist, where do you go?'

'I was hoping you would tell me.'

'So what university was he at?'

'That's what I don't know.'

'That,' said Fullalove, 'is going to make it difficult.'

Plant conceded that it might.

Fullalove sat and brooded in his squalor. He was a creature of the night and lived like an owl lived, his nest surrounded by detritus. Not so much the bones of small animals and rodents, though there could have been for all Plant could see, buried beneath the litter of newspapers and magazines and print-outs and books. Books covered the walls and floor and table of the seedy flat. Amidst the inner-city gentrification, this was like a preserved historic site, bohemian accommodation from the 1960s, heaped ashtrays, unwashed glasses filled with cigarette butts and roaches, the paper Japanese lantern discoloured ochre from decades of smoke, circles of red wine from bottles and glasses superimposed on the sheets of paper strewn over the floor, books spread open on the floor, their bindings cracked, or stacked in heaps against the wall and stuffed haphazard in the unpainted, chipboard and melamine bookshelves, a complete library of paranoia and conspiracy, spies and counter-spies, information and disinformation, wars and rumours of wars. Philip Agee, Victor Marchetti, Chapman Pincher, Nigel West, Christopher Andrew, David Dilks, Desmond Ball, Richard Deacon, Richard Hall, Philip Knightley. *The Politics of Heroin in SouthEast Asia*, *Spycatcher*, *My Five Cambridge Friends*, *The Climate of Treason*, *The Search for the Manchurian Candidate*, *Wilderness of Mirrors*, *The Spying Game: An Australian Angle*. Plus the historic stuff, lives of Francis Walsingham and Henry Wotton and Dr Dee and Giordano Bruno and Christopher Marlowe and Andrew Marvell and Richard Thurloe. Shelves of Dennis Wheatley and Len Deighton and Ted Allbeury and Ross Thomas and Ian Fleming and Richard Harling and Graham Greene and Compton Mackenzie and John le Carré and Robert McCrum and William F. Buckley and Frederick Forsyth and David Ignatius and Charles Cummings. Jim Jones in Guyana, Jim Thompson in Thailand, Jim Cairns and Junie Morosi in Australia. Mata Hari and Richard Sorge, Alan Turing and multiple accounts of Bletchley Park. *Ashenden*, *Kim*, *The Secret Agent*, *Under Western Eyes*, *Stepper* and *The Complete Richard Hannay*. Kim Philby and Greville Wynn and George Blake and Anthony Blunt and Colonel Abel and the Petrovs and the Krogers and the Rosenbergs. Shelves on the Kennedy assassination and Robert Kennedy and Marilyn Monroe and Martin Luther King and John Lennon. J. Edgar Hoover and COINTELPRO and Watergate. The Oklahoma bombing and KAL 007 and September 11, both Chile and the USA, and October 12 in Bali, and November 11 in Australia and November 5 beneath the House of Commons.

'How do you sleep at night with all this stuff around?' Plant asked.

'Amazing dreams,' said Fullalove. 'Things come to me.'

'I can imagine.'

'I doubt it,' said Fullalove. 'Way beyond imagination what comes to me.'

He offered Plant the spare room. A narrow bed amidst the stacked document boxes stuffed with files.

No more expenses, no more happy hour, not a lot of choice.

'You might enjoy it,' Fullalove said.

'I might,' said Plant.

But it was terrible.

'Sleep well?' Fullalove asked.

'No.'

'That's good. Anything come to you in the night?'

'Nothing I care to remember.'

His eyes were gritty from the long drive, the lack of sleep, the appalling dreams. He drank some of Fullalove's particularly foul instant coffee and it did nothing for his stomach or his head. He had looked in the fridge and the breadbin and there was nothing that he cared to eat. He repressed all memory of it. He was not sure that he cared for the coffee, either.

'Ah well,' said Fullalove. 'Something came to me. Never fails.'

'Yes?' said Plant.

'First thing we go to the university, check out your friend Starr in the library. We go to the reference section. Open shelves. We don't have to ask a librarian. We don't have to borrow anything. No record, no personal contact. Forget the web. Forget electronics. That's all monitored. We just take a pen and paper, whiz in, whiz out, then you buy me breakfast. And no one need ever known we've been there.'

'And what do we look up?'

'Whatever's there. We start with the Marquis *Who's Who in the World.*'

'What if he doesn't have an entry?'

'You told me he was a data publisher, right? Right. He'll have an entry. Data publishers are into data. So they all make sure they get themselves listed. Data's their basic product.'

'If only it were so efficient,' said Plant.

'It is. And once you factor in personalities, you've got a reinforcement of motivation. People want to be accepted by society. Data publishers want to be like publishers of influence, dining with the rich and powerful. So they make sure they include themselves in the directories as a matter of principle. Preferably *Burke's Peerage* or the *Almanach de Gotha*. But if they can't make them, *Who's Who in the World* will do.'

'You sure?'

'Positive. They see the way their writers get listed in directories of novelists and dramatists and poets. So any chance to get themselves listed somewhere, they take it.'

'What if he's like the silent number type? Prefers to keep out of the public eye.'

'He'll still be listed. Data publishers all collect data on each other.'

'Do they?'

'They'd be mad not to. Know who your competition is. The information will be out there somewhere. Just a matter of thinking of the obvious place.'

They set off eventually. First thing. Fullalove's first thing. Eleven a.m. Not especially bright. But eager. Bushy-tailed like the possums in the Moreton bay fig trees in the university grounds. They cut through the quadrangle. The carillonist played 'Gaudeamus Igitur'. A parade of academics with nothing better to do filed into the Great Hall in their black and scarlet robes for degree day.

'Deep cover,' said Fullalove.

'Deep cover?'

'All those fancy gowns. Underneath them lies your everyday ordinary spook.'

'Is that so?' said Plant.

'The first lectureship in Oriental Studies at this revered institution was funded by the Department of Defence,' said Fullalove.

'How do you know?'

'The alumni magazine. There was an article about it. They seemed quite proud of the fact. The first professor of Oriental Studies was funded by the Department of Defence, too. This Professor Ackerman you were pursuing, he could've been some kind of spook.'

'You think?'

'In Asian Studies, could easily be. You've been paddling in murky waters, Plant.'

'I kind of figured that.'

'But you never figured how murky.'

'No.'

'Well, that's what we're about to find out, I guess.'

Groups of Asian graduates posed in their gowns and squares for photographs.

'Reckon they've all been recruited?' Fullalove asked.

'No idea.'

'Sure look like a lot of honey traps to me,' said Fullalove.

Trestle tables with white cloths and white cups and tea urns and sandwiches spread over the sacred lawns.

Fullalove eyed it all hungrily.

'Let's get this over with and grab some breakfast,' he said.

They left the repro-Gothic quadrangle and walked across to the disfunctionalist library. There was a huge open area of students sitting at computer terminals, clicking away at keyboards. But over at the reference shelves all was peace. No one was consulting anything.

Fullalove took the *Who's Who* down from its shelf and carried it across to a desk by the window. Sure enough he had been right. The entry was there. Starr, David. And between the Yale Law School and the publishing directorships, there it was: military service, Special Operations, Vietnam, 1971-74. Along with hobbies: collecting art, Asian exotica.

Plant looked out on the university lawns. The young in one another's arms. Mynah birds scavenging around them for crumbs. It was all too easy. All too hard. The eleven-hour drive and then, open sesame, public information. He could have wept.

Fullalove grinned happily to himself.

'Now you can buy me breakfast,' he said.

'You're a magnificent resource,' said Plant. 'A great data bank. Brilliant.'

'Like all the other banks I'll be putting up my fees.'

'I'd put up mine,' said Plant, 'but since I don't have any clients it wouldn't make much difference to my life.'

'If ever you do get any more,' said Fullalove, 'maybe you could point them my way for a spot of consultancy. Recommend they get a second opinion. It could make a difference to my life. Could make a difference to theirs.'

'When I do, I will,' said Plant. 'As it is, this is just a threat against my life, not a revenue generating item.'

'Not good,' said Fullalove. 'And the last time you came for information I seem to remember you were investigating your own client. The person who hired you.'

'Just taking precautions,' said Plant.

'Shows an admirable lack of trust. But you felt you couldn't charge that item to his account.'

'I've thought of a way since,' said Plant. 'So next time.'

'Next time, sure. I'm thinking about this time. The here and now,

Plant. Figure out a way you can charge menaces to your life and well-being and pass me along a slice, would you?'

'I will put my mind to it,' said Plant. 'I promise.'

Fullalove grunted. Sceptical grunts. Grunts rising from a deep uncharted ocean of scepticism.

39

Fullalove refused to eat anything on campus on the grounds that it would all be contaminated by the germ warfare and chemical weapons research that was inevitably going on there. He insisted on a café in Newtown. If he was to be around in daylight, and early, noon light at that, then it had to be amidst narrow streets and milling crowds and heavy traffic and clouds of diesel exhaust and carbon monoxide and parking problems.

'You could have looked that up in a local library,' said Fullalove. 'At the worst you would just have had to drive to Brisbane.'

'Yes,' said Plant.

'Ninety minutes.'

'Yes,' said Plant.

Fullalove laughed happily.

'You're losing it,' he said.

Plant didn't argue. It was all too true.

Fullalove ordered a cappuccino. 'You should only have these for breakfast. It's like a solecism to drink cappuccino in the afternoon or evening.'

Plant wondered whether to say 'I know' or 'is that so?'

'But there again,' Fullalove went on cheerily, 'if you'd gone to your local library you wouldn't have had the benefits of my advice.'

'Give me more while I'm here,' said Plant.

'So fill me in. What exactly are you up to?'

'I told you. I was hired to look for Ackerman. By his wife.'

'And now the case is closed.'

'I suppose so.'

'But you found Ackerman and you're off it.'

'Yes.'

'Mrs Ackerperson no longer retains your services.'

'No.'

'So why not leave it alone?'

'I felt Starr was kind of menacing me.'

'And how does he get into the picture?'

'Starr's company Lavi took over the series of books Ackerman and Ghosh edited. Ackerman might have gone on board with Starr and be mixed up in whatever Starr's mixed up in. Or he might have been investigating them when he disappeared.'

'I thought you said you found him.'

'I lost him again. But I got the impression Starr could have been looking for him too.'

'So Starr was menacing you to get you to leave it alone.'

'Could be,' said Plant.

'But you won't.'

'No.'

'You're an idiot.'

'Well, maybe I'll leave it alone when I know what it's about.'

'That could be too late,' said Fullalove. 'Tell me, how did you get this interesting commission?'

'I was recommended to Mrs Ackerman.'

'Recommended,' Fullalove laughed hollowly. 'Come on, Plant, who would recommend you?'

'A professor called Oates. I bumped into him on a job I was doing once.'

'Bumped into him or trod on his toes? Didn't that job have some security angle?'

'It was never clear.'

'Of course not. So we can take that as meaning yes. And now he recommends you on this dodgy business. Nice of him.'

'These things work by recommendation.'

'I'm sure,' said Fullalove. 'You reckon he recommended you because he thinks you're good?'

'Why else?'

'Or because he thinks you're hopeless and you won't find anything out?'

'Thank you,' said Plant.

'I'm not finished,' said Fullalove. 'There's also a third way, as American liberals used to believe in the Cold War.'

'Go on,' said Plant. 'I'm waiting.'

'Not that I ever found the idea of a third way persuasive.'

'Get to the point, Fullalove.'

'Not much to say really,' said Fullalove. 'Just the possibility that he thinks you're disposable.'

'Disposable?'

'Yeah, disposable. You know. You've got no dependents or anything. No significant assets. So if there was some kind of problem and you blundered into it, no one would notice if you just kind of disappeared. Would they, now?'

Plant looked at the shaven-headed, body-pierced, black-clad denizens of Newtown milling around him. It had touches of a late-medieval vision of the underworld. Sometimes he felt he already had disappeared, and the good times with him.

'With someone like your Professor Oates in the picture, you've got to ask who Ackerman was working for. Not that he needed formally to be working for anyone, of course. He could just have been an academic with progressive sympathies and good contacts. It would suit everyone just as well if he was on his own. They'd simply follow him and monitor him. Probably get better intelligence, that way.'

'Who would?'

'Everyone who wanted to. Hack into his computer, tap his phone, intercept his mail, put a microchip in his spectacle case, keep him under surveillance, get all the data that way. All his contacts. Everything he ever heard or talked about. Wired for sound. He would be like a remote-control robot, like one of those robots they use for bomb disposal. Or a pilotless drone. If it gets blown up, too bad, but no one else gets hurt. You're far enough back. Quite safe.'

'So he mightn't have been working for the government?'

'Maybe not. Not as far as he knew.'

'On the other hand, he might have been.'

'Them's your choices,' said Fullalove. 'What you've got to ask, if he was working for them, is why didn't they use one of their own people to look for him if they'd lost him. So the possibilities are he wasn't ever lost, or they didn't want him found, or it was too risky to use one of their own. Oates could be using Mrs Ackerperson to run you to see what you flush out.'

'That's what you suggested they were doing with Ackerman.'

'There's only so many plots,' said Fullalove. 'If you believe Vladimir Propp.'

'A disposable target. Like a surveillance drone.'

'There you are then,' said Fullalove.

'Where?' Plant asked.

'Where you wouldn't want to be, if you had any sense.'

There didn't seem to be a lot to say.

'So what would Starr's Special Operations in Vietnam, have been?'

'You know all this stuff, Plant. You've heard it all before. Sometimes I think you're like one of those kids who just likes to hear the same bedtime story over and over again. It gives them a feeling of reassurance. Is that what it's like?'

'Yes,' said Plant, 'that's what it's like. Give me reassurance, Fullalove.'

Fullalove sucked up some coffee and wiped the aerated froth from his lips with the back of his hand. He hadn't wiped away the grin. He sat back and smiled and held forth.

'Could be anything,' said Fullalove. 'He could have been working in the PX or he could have been working on some undercover programme for one of the agencies.'

'Which one?'

'What does it matter? They were all there, army intelligence, navy intelligence, CIA, NSA, DEA, secret service. He could have joined the CIA so he wouldn't be drafted into the army, and still ended up in Vietnam. You could take the fact that he lists it publicly to mean he's got no connection with that world now. Or it could be a bluff and he's working on the assumption that you wouldn't think if he was still working in the shadows he would say he worked in them before. Or it could be he was just an office boy in the catering corps but he wants to look like the traditional gentleman publisher. Yale and OSS. With his time in intelligence. Like Graham Greene. Or Robert Maxwell. Which raises the issue of credibility, of course. Let alone the issue of what is a gentleman. So we have to ask, is it true? Is it significant? Maybe he just spent a couple of years as a messenger boy and is trying to big-note himself.'

'But he could still be on someone's payroll.'

'Of course. Or he could have picked up some tips or profitable sidelines while he was there and struck out freelance.'

'Like drugs.'

'Or army surplus. Guns. Rockets. NBC.'

'The television network?'

'Nuclear, biological and chemical. Or he could just be running a publishing company and getting a subsidy for publishing certain sorts of product. And not publishing others. As you say, like a television network.'

'I'm surprised he listed it.'

'That's because you have a distorted view of social reality,' said Fullalove. 'He's proud of it. People are proud of doing the state some service.'

'I suppose so.'

'Never forget it,' said Fullalove. 'Apart from that, you're no nearer knowing what you want, are you?'

'Not much. Except we've got danger signals. Which is the most important thing. We've been warned.'

'You've been warned,' said Fullalove. 'Not me. Keep me out of it. Nothing to do with me.'

'How could I find out if he's still linked up with any of the agencies?'

'You could write and ask,' said Fullalove.

'Ask who?'

'Ask the agencies.'

'Without them knowing.'

'You try and do it covertly, they'll find out. You know that. Either way, covertly or openly, they're probably not going to be thrilled at your question.'

'Probably not.'

'Even if Starr's not working for them, they're the sort of people who resent questions. So you start asking and they'll start asking about you. And worse. If they're not already. Which they probably are. Since you've been pursuing Ackerman and sure as eggs he has to be either in the game or a subject of interest to them. Anyway, the point is Starr probably worked for them once. And once you've worked for them you're always going to be working for them. Full time, part time, freelance, maverick, rogue, whatever. Once you've worked for them they can always call on you and you can always call on them. Or call on someone you knew then. He's probably under contract, or his company is, one of his companies. Suits them, suits him. Good for business. Everything's done through cutouts and money-laundering anyway. Drugs for arms, what other currencies are there? So whether the government is running some operation or the government gets Starr to run it and doesn't want to know the details, is irrelevant. Best thing is to keep it that way. Irrelevant. Personally, I wouldn't ask anything more. I'd just take it that Starr's got connections and Ackerman's probably got connections and even if he doesn't, Oates does. All of which I'd try to avoid encountering, if I were you.'

'I think I already encountered them,' said Plant. 'When they kidnapped me.'

'Kidnapped you,' said Fullalove. 'Now that's something. What an exciting life you lead. Tell me. Buy me another cappuccino and another almond croissant and tell me.'

Plant did what he asked.

'So you had your warning,' said Fullalove. 'So leave it alone.'

'I don't think it was me they were after. I think they thought I was Ackerman.'

'You reckon? Why would they want to grab Ackerman?'

'Could be they're worried about the memoirs he's writing, or they think he's doing something he shouldn't be.'

'Like what? Whoever heard of an academic doing anything?'

'True,' Plant agreed. 'Unless of course the academic bit is just his cover and he's basically a spook. Maybe that's it. Maybe he's not doing what he's supposed to be doing. Maybe he's gone soft on terrorists. Or maybe he's a maverick, running some dope smuggling operation.'

'Or maybe he's just running away from his wife with his floozy and nobody cares a toss. Except Mrs Ackerperson, and she plans to put out a contract on him. She just wants to find him dead so she can get whatever assets he hasn't liquidated.'

'So why did they try and grab him?'

'They didn't. They grabbed you.'

'Why grab me?'

'Maybe because Starr felt you were bugging him. Or maybe Ackerman was out there doing some dirty tricks and someone didn't want you to find him. Or maybe they're just running some free enterprise drugs operation. You must have been in someone's way and they wanted to give you a fright, without letting on that they were looking for you. You're nosing around asking questions and they don't like lone nut investigators and they want to warn you off. You're trampling around in sensitive areas, getting in the way, muddying the waters. So leave it alone.'

'So what do you reckon is going on?'

'Nothing you need to know about,' said Fullalove. 'Whatever it is, let me tell you now so it doesn't come as a surprise, you're never going to find out. Not the truth. So there's guerrillas, terrorists they call them now, and so there's guns, they still call them guns, and so there's drugs and so there's intelligence agencies and they all work together in a symbiotic relationship to maintain the new world order, and more than that you wouldn't want to know, and never will know. Think yourself lucky you're still alive. Take the warning. No one ever finds out the truth in things like this, and why would you want to? You're like those crazies who keep on about the Kennedy assassinations, or Jim Jones in Guyana, or Lockerbie, or Port Arthur, or the Oklahoma bombing, or sweet September or Bali. You'll never find out the truth by digging around. These are conspiracies, man. And they can't be resolved. You're not meant to find out. Not the detail. The details are all contradictory and they're just meant to confuse. And you don't need the detail anyway. You just need the one question. Who benefits? And don't even ask it out loud. You know the answer. Who always benefits? You know it goes on. You're not going to stop it. You don't even know who anyone's working for any more. As if it would make any difference. Say Starr's a maverick or Ackerman's a maverick, aren't they all mavericks, anyway? Selling arms for drugs to everyone. The more the merrier. Keeps everything in flux. Keeps the blacks and the unemployed narcotised at home, arms the rebels so the Philippines government can get more military aid, which helps business, more armament contracts. The emergency serves to bolster ruling class rule, close down dissent, prevent land reform, impoverish the peasants, repress the unions. So you've got cheap labour. Good environment for global capitalism.'

'Are you warning me off?' Plant asked.

'Sure am.'

'Why?'

'For your own good,' said Fullalove.

'Yeah?' said Plant. 'So whose side are you on, Fullalove?'

'Whose side?' said Fullalove. 'What are you talking about, man? When are you going to realise there aren't any sides any more, Plant, even if there ever were? There's only one side now.'

40

The dawn chorus continued well into the morning. The kookaburras kicked it off before light broke, then the currawongs and crows took up the challenge. This was one of the mornings the crows really got into it. Plant could not tell whether they were cries of derision or cries of delight. Sneers of superiority from the high treetops. Or had they spotted some dead animal and were singing a lengthy graceless grace before sticking their beaks in and tearing it apart. In the bushes the honeyeaters and fly-catchers fluttered and darted around, adding their own chirruping. But none of it was loud enough to drown the sound of the phone.

He needn't have answered it. Apart from the necessities of work and income. He could just have pretended that he didn't hear it. He could just have disregarded it, not even bothering with pretence. Who was he pretending to other than himself? But he answered it.

'Ghosh here. You are needed most urgently in Singapore.'

'Am I, by golly?' said Plant.

'You must come straight away,' said Ghosh.

'How do I do that?'

'We will reimburse your fare.'

'Not on,' said Plant. 'Ticket in advance. No reimbursement.'

'All right, ticket,' said Ghosh, impatiently, gracelessly, as gracelessly as the crows.

'A return,' said Plant, to be sure.

There was a delay, and then a reluctant, 'If you insist.'

'I certainly do,' said Plant.

Ghosh grunted.

'Did I hear that correctly? You were just going to get me a single?'

'You might have wanted to go on to London. Or somewhere. Athens. Kolkata. Take a holiday. Go sightseeing.'

'I'd still need to come back.'

'Perhaps,' said Ghosh, doubtfully.

The wompoo pigeons pecked around beneath the trees. The scrub wren sat on the wooden garden bench. The honeyeaters ate honey from the bottle brush. Why would he want to be anywhere but where he was?

'Why would I want to be in Singapore?'

'You are needed at this very moment,' said Ghosh.

'Why's that?'

'Mrs Ackerman is in gaol.'

Plant pondered the correct reply. He eschewed irony. He suppressed the joy from his voice. He avoided hilarity.

'In Singapore?'

'No, in Bangkok.'

'So why am I wanted in Singapore? Who wants me?'

'She does. I do. Professor Ackerman does.'

'Is he in gaol too?'

'No, he cannot be found.'

'So why Singapore?'

'I am in Singapore,' said Ghosh.

'And what am I wanted for?'

'To discuss the situation.'

'Just to discuss it.'

'To discuss a course of action.'

'Action?' said Plant. He was not sure he liked the sound of action. 'I don't do gaol breaks.'

'Legal action,' said Professor Ghosh.

'Meaning what?'

'Arranging her defence.'

'Can't Professor Ackerman do that?'

'I have already told you, he cannot be found.'

'Why not get a lawyer?'

'She needs to talk to you.'

'So why don't I fly to Bangkok?'

'I will explain when I see you.'

'That will be the day,' said Plant. 'Why can't you explain now? Why is she in gaol?'

'She was arrested at the airport.'

'Don't tell me she was smuggling drugs.'

'No, good heavens no,' said Professor Ghosh. He sounded quite shocked.

'Art works?'

'No, no, not at all, nothing like that. Someone was found dead.'

'Dead?' said Plant. 'Murder? Who did she murder?'

'Mr Starr.'

'Starr? She murdered Starr.'

'Yes. But she didn't do it.'

'She murdered Starr but she didn't do it.'

'No, no, don't be ridiculous. Starr was found dead. But Mrs Ackerman would not have done it.'

'Would not, now,' said Plant. 'So who did?'

'It could have been anybody.'

'I suppose it could,' said Plant.

It was not long ago that Ghosh had threatened to do it, Plant recalled. But that was not the sort of thing to mention on the phone.

'It may not have been murder,' said Ghosh.

'But Mrs Ackerman is in gaol for it.'

'She is being held as a witness.'

'She watched it happen?' said Plant.

'I will explain when you come here,' said Ghosh.

The kookaburras gave a raucous laugh from the trees. They may not have meant anything by it. They may just have been signalling it was going to rain.

Ghosh met him at Changi airport. A quaint old world courtesy; or a neurotic anxiety to make sure he arrived and to make sure where he was staying.

'You haven't booked accommodation?' Ghosh asked.

'I thought you would be arranging that.'

'Yes, of course, as we arranged,' said Ghosh. 'No problems.'

'So what is the problem?' Plant asked.

'We will find a taxi and I will tell you.'

Finding a taxi meant standing outside the terminal at the taxi rank and getting into one. It sped into town. No traffic jams. Were there just fewer people than other cities or was it better organised, or had he come at a good time of day?

'So tell me what's happening,' said Plant.

Ghosh put a conspiratorial finger to his lips.

'Later,' he said.

'In the fullness of time,' said Plant.

'It is very serious,' said Ghosh, censoriously.

'I figured it might be,' said Plant.

'You should know the taxi drivers listen in to everything. They are all security or police or army reserve. They can be summoned at a moment's notice on the taxi radio. Mobilised immediately.'

'I got mobilised pretty fast,' said Plant.

'There is not a moment to lose,' said Ghosh. But he still didn't tell Plant anything.

The taxi took them onto the National University campus and pulled up at the Visitors' Lodge.

'I have put you up on campus,' said Ghosh. Somewhat self-evidently.

Was it because Ghosh could not drag himself away from the ambience of learning, or because it was cheaper?

'I thought you would prefer that.'

'Thank you,' said Plant. Though if Ghosh had had Plant's preferences in mind, wouldn't he have consulted what they were?

'Not a hall of residence full of noisy Chinese students, never fear. You cannot imagine how much noise they can make.' He laughed, blackly. 'I would not wish that on you. No. I would not wish that on you. No. The Visitors' Lodge. It is quiet. Away from the noise of the city.'

Plant wondered if he wouldn't have preferred the city. But it was too late.

'I can eat there?'

'No. Not there. Unless you cook. There are cooking facilities. I am sure you will be very comfortable. It is cheaper too. Not that that concerns you. Since you are not paying.' He said it almost resentfully, more than almost, definitely resentfully.

'Is there anywhere to eat?'

'Of course there is. Lots of places.'

'On campus.'

'Of course. The student cafeterias.'

'Anywhere else?'

'The student cafeterias are excellent. Very good. Very cheap. Or there is the faculty club. But they might not admit you. Or there is the Guild. They will probably admit you there. It is the alumni club.'

'Are you staying at the Visitors' Lodge too?'

'No,' said Ghosh.

'Too expensive? Or not good enough?'

'I am staying with a colleague,' said Ghosh. 'He is a professor here.'

Ghosh checked him in and came along to his rooms. A bedroom. A living-room. Cooking facilities. Television.

'This is a disaster,' said Ghosh.

'It will do,' said Plant.

'Not this. This is excellent.'

'Whatever you say,' said Plant.

'But this other business. It is a tragedy.'

Plant nodded. He was not sure of Starr as a creature of tragic dimensions.

'I came here immediately. It was a matter of calling a meeting of the board at the first opportunity,' said Ghosh.

'The board?' said Plant. 'Of Legal and Visual?'

No doubt somebody would have to. But it hardly seemed Ghosh's business. Or his own. Indeed, it seemed nothing to do with him. Or Ghosh, for that matter.

'Legal and Visual?' said Ghosh. 'What on earth are you talking of? How can that be our responsibility?'

'That was what I wondered.'

'Wondered?' said Ghosh. 'What were you wondering? Our editorial board, of course.'

'Your editorial board?' asked Plant.

'Yes, of course. The South East Asian Library of Current Affairs. Our monograph series. We must reconvene it. Ackerman is missing. Bowles is dead, of course. But there is this excellent fellow at the National University. He is willing to come on board. I have spoken to him. I have spoken to them all.'

'All?'

'The new board.'

'I thought you were no longer on it. I thought Bowles had dropped you and Ackerman.'

'But he is dead now,' said Ghosh, with undoubted satisfaction. 'And Starr too. Somebody must take control.'

'I suppose so.'

'There is no doubt. It is a matter of public responsibility.'

'So who owns it now?'

Ghosh dismissed the question with an airy wave of the hand.

'That is not important. What is important is to maintain editorial continuity. I have found a publisher in India who will take it on. I was at school with him. I remember him as a little boy in short trousers. Even earlier. Just a bare backside. Now he controls a publishing empire. For a small subsidy he has agreed to take over.'

'And Ackerman agrees?'

'That is why we are meeting.'

'But does he agree?' Plant persisted, Ghosh's airy assumption of responsibility wafting round him like mesmeric ether.

'He will see reason,' said Ghosh, 'when he reappears.'

'And if he doesn't?'

'Doesn't what?'

'See reason. Or reappear.'

'Of course he will,' said Ghosh.

'I guess it would be a way of publishing his memoirs.'

'Absolutely,' said Ghosh.

'But can you do that?' Plant asked. 'I thought you had handed the series over to Starr.'

'But now he is dead we cannot let it just lapse. We must resuscitate it.'

'Unlike Starr,' said Plant.

Ghosh said nothing.

'So who actually owns the series?'

Ghosh gave an airy wave.

'What is there to own? Anyone could own it. Ownership is not the issue. It is the team. The editorial board. That is what matters.'

'What about your agreement with Starr?'

'What about it? Nothing has been signed.'

'Really?'

'Of course not. There is no necessity to sign unless you have to. There was no urgency. It was a matter of seeing how things developed. Ackerman may have handed the series over but I signed nothing.'

'I see.'

'If things were not done correctly, it is for us to take it back.'

'Was that in the agreement?'

'There was no agreement.'

'I am beginning to get the picture.'

'And things were not being done correctly. Bowles, for instance. That was a disaster. A tragic disaster.'

'It was a sad way to go,' said Plant. 'Dying like that.'

'Death?' said Ghosh. 'There was nothing tragic about that. Anyone can get himself killed. The tragedy was in appointing him general editor. An appalling move. To such a sensitive position. I realised then that we had to act.'

Plant looked at him with alarm. Did act mean what he hoped it didn't mean? Had action been taken with Bowles and Starr? And Ackerman, too, missing again? All for the publishing project?

'So what action did you have in mind?'

'Calling a board meeting, of course,' said Ghosh. 'At the earliest opportunity.'

'And you've called it?'

'That is why I am here.'

'What does Ackerman say?'

'Ackerman? How can he say anything since he has disappeared?'

'So you don't have his agreement.'

'I have his proxy.'

'About calling the board?'

'For everything.'

'So how does this involve me?' Plant asked.

'Involve you?'

'What do you need me to do?'

'I do not need you to do anything. It is Mrs Ackerman who needs you.'

'So why am I here?'

'You will be on hand for when we finish our editorial meeting. That is why I asked you to come to Singapore before going to Bangkok.'

'That's number one priority, is it? Your meeting.'

'What else?' said Ghosh.

'And Starr?'

'He is already dead. No amount of haste will save him. Let the dead bury the dead.'

'I'll make a point of it. And Mrs Ackerman?'

'We shall see if Professor Ackerman comes to the meeting. Then he will brief you. If not, I shall.'

'Why not brief me now?'

'I have much too much to do. Indeed, I must rush off now. This very instant, if not before. Mrs Ackerman will keep. She will not be going anywhere. When we have established the new board and our future direction, then I will call you.'

And off he rushed.

Was this rabid insanity or the academic norm? Plant reflected. He reflected without anxiously searching after a decision. Were they exclusive categories, anyway? Ackerman having handed over the series, Ghosh was now blandly setting about repossessing it by moral right, like some sort of United Nations intervention. Maybe it was the thing to do. Maybe it was how things were done. Maybe decisive action in the world of captains of industry, or whatever Starr had been, was the only way to go. It might work. Who would want to stop Ghosh? Who would want to keep the series? Would Ackerman welcome it back? Would Ackerman reappear, for that matter? The mere fact of Starr's death and Mrs Ackerman's incarceration seemed as nothing before Ghosh's imperatives.

Plant put the air-conditioning on medium, lay on the bed, and thought about the situation. He was soon asleep.

41

When he awoke it was dark and he was chilled from the air-conditioning. He opened the fridge hopefully. There was nothing in it. He went up to the lobby. There was no one there. He called out but no one came. He went outside and the heat and humidity overwhelmed him. He went back inside and sat on a lobby chair. He thought about Ghosh. How come no one had killed him?

A taxi drew up and dropped off a couple of people. They came into the lobby and headed for the staircase. The taxi drove away.

'Excuse me,' Plant asked. 'Is there anywhere to eat round here?'

They suggested he went into town.

'How do I do that?' Plant asked.

'Get a taxi,' they said.

'How do I do that?' Plant asked again.

They suggested he waited until one dropped someone off, and then grab it. Plant waited.

In the end one came and Plant got in.

'Where you go?' the driver asked him.

'I don't know,' said Plant. 'Somewhere to eat.'

'You want somewhere expensive or not expensive?'

'Not expensive,' said Plant. He could see trouble with Ghosh over expenses already.

'You try hawkers' market?'

'Sounds good,' said Plant.

It was. A central space with chairs and tables, and round the edges the food stalls, Chinese and Malayan and Indonesian and Indian and seafood, and a stall selling beer. He did a preliminary walk round. The food was cheap, amazingly cheap. The beer was expensive. He ordered Singapore noodles since he was in Singapore. And a Tiger beer. For a while what he saved on food prices compensated for what he spent on beer. Until he drank more than he was eating. And why not? He sat in the sultry evening and drank more.

Ghosh phoned.

'We must talk.'

It was mid-morning and Plant was lying in bed, jet-lagged and hung-over.

'Sure,' he said. 'I'm at the Visitors' Lodge.'

'I know that,' said Ghosh. 'Come up here to the Guild.'

'I don't know where it is,' said Plant. 'Couldn't we meet here?'

'No problem,' said Ghosh. 'Go out of the front door, turn right. A couple of minutes. I will be waiting for you.'

He hung up.

Perhaps he wanted to avoid surveillance. Perhaps he wanted to avoid a tracer on the phone call. Perhaps he was just a peremptory, arrogant old bastard. And still alive, Plant reflected. It was amazing how some people survived.

Plant walked out into the equatorial humidity. He turned right. The air was like soup. Thick, warm soup. Minestrone, maybe. Or mulligatawny. Within half a dozen paces every pore was dripping sweat. Half a dozen more and he was awash. He trudged along the paths, marveling at how the students seemed to walk past unaffected by the heat. He tried to keep in the shade but it made little difference to the humidity. No wonder Ghosh suggested Plant do the walking. Cunning old bugger.

The grounds were rather splendid. Rolling lawns. Spreading trees. And men in masks and goggles, their heads wrapped with a cloth, looking like terrorists, whipper-snippering the grass. They looked extraordinarily menacing. He felt like hiring one to run the whipper-snipper over Ghosh.

Ghosh was waiting in the lobby, all impatience and solicitude.

'Where have you been? You didn't walk? Poor fellow, you should have got the shuttle, it costs almost nothing, it drops you off right here.'

'You didn't tell me there was one.'

'Everyone knows there's a shuttle. Ah well, you know now, you can take it back, come and buy yourself a drink.'

They sat on the terrace overlooking the swimming pool.

'Ackerman did not come to the meeting,' said Ghosh.

'I thought you said he'd disappeared. Again.'

'Yes, I did. He has.'

'So why did you expect him to come?'

'I didn't expect he would,' said Ghosh. 'But he might have come. It is a matter of importance to resume publishing.'

'How would he know the meeting was on if he's disappeared?'

'I left him a message.'

'So you know where he is?'

'No, I have no idea where he is. He has an answering service.'

'Now you tell me.'

'It is confidential.'

'How long has he had it?'

'I am not sure exactly.'

'Long?'

'A while, why?'

'When I saw you in Kolkata, did he have it then?'

'Quite possibly.'

'But you didn't tell me.'

'It was given me in confidence. It was not to be disclosed to anyone.'

'His wife had hired me to find him.'

'Especially not to his wife.'

'I need another beer,' said Plant.

'Go ahead,' said Ghosh, polite as ever.

Plant went.

When he came back from the bar he began again. Put frustration behind you. Stay detached. The wisdom of the East.

'Tell me about Mrs Ackerman,' he said.

'It's appalling,' said Ghosh. 'They have arrested her.'

'Who have?'

'They say they haven't arrested her, they're holding her, but it's the same thing.'

'Who arrested her?' Plant tried again.

'The Thai authorities.'

'Authorities?'

'Police, of course,' Ghosh snapped. 'I don't know which ones. At the airport when she was leaving. It's appalling, she had nothing to do with it, it is sheer mischievousness. Malice.'

'Nothing to do with what?'

'With Starr.'

'So what happened to him?'

'He was found dead. In a hotel room. He hanged himself, poor fellow.'

'Hanged himself?' said Plant. 'So why are they holding Mrs Ackerman?'

'Absolutely,' said Ghosh, 'it's ridiculous.'

'Was she there or something? You said she was a witness.'

'She was the last person to see him alive. Or the first to see him dead. One or the other.'

'But if he hanged himself?'

'I know. As I said, it's ridiculous, it's a set-up. I got out right away. You must help her.'

'You were there?' said Plant.

'In Bangkok, yes,' said Ghosh. 'I was hoping to meet Alec but he did not turn up. There was nothing I could do there. Better to be a free man helping from here than in gaol and unable to do anything over there.'

'Why were they going to put you in gaol?' Plant asked. 'Did you see him in his final hours, too?'

'I could not afford to take the risk.'

'You figured there was a risk?'

'There's always a risk in those sorts of cases,' said Ghosh.

'What sort of cases are those?'

'You think I should have stayed in Bangkok, visiting the women's gaol twice a day, in that traffic, camping out there maybe until maybe after a day or two I'd be in the men's gaol, so not visiting her twice a day, not visiting anyone at all, not able to do anything, is that what you are recommending?'

'Put like that,' said Plant, 'I can appreciate your estimation of the situation.'

'Estimation of the situation,' Ghosh growled. He looked at Plant like he'd like to fail him. One of those firm, fail marks. Nothing borderline. A mark to ensure he was out of history forever and could never return. But he needed him.

'Look,' said Ghosh generously, 'let's not worry about me, let's worry about you. You must go to Bangkok and sort this out.'

'Sort it out?' said Plant. 'That could be kind of difficult.'

'Find out about lawyers. She needs help.'

'You want me to visit Mrs Ackerman.'

'If you would.'

There were people, he knew, who would find the idea of visiting a Thai women's gaol a turn-on.

'Why me?'

'Because I cannot find Professor Ackerman.'

'Have you looked for him?'

'Of course. I cannot find him anywhere. Where would I begin to look? And immediately there are other things to be done. Immediately someone must speak to Mrs Ackerman and find out what is going on.'

'And your idea is it should be me.'

'I cannot possibly do it,' said Ghosh. 'And she knows you. You worked for her before.'

'I'm not sure how well we got along by the end,' said Plant.

'Who is sure with Mrs Ackerman?' said Ghosh. 'Who ever is?'

Plant gazed idly at the swimmers in the pool.

'Have you eaten?' Ghosh asked. And without waiting for a reply told Plant that the best place was where the students ate.

'And staff for that matter. Excellent value. People come in especially for one of the noodle stalls.'

'And it's good?'

'Excellent value.'

'Is it far?' Plant asked warily.

'Just across the road. Come, I'll show you.'

He took Plant out through the air-conditioned cool of the lounges, back into the heat and glare.

'Just up the hill there, along the track, up the steps, where those roofs are.' He gestured with his walking stick.

'Right,' said Plant.

He stood there. Ghosh showed no sign of movement.

'Keep in touch, then,' he said.

'You're not eating?'

'No, no, I have to see someone, the editorial board, you know.'

A taxi dropped someone off and Ghosh leapt into it, surprisingly agile for a man with a walking-stick.

There was an even greater variety of stalls than at the hawkers' market. Noodles, curries, stir-fries, hot-pots. Juices, teas, cakes. Ghosh had neglected to tell him which was the stall people came to visit from miles away. But they all looked appetizing. He walked along the line of them and round the corner and back again. He found one that was totally vegetarian and then just pointed at things that looked good. It was all good. He had to concede that Ghosh knew what he was talking about. In this context, at least.

Then there was a crash of thunder and the heavens opened and the rain poured down. It was dry beneath the roofing, though scuds of rain blew in at the tables near the edges. There was no way of leaving without getting totally drenched. Plant went back along the line of stalls. No one served beer. He ordered tea and it came blacker than any tea he had ever seen, with a spoonful of condensed milk added and stirred in before he could protest. He told himself it was an experience. And the thunderstorm was an experience too. It was all an experience. But he would still like to have Ghosh whipper-snipped.

In the end the rain stopped as it always did. The clouds dispersed. Plant walked back down to the Visitors' Lodge, plumes of steam rising from the road and paths as the equatorial sun evaporated the moisture. He opened his duty-free bottle of wine and drank a couple of glasses, lay on the bed and fell asleep. Until he was woken by Ghosh phoning him with details of his flight to Bangkok the next day.

42

It was an experience visiting the women's gaol. More experience. Much as he had expected. The inmates whistled and waved at him. 'Hi man,' they called, 'you wanna fuck? You wanna joint, man? You wanna fuck for a joint? You wanna joint for a fuck?'

Mrs Ackerman was her usual gracious self, if somewhat more importunate.

'You have to get me out of here,' she said.

No 'Thank you for visiting,' no 'Did you have a good trip?'

'Did you kill him?' he asked.

It was a brusque opening, he realised. But he wanted to get things straight from the beginning. So he tried straight questions. There was no reason to expect results, but it at least saved time. Skipped the polite conversation. Not that there was much sign of any of that.

'Don't be ridiculous,' she said. 'Why would I kill Starr?'

Plant shrugged.

'Anyway, why would I tell you if I had?'

Plant tried a calming smile.

'You're not a lawyer,' she said.

'No,' he agreed. 'I'm not a lawyer so I can't see that I can be much help.'

'Yes, you can,' she said.

'So who killed him?'

'No one killed him. He killed himself.'

'Suicide?' said Plant. 'He didn't seem the suicidal type to me. Quite the opposite. More homicidal.'

'Shut up, Plant,' said Mrs Ackerman. Gaol had not shaken her imperious authority.

'He was into' – she gestured – 'you know, weird stuff. You know.'

'Not really,' said Plant.

'Bondage, flagellation, hanging.'

'Is that so?'

'Everybody knows,' she snapped. 'What do you think he came to Thailand and the Philippines for? The climate?'

'I didn't know,' said Plant.

'I can't help your ignorance of the world,' she said. 'Just take it from me, it was well known. He had people on twenty-four hour standby round the world. Ready to come to his hotel room and whip him. Tie him up. Help him hang himself.'

'So he called someone up and they topped him?'

'It was an accident.'

'Sure?'

'It's risky stuff, what he was into.'

'Clearly.'

'Don't be glib,' she said.

There were other conversations going on. Some were affectionate, couples gazing into each other's eyes. Others seemed fraught and combative. The warders looked on impassively.

'So why did they pick you up?'

'I was staying in the same hotel. I'd arranged to see him. I got this call to go to his room. I knocked. He didn't answer. The door was unlocked. When I went in he was already dead. Hanging there. There was nothing I could do. So I took his address book and left.'

'So who called you?'

'I thought it was a secretary. But it was probably some little bar girl. Setting me up so they got me on CCTV.'

'You took his address book?'

'Yes.'

'Why did you do that?'

'It was out on the table by the phone. I thought it might have Alec's number. It didn't. But it has all Starr's bar girls in it. You've got to call them. Get them to make sworn statements. That Starr was into weird stuff. If we can show the investigating authorities a bunch of statutory declarations that Starr was into risky sex, they'll stop treating it as anything other than an accident.'

'And let you go.'

'Yes.'

'So where's the address book?'

'I put it in the mail. I sent it to Prem and told him to hold onto it till someone collected it.'

'Why did you do that?'

'I didn't want anyone finding it on me. I knew I'd been seen. It seemed the safest thing to do.'

'Why Prem?'

'Because he was in Bangkok. I wouldn't want to send it back to Australia, would I?'

'So why not get Prem to fix the affidavits?'

'Because he lives here.'

'That should make it easier.'

'Not necessarily. He wouldn't want to get involved. It's too risky.'

'But it's not risky for me?'

'It's what you do,' she said.

Maybe it was. But he noticed she hadn't answered the question.

'So you want me to pick up the address book and make a few calls and organise a few affidavits.'

'Precisely.'

'Why were you visiting Starr?'

'I thought he would know where Alec was.'

'You're still looking for Alec?'

'He's my husband, isn't he? I wanted to find out what his intentions are.'

'And that's all?'

'What else would it be?'

'It still doesn't explain why you were checking up on Starr.'

'I wasn't.'

'Searching his company records. In my name.'

'Oh, that.'

'Yes, that.'

'I wasn't checking on Starr. I thought Alec might be on one of his company boards or something.'

'And?'

'And that would give me an idea where he was hiding out.'

'Why do it under my name?'

'I just happened to have your Amex card on hand at the time. I thought I'd keep it all on the same set of accounts.'

'Really?'

'And I didn't want to alert Alec.'

'Why? You were planning to serve divorce papers? Or string him up too?'

'Just get the address book and organise the stat decs,' she said.

'They're quite fetching, those overalls,' he said. 'They suit you. Are they prison issue?'

'As a writer,' said Prem, 'perhaps I see things academics are unable to see. Or prefer not to see. A training in selective vision is the basis of academic life, or so it seemed to me in those years when I was a university student.'

'And that was a lot of years.'

'Indeed.'

'I can think of writers who have selective vision, too,' said Plant.

Prem laughed.

'Only the successful ones,' he said.

'So what do you see that Ackerman and Ghosh might miss?'

'Where to begin?' said Prem. 'Where to begin?'

'What about Starr?'

'One step ahead till the very end.'

'Ahead of what?' Plant asked.

'The tax authorities.'

'Were they after him?'

'Oh yes. Mr Starr was under investigation. Had you not heard?'

'No.'

'Perhaps it was not reported in the English language press,' said Prem. 'It was widely reported here. Once he was found dead.'

'So what does that mean?'

'That he made a lucky escape?' Prem offered. 'What it usually means is that when the authorities find difficulty in proving your crimes, they examine your tax returns. Al Capone, Edmund Wilson. If they cannot get witnesses to say you smuggled drugs or ran guns or laundered money or bribed politicians or thought forbidden thoughts, they can get accountants to calculate you underestimated your tax liability.'

'So they were after him?'

'Perhaps. Or perhaps his name came up in the course of some wider investigation. One of our periodic crackdowns. If he had been lower on the pecking order he might have been peremptorily shot.'

'Really.'

'It has been known to happen.'

'So he chose a good moment to make an exit.'

'Perhaps,' said Prem. 'If he chose. Or perhaps he was helped to the exit before he could help the authorities with their inquiries. Strangled by some thug and then strung up.'

'When you say some thug,' said Plant, 'you don't necessarily mean an Indian.'

Ghosh as a thugee performing ritual strangulation. Was it impossible?

'Just a manner of speaking.'

'So it's not exactly clear what happened.'

'Would you expect it to be?' Prem asked.

'Well,' said Plant, 'at least we know now he was up to something.'

'Did you ever doubt it?' Prem asked. 'Even if he was only being creative about his taxes.'

'That was his business,' said Plant, 'tax law. I'm surprised he got caught.'

'He was only under investigation,' said Prem. 'Perhaps he would have been exonerated. Honourably. The story only came out because he was found dead.'

'And are we sure he is dead?'

'So Mrs Ackerman says.'

'She saw him.'

'So she says.'

'Why did she entrust his address book to you?'

Prem flattened the back of his hair. Nothing was out of place.

'I imagine because her husband would have wanted no part of it. Ever the self-effacing academic, he seems to be missing again. Or so you tell me. She couldn't give it to Bowels, alas poor Bowels, also missing. Terminally. Who else? She knew of me through Alec.'

'Of you,' said Plant. 'You never met her.'

'Maybe once or twice. I cannot be sure. European women all look alike.'

'Really,' said Plant.

'It is like wine tasting. You have to develop a palate. You have to learn to discriminate. But if, say, you are not a wine drinker, you have no motivation to develop your powers of observation and comparison and discrimination. Let alone taste.'

'Is that true?'

'Never trust the teller, trust the tale, as your D.H. Lawrence put it.'

'One of the sayings of my people,' said Plant.

'Then we understand,' said Prem.

'I'm not sure that I do.'

'No matter. The important thing is that you take possession of this wretched address book. As of now.'

He pushed it across the glass table with an outstretched finger.

'Then perhaps I can sleep peacefully in my bed. While you sample the delights available at the mere call of the telephone. And an adequate credit card limit. I wouldn't think any of them would come cheap.'

'You know what's in it.'

'Of course. Everyone knew Starr's tastes. It is to be assumed his private address book would record such phone numbers as he did not want in his office data base. Or his home one. Why else would he maintain such a retro affectation? Because of a sentimental attachment to the book in the electronic age? Or because he wanted something that could not be hacked into electronically? Why else would he carry it around?'

'Even if everyone knew his tastes.'

Prem shrugged.

'They might know his tastes but not the numbers. Or not all of them. So whenever he felt the urge he pulled out his little black book and asked himself "Where am I?" and looked under Bangkok and dialed Mimi or Fifi or Moo Moo or Frou Frou.'

'Mimi or Fifi,' said Plant, 'Moo Moo or Frou Frou. I like that. They sound delightful.'

'Enjoy,' said Prem, 'as they say in your country.'

It was a neat little address book. Bound in some dead animal's skin. Probably an exotic dead animal. Or bird. Or reptile. A threatened species. He had asked Mrs Ackerman was she sure it was Starr's notebook.

'Of course,' she snapped, 'It was the same leather as his boots.'

'You checked?' he asked, somewhat incredulously.

'Just get it and do what you have to do, please, Mr Plant. I am not in the mood for pleasantries.'

'Fair enough,' said Plant.

Plant sat in his hotel room and opened the address book. He started at the beginning. At A. Anna. No surname. A number with a Thai prefix. He flicked through to I. Imelda. Philippines prefix. Of course they might be different girls. Not uncommon names. He tried B. Bangkok. Prem was right. Mimi. Fifi. Moo Moo. Frou Frou. Bingo. There they were.

It had seemed like the assignment any adolescent would drool over, phoning up working girls and semi-professionals round the world and asking them about what they specialised in. Describe the weirdest sex you do. How much do you charge? When can I come and interview you? Or do you prefer to make house calls? About Mr Starr, but we don't have to confine it to that.

Once he would have thought it was a great idea. Now he was not so sure. Now he could probably just phone Anna-Imelda. She would no doubt know the other professionals and part-timers in the trade. How many affidavits did it have to be, anyway? If she gave one under each name she used, how many would that make? Enough, probably. Assuming she hadn't disappeared along with Professor Ackerman.

He went down to the bar and there she was. In full voice. Miss Anna. Happy hour was here again. He sat down and ordered a beer, buy one, get one free, and waited till she finished her set.

43

Anna-Imelda was singing 'Smoke Gets in Your Eyes.' Plant sat there with his beer and his peanuts in a cloud of unknowing. At the end of her set he held up his glass in greeting and fabricated a smile. She walked over.

'You left Manila without saying goodbye,' she said.

'I could say the same about your departure from Baguio City. That's twice you've drugged me.'

She pouted her lips.

'Nobody has to drug you, Plant, you drug yourself perfectly willingly and absolutely voluntarily every time.'

There was an element of truth in it, he could not deny.

'Eagerly,' she added. 'Greedily,' she tossed in for good measure.

He sipped his beer.

'I expected to see you in Manila. I looked for you every happy hour.'

'But no joy was to be found,' he said. 'I was put on a plane and sent home.'

She pouted again.

'Have a seat, have a drink,' said Plant.

'I don't drink when I'm working.'

'Ah, you're working,' said Plant. 'I thought this might have been the recreation part. Kind of like karaoke after a hard day knocking out tourists.'

'You're not a tourist,' she said.

'True enough,' said Plant.

'What brings you here?'

'You don't know?' said Plant.

'I can guess.'

'I'm sure you can,' he said. 'Or someone keeps you informed. You got time for a talk?'

'You know the drill,' she said.

He was not sure that he did. But he knew how to put a bold front on things.

'Afterwards?'

She nodded.

'Not the Eternal Night again,' said Plant. 'If possible.'

'Everything is possible,' she said.

'If you can afford it.'

'If that is how you want to look at it,' she said, 'that will be the reality you create.'

Reality, said Plant, chewing his peanuts, drinking his draught beer. He said it to himself. Anna-Imelda was back with her microphone and the keyboard player was back at the keyboard. Reality seemed a very alien concept. What could have led anyone to create all this?

She launched into 'Bewitched, Bothered and Bewildered.'

Plant entertained himself by dozing in his room in front of the television until it was time to go down and face the music again. It was no longer happy hour, just one beer for the price of several, hotel prices. He ordered one and sipped at it as she sang her way through the usual numbers. They were familiar enough now for him to have sung along with them if he had been a singing man, but he wasn't. He just tapped his foot once in a while to keep the blood flowing through his legs. But even bad things all come to an end, and there she was, standing in front of him, waiting impatiently as if he had been holding her up.

'Let's go,' she said.

He had expected a taxi and a nightclub, but she headed for the lift and down to the car park and across to a black Isuzu Mysterious Utility. It looked like a serious four-wheel drive, not just a toy sports and recreation vehicle, but one that would handle off-road conditions. He wasn't sure he liked the implications. He tried to tell himself they had bought it for the name. Just the sort of vehicle for a whimsical retired academic and his unsmiling chanteuse.

'So what low dive is it tonight?' he asked. Playfully. To set a playful tone and reduce the tension. Plant's tension.

'You want to fuck around or you want to talk?' said Anna-Imelda.

'I think we need to talk.'

'So don't fuck around.'

She drove up the ramp and out onto the street.

'Where are we going?'

'You'll see when we get there,' she said.

'And when will that be?'

'Hour and a half,' she said.

'That long?'

'Uh-huh.'

'We talk on the way?'

'Save it till we get there,' she said.

They were in the Bangkok late night traffic. Crawling along. No radio, no tapes, maybe she'd had enough music. No conversation. No sleep either, the suspension was too hard. It let you know this was a serious vehicle.

Plant had no idea where they were and Anna-Imelda wasn't talking. The city gave way to suburbs, squatters' slums, golf courses, country. Small towns, villages, rows of shop-houses, bill-boards, picked out in the headlights. He tried a couple of times to start a conversation but she wasn't having it. He reconciled himself to hurtling through the darkness. The soul is like a bird flying through the dark night into a lighted hall and out again at the other end, as the Old English poet put it, a millennium and more ago. Plant waited for the lighted hall.

And the lights appeared. Billboards. Shop-houses. Ferro-concrete development. Pattaya. They came to a high wall, pulled up at the gates. It looked like the entrance to some military compound. A bandit chief, maybe. She stuck a smart card in a post and the gate opened. From a sentry hut a security guard watched them impassively. And then inside the walls there were lines of villas and at the end of the driveway a condominium tower block and an underground car park.

'Not what I expected,' said Plant.

'The story of your life,' said Anna-Imelda.

They took a lift and roared up fifteen storeys. The number of the steps to the temple. She opened the door to a large room with a large picture window looking out onto the night.

'Good view?' Plant asked.

'What you see is what you get.'

He couldn't see anything. Just darkness.

'What's it like in daylight?'

'The same.'

'Really?'

'The cruel sea,' she said, disappearing through one of the doors that led off the room.

He turned around, took in the furnishings, a couple of chairs, a long low couch. It had a familiar feel. Maybe just modernity. The feel of concrete and glass. Pastel shades. Polished parquet floor. Rugs. Like the Gold Coast and Mrs Ackerman's apartment. Very like.

'How's Alec?' he asked.

'Alec's dead,' she said.

He hadn't expected that. It hit him in the stomach.

'Dead?' he said. 'When? How?'

'Couple of months ago. Natural causes.'

'What happened?'

'He died.'

'I can't believe it.'

She came back in. She had taken off her shoes and was bare-footed. She looked very small.

She gestured at an urn on a side table.

'There he is.'

'I'm sorry.'

'Yeah, well,' she said.

'I had no idea.'

'Why should you?'

'It's hard to take in.'

She shrugged.

'So if you've come looking for him again, it's too late. You missed him.'

'I came looking for you, actually.'

'Did you actually?' she said. 'Who you working for this time?'

'You know his wife's in gaol.'

'You don't say,' she said. Without saying whether she knew or not.

'Yes.'

'So? You want I should go visit her? Prison visiting is not one of my services.'

'Tell me what are your services.'

She shrugged. 'Maybe you tell me what you got in mind and we see,' she said.

'You know Starr is dead?'

She nodded.

'Your name was in his address book.'

'Was it now?'

'All your names.'

'All of them?'

'Anna, Imelda.'

'Uh. Just those names.'

'What were they doing there?'

'What were you doing looking in his address book?'

'Mrs Ackerman gave it me.'

'So?'

'She found it on him when she found the body.'

'Found the body. That's one cute way of putting it.'

'She says she didn't kill him.'

'Well she would say that, wouldn't she?'

'Why?'

She shrugged.

'What do you think?' he asked.

'Why should I think anything?'

'I understand Starr was into weird stuff.'

'So what's weird?'

'You don't know?'

She looked at him steadily.

'I find you pretty weird, if you want to know.'

'Apart from me,' he said.

She said nothing.

'You knew Starr?'

She didn't reply.

'Did you meet him through Alec? Or did you know him before?'

'Before what?'

'Before you knew Alec.'

'Oh, man,' she said, 'you sound like some jealous lover. What's the deal? Just lay it on the table.'

'OK. Mrs Ackerman is being held in gaol while the authorities investigate Starr's death. If someone can tell the authorities Starr was well known to be into weird stuff and his death was an accident, then they'll let her out.'

'Let her sweat,' said Anna-Imelda. 'Get some of that flab off.'

'I think she's sweated enough.'

'Nah, nowhere near.'

'I was hoping you'd cooperate.'

'And go along and put my neck in a noose. No way.'

'It's just a matter of affidavits.'

'Bullshit it is.'

'Apparently he had people all round the world he'd call up.'

'You implying I'm one of them?'

Plant stayed silent.

'I should fix you,' she said.

'You already did a couple of times.'

'Permanently,' she said.

'Like Starr?'

'You implying I fixed him?'

'What happened?'

'How would I know what happened?'

'What was the deal between him and Alec?'

'No deal. He took over Alec's publishing. End of story.'

'I don't think so.'

'You're a persistent fucker, aren't you?'

Plant nodded.

'You've got the wrong end of the stick. You're as bad as Mrs Ackerfuckingwoman.'

'Go on.'

'She thought Starr would lead her to Alec. That's why she was stalking him.'

'Stalking who? Alec or Starr?'

'Both of them.'

'And did it?'

'No, fuck her.'

'Why not?'

'You don't fuck around with people like Starr.'

'Why not?'

She shook her head. 'Oh, man. You putting me on?'

'No,' said Plant. 'I'm just asking.'

'Well don't,' she said.

'Don't what?'

'Don't ask.'

'He's got connections?'

'Of course.'

'What sort?'

'The sort you don't ask about.'

Plant could believe that. There wasn't much he could believe, but that was one item that coincided with his own perceptions. He thought back to the stretch limo and Starr's heavy presence. And now Starr was without presence, at least in any earthly dimensions. Likewise Ackerman. The apartment felt chill and unwelcoming, the aura of death or absence settled in there, expanding to occupy it, repelling the living, silent as the grave.

'So she came over and saw Starr. Then what happened?'

'How would I know what happened? Maybe she was turning tricks on the side.'

'So Alec didn't see her?'

'Too right he didn't. He was dead.'

'How did he die?'

'I told you. Natural causes.'

'What sort of natural causes?'

She looked at him in disbelief. Or horror. Or disgust.

'You want to see the death certificate?'

'It might be an idea.'

'Schmuck,' she said. But she went into one of the rooms that led off the living-room and came back with a piece of paper. She handed it over to Plant. It was in Thai.

'Satisfied?'

'Could I get a copy?'

She flounced off again. When she came back she was carrying a spade. Maybe it came with the four-wheel drive. One of the off-road accessories.

'You want to go see the grave?' she said. 'While the photocopier warms up? You want to go dig up the body and make sure?'

'There's a grave as well as an urn?' said Plant.

'So?'

'Isn't that like overkill?'

'Overkill?' she said.

She held the spade as if she was about to swing it at him. To Plant it seemed touch and go. But she put it down and went across to the urn. She opened the top.

'How dead do you want him to be?' she asked.

Plant tried conciliatory noises.

'You wanna see? You wanna take a matchbox full and get it analyzed? Have a taste?'

Plant declined.

'So shut up about it,' she said. 'This is my man you're talking about.'

'I'm sorry.'

She opened a door.

'This was Alec's study. You wanna look?'

He walked across. A chair, a bare desk, an empty bookcase. The photocopier warming up from its big sleep, as if it might produce a simulacrum of the late Ackerman.

She opened the door next to it. It was a bedroom. A king size bed, with a single table and single lamp to one side of it. A built-in wardrobe. A dressing table. A chair.

'This is where we lived together,' she said. 'We bought this place to be together. For his retirement. Then he died.'

'I'm sorry,' said Plant.

'You wanna look under the bed to make sure he's not hiding?'

He shivered. Was it the chill and stillness of death or of absence, the grave or the empty grave? She had driven him all the way down here for what? To show him Ackerman wasn't there? Was absence a proof? Of what? That he had ever been there? That he would never be there again? A long drive, and a long drive back, to show him nothing. A lot of effort, certainly. If only to have emptied the room of what might have once been in there. And to have put it somewhere else. But proof? How could he say it was proof? The long drive, the force of her will, the feel of emptiness. Maybe it had never been lived in. Maybe this was just theatre, the apartment rented for the night, while Alec wasn't in the urn, or the grave, but living in some fisherman's thatched hut and catching prawns and waiting till she showed up again. Maybe he was following Prem's example and had become a landowner in some remote village. A reluctant landowner. Or cultivating opium poppies in Laos. Better than hanging from a leather strap in a hotel bedroom in Bangkok. Of course, he hadn't seen Starr's body either. Was there the possibility of another miraculous survival there? Bowles, too. Another body he had never seen. He could see Doubting Thomas's point, wanting to stick his fingers in the nail holes. Up to a point. Some things he was happy to pass on. He felt he was happy to pass on all of this.

'You wanna fuck?' she said.

It was not what he'd been expecting. It came as a shock.

'What you looking like that for? If he was still alive you think I'd fuck someone else? Fuck you? So you wanna fuck me just to make sure?'

'It's all right,' said Plant.

'Don't ever say I didn't offer,' she said, closing the bedroom door.

44

They sat in silence. Plant on the couch, Anna-Imelda in one of the chairs. She curled her legs up beneath her. They sat there a long time. Nothing disturbed the stillness. Not even the sound of the sea through the wide window. No sounds at all, until someone raised a voice in the corridor outside. Another voice answered it. The voices were loud to penetrate the substantial security door. They were raised in something above ordinary conversation. Impassioned, argumentative, angry. Anna-Imelda sat there saying nothing. She might have been listening, she might have withdrawn into reverie. Plant did not find it comfortable, the silence between them, the voices outside, the urn on its side-table, the spade lying on the polished floor.

The voices went on, ambiguous, sometimes there seemed to be laughter, though not necessarily of a mirthful kind. Not knowing Thai, Plant could only listen to the rhythms, rising and falling, surging and dying away, and they made no sense to him. They might not have been in Thai for all he knew.

'What's going on?' he asked.

'I don't know.'

'Should we have a look?'

'No.'

'What is it, a fight, or just a farewell?'

'I don't know.'

The voices surged, impassioned. Plant stood up.

'Don't,' she said. 'Leave it.'

'You don't think we should see?'

'No.'

'Why not?'

'Because that might be what they want. They make a noise to get us to open the door, then they break in. Or just kill us.'

'Really?'

'I don't know.'

'Does it often happen?'

'No. It shouldn't happen now. There should be a security guard.'

'Why not call him?'

'No,' she said. 'Just do nothing. It could be nothing, it could be a set up, we do nothing, that way we give nobody any excuse to do anything.'

'Who would want to do anything?'

'You're the investigator, why ask me? Burglars. Rapists. Police. Your Australian security people. Who knows who you've stirred up. Best not to know.'

'You think I've stirred someone up?'

'Best not to know.'

'Makes sense, I guess.'

'Good,' she said.

She got up. 'You want a drink? A smoke?'

'Sure.'

She brought him a beer from the kitchen and a mineral water for herself. She rolled a smoke, lit it, took a couple of drags, passed it across. He figured if she smoked it herself it should be safe. Though he could be wrong. He'd been wrong before. Maybe she'd rolled something lethal into the middle. But by the time he'd thought of that the joint was over halfway down.

She handed him the copy of the death certificate.

'Convenient having a photocopier,' he said.

'It belonged to Alec. He bought it with some research grant.'

'What did he use it for?'
'He didn't much. He bought it years ago.'
'And you've kept it?'
'Why wouldn't I?'
'Ugly brutes. Take up a lot of space.'
'Speak for yourself,' she said.
'What happened to the memoirs?' Plant asked.
'The what?'
'Alec's memoirs. The book he was writing.'
'He wasn't writing any book.'
'He talked about it in Baguio City.'
'Oh, he talked about it all right, maybe. His talk was one big memoir. But he wasn't writing anything. He was retired. Once he left that university and that wife he never wrote anything again.'
'He never wrote a lot before,' said Plant.
'Is that so?'
'Yes.'
'He was through with all that, anyway. He just wanted to live.'
'And he died.'
'Yeah, well. He wanted to live before he died. And he did.'
'So there's no manuscript stashed away.'
'You never give up, do you?' she said. 'No, there's no manuscript, no memoirs.'
It could have been true. Like it could have been true he never used the photocopier much. And wasn't figuring on using it again.
'Who has Starr's address book now?' she asked.
'I do,' said Plant.
'Not Mrs Ackerman.'
'No, I have it.'
'With you?'
'No.'
'Where?'
'Somewhere safe.'
'Uh-huh. What do you plan to do with it?'
'Work through the names till I find enough people who will swear to affidavits that he was into weird stuff and liked to be strung up.'
'Stringing himself up would be better. For your purposes.'
'I stand corrected.'
'And then what?'

'Then Mrs Ackerman gets out of custody and we can all go home.'

'And the address book?'

'I guess I hand it over to the police.'

'Why would you do that?'

'I don't need it.'

She drew on the joint reflectively, her eyes narrowed.

'Maybe we could do a deal.'

'Maybe,' said Plant.

'You give me the address book, maybe I can arrange some affidavits. Get a lawyer. It might cost.'

'Maybe you arrange the affidavits first.'

'You don't trust me?'

'Not a lot.'

'Why don't you trust me, Plant?'

'I don't trust most people.'

'So it's nothing personal.'

'It's personal all right.'

'That's not nice.'

'That night at the Eternal Night club wasn't nice.'

'Oh, but it was,' she said. 'You kept saying how nice it was at the time.'

'At the time.'

'You were cute,' she said. 'You were very trusting then.'

'Yeah, well. And Baguio City?'

'I had Alec with me then,' she said.

'So you did.'

'You're not afraid of me, are you, Plant? You don't think I'd do anything terrible to you.'

'There is a trail of corpses,' he said.

'What trail?'

'Bowles.'

'Bowles? You think I killed him, do you?'

'I hadn't. But since you mention it, did you?'

'Bowles was a snitch. He was snooping around the drug trade. Gave him an excuse to hang out in the bars and get laid. He invited Alec over to give that lecture so he could quiz him about Starr's publishing operation. Starr must have found out and had him pushed in a canal.'

'How do you know that?'

'In my business you hear things.'

'What business is that?'

'I'm a singer, in case you forgot.'

'Is that all?'

'You don't want to believe it, don't believe it. You asked.'

'And Alec knew this?'

'Knew I'm a singer?'

'Knew about Bowles.'

'Everybody knew it.'

'Everybody?'

'Everybody who knows anything.'

'So was Starr in the drug business?'

'Of course.'

'And intelligence?'

She shrugged.

'It goes with the territory,' he agreed.

'There you are then.'

'Is that why Alec disappeared? Because he knew? Because he knew they knew he knew?'

'Alec was disappearing from his wife.'

'Is that all?'

'Isn't that enough?'

She gave him a blank, impenetrable look.

'That's your story and you're sticking to it?' Plant asked.

'He just wanted to get away from her.'

'And be with you.'

'You've got it,' she said. 'Case solved.'

'Maybe,' he said.

'And now you're trying to drag him back to her. You think about it. Now she's had a taste of gaol, she's going to use that experience. She's not going to be satisfied with just keeping him under house arrest after that. Think what you'd be sending him back to.'

'So there's no drug-trafficking, no money-laundering, no secret services, no guerrilla armies, no terrorists.'

'Well, there are,' she conceded, 'but Alec had nothing to do with them.'

'I see,' said Plant. 'But you'd say that anyway if he were involved with them.'

She shrugged.

'And how could I be dragging him back to his wife if he's already dead?'

She picked up the urn and held it out to him. He kept his hands at his sides.

'I'll tell her I saw it,' he said. 'I wouldn't want to take it away from you.' Last thing he wanted was to be flying back with an urn of Ackerman's or someone or other's ashes.

'And was Alec working with Bowles?' he asked.

'Of course not.'

He wasn't sure he believed her, but it was all she was going to give him.

'When I spoke to Bowles he said there was nothing suspect about Starr's operation.'

'Well, he would, wouldn't he? He wouldn't go around telling people what he knew.'

'But you said everybody knew anyway.'

'So what? Bowles was a schmuck. He never gave away anything for free.'

'And Starr?'

'What about Starr?'

'Who killed him?'

'Accidental. Dangerous sex.'

'Is that the story?'

'That's the story.'

'So we're agreed on that.'

'No problem.'

'Good.'

'And is that it?'

'There's Alec.'

'Alec? You don't think I would have killed Alec. That's terrible, Plant.'

'Terrible,' said Plant. 'No.'

'No what, Plant?'

'I don't think you killed Alec.'

'That's nice of you to say so.'

'So we've got a deal?' he asked.

'She pays for the lawyer for the affidavits.'

'Sure.'

'Good.' She stubbed out the joint and looked across at him. 'So. Is that it?'

'I was told you were a terrorist,' he said.

'Do I look like a terrorist?'

'I don't know what terrorists look like. I was also told you might be an undercover agent.'

'Well,' she said, 'which would you prefer?'

'I don't know.'

'That's interesting in itself,' she said.

'In what way?'

'That you don't automatically go for the forces of law and order.'

Caught on that one.

She leaned across to him.

'Shall I tell you what I am, Plant?' she said. Sweet and low.

'Go on.'

'I'm just a girl who can't say no.'

'I already heard you sing it,' he said. 'Several times.'

'So who gets to write their own lines any more?' she asked.

'You sing it well,' he said.

'Thank you.'

'With conviction. Like you really believe it.'

'You're a smart-arse, Plant, you know that? You're a smart-arse, but it doesn't hide the fact that you're still uneasy, aren't you, Plant?'

'Uh-huh.'

'That's why you won't fuck me, isn't it? You're afraid you mightn't live to tell the tale.'

'Something like that.'

She laughed.

'Only one way to find out,' she said.

Outside in the corridor the voices had gone away.

45

'Quite honestly, Plant, I don't give a toss. The certificate says he's dead, so he's dead. That's good enough for me. He wants to come back to life he's got a problem proving it. His passport will be dead, his driving license will be dead, his bank account will be dead. How much deader than that do you want to get? He comes back here, he doesn't exist. Nor his house nor his car. The man who never was. Just be thankful you came back with this and I didn't have to hire you to kill him.'

The Ackerwoman looked distinctly fetching all in her widow's weeds. The black made her slimmer. Or maybe she'd sweated off a bit of weight in gaol. Anna-Imelda had been as good as her word. She'd got a lawyer to fix the affidavits and she'd kept the Ackerwoman sweating a couple more weeks while it was being done. And Plant too. Plant had been the prison visitor, suffering the harangues and complaints and threats and menaces about the delay. There was no way he could say it was just part of the deal. He didn't know for certain that it was. But he suspected it. So did the Ackerwoman. She knew she was being strung along and she resented it. Vocally. But back on the Gold Coast, sipping a chilled white wine as she looked at her ocean view, she didn't look any the worse for wear. Better, in fact. Though he didn't think it would be smart to say so.

They'd taken her straight from gaol to the airport. No messing around. She complained, of course.

'If I'm not being charged, why am I not being let out?'

'You are being let out,' they said. 'At the airport. As soon as you are through passport control.'

Plant had broken the news about her husband's death to her in gaol.

'I don't believe it,' she said.

'Here's the certificate,' he said. 'Or a copy of it.'

'I don't believe that either.'

'I'm not sure I do,' he said. 'Do you want me to look into it further?'

'No,' she said. 'The certificate will do.'

Plant had figured it might. Get the properties and the pension. What was left of the pension after Ackerman had taken out the lump sum. The half-pension.

'If he wants to live in a hut on water and a crust with a bar girl, let him,' she said. 'Don't let him think he can come crawling back. I'll cancel his passport. He'll see what dead means.'

Plant believed her.

Back on the Gold Coast he went through it with her. She was well into the bottle of Verdelho when he arrived. She poured him a glass.

'Your husband could have been doing some undercover operation with Anna-Imelda,' he said, for no good reason other than it was one of the things he'd thought of. One of the many things he'd thought of.

'Under what cover?' she said. 'Under the fucking sheets?'

'Like they say; lying abroad for the honour of his country,' he said.

She snorted. Like a young racehorse. Youngish.

'So why should I care?'

'You don't think he was?'

'How would I know?'

'He never said?'

'He wouldn't have, would he?'

'Probably not.'

'And if he was, you're never going to find out. So you can forget research and investigation.'

'It might have explained the trips he made.'

'Screwing bar girls explains enough,' she said.

'Starr was almost certainly working for some agency too.'

'The only person Starr ever worked for was Starr,' she said. 'He was just a crook.'

'No doubt,' said Plant. 'Like many a businessman. But he had undercover connections too.'

'And they got him killed,' she said. 'That's what comes of getting undercover with sluts like that.'

'Sluts like what?'

'Like your bar girl,' she said.

'She wasn't my bar girl.'

'You trying to tell me you weren't screwing her?'

'Yes.'

'Yes what?'

'That's what I'm trying to tell you.'

She snorted again.

'Pull the other one,' she said. 'You're lucky she didn't kill you too.'

'Too?'

'Like Alec and Bowles and Starr.'

'I thought Starr and Bowles were supposed to be accidents, and you thought Alec was still alive.'

'Who cares?' she said. 'You believe those were an accident you'd believe anything.'

'I'm just giving you the official findings.'

'You don't believe them.'

'Can't say I do.'

'That's something.'

'You didn't kill Starr, did you?'

'Plant!'

'You're sure?'

'If anyone killed him it's your little singing girlfriend.'

'Not my girlfriend. Your husband's girlfriend.'

'And she probably killed Alec too. Or do you think I did that?'

'Who knows?'

'She'd do anything for a price.'

'So how much did she cost you?' he asked.

He was on guard for an unfriendly response. Possibly violent. But all she did was laugh. She picked up the wine bottle but it was only to take it into the kitchen. She came back cool and composed with a fresh bottle. She handed it to Plant to open. It was chilled from the fridge.

'You have a horrible mind, Plant,' she said. 'And your body's not that enticing, either.'

'It saves me from a lot of trouble.'

'Don't bet on it,' she said. 'Maybe I don't want you for your body, Plant. Maybe I just want you for your complicity.'

'I was told she had terrorist contacts. I was also told she might have been an undercover agent. But that could just have been disinformation to discredit her.'

'Discredit her?' said Mrs Ackerman. 'Surely that's impossible. How much more discredited can you get than being a bar girl?'

'She wasn't a bar girl. She was a singer.'

'Bullshit, Plant. She was a hooker and a killer.'

'I'm not sure she was a killer. I'm not even sure your husband's dead. Nor are you.'

'Well Starr is, that's for sure.'

'It could have been an accident.'

She laughed, derisively.

'Are you saying it wasn't an accident, now?'

'Now what?'

'Now you're out of gaol?'

'Yes.'

'Why would Starr have been killed?'

'Because Alec and his little tart had some scam going with Starr and they had a falling out.'

'And you're saying she killed him?'

'Her name was in his little book.'

'True.'

'And you gave it her.'

'It was the price of getting you out.'

'The only price?'

'Plus the lawyers' fees.'

'You sure you didn't have to screw her, too?'

'Sure.'

'You're lying.'

'No.'

'She wasn't having any?'

'She would've.'

'Really?'

'Well, she offered.'

'Tell me.'

'She offered to sleep with me to prove your husband was dead.'

'Is that a mark of proof?'

'Apparently.'

'So did you?'

'No.'

'Why not? You were too scared, was that it? You chickened out. Afraid you'd end up like her other boyfriends. Strung up from a doorframe or pushed into a canal. Or burned to ashes and stuffed into an urn.'

'It was a consideration,' Plant admitted.

She laughed.

'Any regrets?'

Plant shrugged.

'You're a lousy liar, Plant,' she said. 'You're like my late husband.'

'I thought you thought he was still alive and living with his bar girl, as you call her.'

'And am I expected to make you the same offer your bar girl made? To show my belief in my husband's demise?'

'It's not required,' he said.

'Would you like me to?'

Plant said nothing.

'Tell me, Plant, are you afraid of me?'

He considered.

'You think I killed Starr, don't you?'

'It's possible,' he said.

'And you think your little singing friend might have killed him too.'

'Possible,' he agreed.

'Make up your mind, Plant,' she said. 'Which of us is it going to be? Or do you think we did it together?'

'I honestly don't know.'

'And you never are going to know for sure, are you?'

'Possibly not.'

'But you're sure it was a woman.'

He shrugged.

'Are you afraid of women, is that it, Plant?'

'I could be getting that way,' he conceded.

'Because you think I killed Starr.'

He stayed silent.

'And it turns you on.'

'No.'

'Not even a little bit?'

'No.'

'You're a liar, Plant. But I don't have any problem with that. You're like my fucking husband. You're a liar and you're turned on.'

'I might be turned on,' said Plant. 'But not by the thought that you're a killer.'

'Uh-huh,' she said. 'Well, at least you're turned on, that's something, isn't it?'

'It could be.'

'So let's see,' she said.

It seemed like a time to remain silent.

'I'm not sure how suited you are to your current occupation, Plant.'

'Nor am I,' he agreed.

'You just don't seem that eager to investigate.'

He opened his mouth but nothing came out.

'Have you ever thought of trying something else?'

'Like what?'

'Like working in an art gallery.'

'An art gallery? Doing what?'

'Oh, this and that.'

'This and that?'

'This and that.'

'I don't know,' he said.

'So let's see,' she said again.

MORE FINE FICTION IN THE PRESS ON SERIES

1. Peter Corris, *Wishart's Quest*, ISBN 978 1 921509 54 4
2. Michael Wilding, *The Prisoner of Mt Warning*, ISBN 978 1 921509 56 8
3. Phillip Edmonds, *Leaving Home with Henry*, ISBN 978 1 921509 55 1
4. Inez Baranay, *With The Tiger*, ISBN 978 1 921509 57 5
5. Ross Fitzgerald & Trevor L Jordan, *Fools' Paradise*, ISBN 978 1 921509 58 2
6. Victoria Thompson, *City of Longing*, ISBN 978 1 921875 36 6
7. Peter Corris, *The Colonial Queen*, ISBN 978 1 921875 31 1
8. Michael Wilding, *The Magic of It*, ISBN 978 1 921875 37 3
9. Morris Lurie, *Hergesheimer Hangs In*, ISBN 978 1 921875 34 2
10. Garry Disher, *Play Abandoned*, ISBN 978 1 921875 33 5
11. Inez Baranay, *Always Hungry*, ISBN 978 1 921875 30 4
12. Ian Callinan, *Dislocation*, ISBN 978 1 921875 38 0
13. Felix Calvino, *A Hatful of Cherries*, ISBN 978 1 740971 67 6
14. James Murray, *Shark City*, ISBN 978 1 921875 35 9
15. Peter Corris, *Standing in the Shadow*, ISBN 978 1 921875 32 8
16. Michael Wilding, *Asian Dawn*, ISBN 978 1 921875 39 7
17. Colin Talbot, *Ah, Sweet Mystery*, ISBN 978 1 921875 93 9
18. Morris Lurie, *Hergesheimer in the Present Tense*, ISBN 978 1 921875 95 3
19. Michael Wilding, *Little Demon*, ISBN 978 1 921875 94 6
20. Félix Calvino, *Alfonso*, isbn 978-1-925003-20-8

Printed in Australia
AUHW021208290922
369328AU00009BA/37

9 781921 875397